CW00347793

INTERNET SHOPPING

in easy steps
.compact

GEOFF PRESTON

COMPUTER
STEP

in easy steps and **in easy steps.compact** are imprints of Computer Step
Southfield Road . Southam . Warwickshire CV47 OFB . England
Web site: http://www.ineasysteps.com
Email: books@ineasysteps.com

Notice of Liability
Every effort has been made to ensure that this book contains accurate and current
information. However, Computer Step and the author shall not be liable for any loss or
damage suffered by readers as a result of any information contained herein.

Trademarks
All trademarks are acknowledged as belonging to their respective companies.

Printed and bound in the United Kingdom

ISBN 1-84078-107-6

Contents

Introduction to Shopping 29

Shopping Around 45

Food Shopping 75

The Home *93*

Things to Wear *133*

Cars and Bikes *187*

Technology *237*

Software *261*

Books *295*

Music *319*

Leisure *349*

Travel *373*

Gifts *411*

Auctions *441*

Personal Services *461*

Index *499*

ReadMe.first

The trouble with many computer books (and in particular, computer manuals) is that they have been written by 'techies'. These people are almost a breed apart: they invariably speak in hexadecimal and have square eyeballs from spending a lot of time gazing at the monitor.

For us mere mortals, such books are about as accessible as a train timetable written by a Martian. To overcome this, Computer Step have developed a simple and easily accessible range of books to help the average human get the most from Computers and the Internet.

What you get

The 'in easy steps' series assumes no prior knowledge, but at the same time tries not to be condescending to the reader. This book is from a new series of 'in easy steps.compact' books exploring one small topic from a huge area of the Internet: Shopping on the Internet.

It explains what equipment you need to shop over the Internet, the pitfalls of online shopping and the things to look out for.

Although most of the websites described here allow you to actually spend money directly over the Internet, some do not but have been included because they provide information to help you, the consumer, make a decision or purchase a product elsewhere.

Over 1000 websites are categorised into 14 topics, each being provided with the name, address and relevant details.

To see the whole range of books by Computer Step, visit our site at: *http://www.ineasysteps.com/*

You can locate 'in easy steps' books by title, subject, ISBN or author. Once you've found a title, you can access details like the contents and description. Then, if appropriate, order it securely straightaway.

What if it doesn't work?

There are over 1000 web addresses in this book and frankly, I wouldn't be surprised if a few do not work by the time you read this. The fact is that the Internet is notoriously transient. A site that exists today, may have vanished from the face of the Earth tomorrow. Many of the sites on the Internet are run by individuals who have been provided with free space to create their own website, but once the novelty has worn off, the sites are abandoned. But even large companies can run into problems. Only a few weeks before finishing this book, *boo.com*, one of the largest Internet sports clothing reseller ceased trading.

Where possible, websites by individuals have been avoided, as for the sites that no longer work, all I can say is sorry. At the time of writing, all sites referred to in this book work.

Help us to keep you up-to-date

If you find one of the websites listed in this book doesn't work, please let us know. Send an email to Computer Step (*books@ineasysteps.com*) and let us know the page, the name and the address of the website and we will remove it in the next edition. You might also care to suggest Internet sites that should be included in the updated book. Using the same email address, tell us the name of the site, the address and a brief description of what it sells.

Although this book was written by a British author, the majority of the sites should be of use to shoppers across the World as many of the sites selected provide international delivery, or are based in countries other than the UK.

What You Need

Your first shopping list

Before you can start shopping on the Internet, you'll need to equip yourself with a few bits and pieces. Some of these you may have but it's worth running through what you need before you go any further. You need six items...

- a computer (including keyboard, mouse and monitor)
- a modem (which may already be installed in the computer)
- a phone line (any BT or Cable phone)
- an Internet account (your way in)
- a browser (to see what you're doing)
- a credit or debit card (to pay for your purchases)

The computer

Although theoretically almost any computer will do, in practice you need a reasonably fast one, especially if you want to be able to use all the multimedia bits. Modern websites contain all manner of goodies such as sound, graphics and even animations and video clips, so you'll need a computer which will be able to download and run these.

The current minimum specification is a computer with 32MBytes of memory and at least a Pentium 1 processor or equivalent, although if you are buying a computer now you should look for at least 64MBytes of memory (to enable you to do things other than use the Internet) and you'll probably now only be able to buy Pentium III or equivalent, as the Pentium II processor is just about obsolete.

You also need a good screen, certainly one capable of supporting SVGA graphics. Until fairly recently computers were supplied with 14" monitors. These should not be considered any longer. Go for 15" or, if you can afford it, and have the space for it, 17" monitors are becoming more widely available.

The latest generation monitors are TFT screens similar to those used on laptop computers. They offer numerous benefits including virtually no flicker, high resolution, and no radiation. They also don't attract the dust like conventional cathode ray tube (CRT) monitors. The downside is that at about 5-6 times the cost of a CRT monitor of equivalent size, TFT screens are very expensive.

You'll need a keyboard and mouse (or equivalent pointing device) which means you'll need an operating system which supports a mouse. That means you'll need a PC running Windows 95, or preferably Windows 98 or the networking equivalent, Windows NT4 or Windows 2000. Older versions of Windows (3.1 or Windows for Workgroups) will work, but you would be well advised to upgrade. All Apple Mac computers qualify, although you should use at least System 7, and preferably a later operating system.

To install the software you'll probably need a CD ROM drive as most service providers now distribute their software on CD ROM. You'll also need some hard disc space to store the software.

Other computers

Most computers used to connect to the Internet are desktop models. The ease of use, quality and size of display and the relatively low cost make them the best choice. But there are two alternatives...

Laptop computers

Laptop computers are perfectly adequate in principle, as long as they satisfy the minimum requirements in terms of memory and speed. The advantage of a laptop is that the screen will be of the TFT type rather than CRT, but the resolution of some older models frequently leaves much to be desired. Screen size is also smaller. Hard disks also tend to be smaller (both in terms of storage capacity and physical size) but that should not be an issue.

Palmtop computers and organisers

Palmtop computers including the so-called Windows CE models, the Palm Pilot hand-held organisers and most Psion models can connect to the Internet and there are even sites that have been specially designed with palmtops in mind. Avoid palmtops that do not have touch-screens as navigating through the Internet with the cursor keys (the arrow keys) can be frustrating in the extreme.

The major advantage with laptops and palmtops is that they are portable which means you can access the Internet whilst away from your desk.

The modem

A MOdulator DEModulator is a device that converts the digital signals generated by a computer into analogue signals that can be sent down the phone line. It also converts the incoming analogue signals to digital signals that can be read by the computer.

For desktop computers opinion is divided as to whether an internal modem is better of worse than an external modem. For what it's worth, an external modem requires a mains socket to provide it with power whereas an internal modem collects its power from within the computer. With all the other bits and pieces you've got to plug into the mains, the introduction of a mains-powered modem might be one too many.

The external modem will also have to be plugged into the computer and frequently the sockets on the back of many computers are in short supply. Internal modems, on the other hand, require an internal connection and these are usually in even shorter supply.

External modems provide a nice array of pretty lights to tell you what they're doing, but the case usually looks unsightly (one was once described as looking like a cheap domestic intercom) and it takes up desk space, which is also at a premium. External modems will work with most computers whether they be desktop, laptop or palmtop. You will probably need to buy any leads that are 'non-standard' and modems that work from batteries as well as the mains are desirable if you intend accessing the Internet away from the office.

What is certain though is that you should try to get the fastest model you can and at present that is a 56k modem. It may also be advertised as being V90 standard. This is the one to get because it will provide noticeably faster access than anything else.

Laptop computers sometimes have modems built into them and are usually top spec. If you haven't got an internal modem fitted, the manufacturer may be able to install one for you. The alternative is a PCMCIA modem which is about the size of a credit card and slots into the side of the laptop computer. There are several types available including ones which will connect to a mobile phone.

Palmtop computers usually have modems either built-in or available as an after sales accessory. Broadly there are two ways to add a modem. The first is to buy an external modem specifically designed for your palmtop, the second is to buy a generic desktop modem (preferably with optional battery power to maintain its portability) and the appropriate cables to get the modem and palmtop connected.

A third option available to some computers (notably Psion) is to buy a PCMCIA adaptor which connects to the palmtop into which you connect a credit card modem used on laptops. If you've already got a PCMCIA modem, this is a good option.

Four alternatives

Rather than using a computer and modem, there are some alternatives which could be considered.

Set-top boxes

The first is an Internet 'set-top box'. These were set to hit the shops in 1998 but some manufacturers couldn't get the price down low enough to compete with the ever-falling price of PCs. NTL are now offering Internet TV as a complete package. A set-top box, as the name implies, sits on the top of your television set. It connects into your television and a suitable telephone point and provides instant access to the Internet.

For more information about Internet TV and set-top boxes visit NTL at *http://www.ntl.com/*.

Internet-ready TV

Just about due to be released is a TV which contains all the equipment required for Internet access. You connect your phone line into the back of the TV as well as the aerial, press a button on the handset and you're on the Internet. In terms of ease of connection, this is probably the simplest, but it's not without some drawbacks. Information is a little sketchy at present, but it looks like you won't have a choice of service provider and it may be possible to be online without knowing.

Games consoles

In late 1999, Sega announced a new Internet capable games machine. Following on from the success of their previous games console, the Dreamcast has a built-in modem so that you can access the Internet. The kit includes a lead to connect it to a phone point and a CD ROM containing Internet access software.

An infrared qwerty keyboard is available at extra cost, but this would be an absolute requirement if you were seriously considering using the console to shop.

With both the games console and the set top box, much of the uncertainty about Internet connection has been removed. You won't need to decide what sort of modem you need, because it's already provided. You don't need to worry about the power of the computer or the amount of memory because that has also been taken care of. In short, what you get is a 'plug-in and go' solution.

But there are some issues that need to be considered before choosing this route. First, all you're getting with the set-top box is Internet connectivity. You won't have a solution that can be used to any great extent off-line. You won't have, for example, powerful word processing or spreadsheet facilities. With the games console, at least you've got a games machine to use when you're not online.

The second point is that you will be relying on a domestic television set to view Internet pages, which frequently contain quite a lot of small print. Whilst TVs are very good for watching TV, they're not always very good for viewing pages of text. The alternative is to buy a computer monitor which will improve the text display, but may not be as good for watching TV. Furthermore, the cost of a monitor added to the cost of the set-top box makes it a less attractive proposition.

Mobile phones

The new generation of mobile phones (WAP – Wireless Application Protocol) means that you can access the Internet directly from your mobile phone, giving access to Internet Shopping as well as other Internet services. The problem is likely to be with the keypad which, as anyone who has tried to send text messages using a mobile phone will confirm, is not best suited to typing words.

The phone line

For the desktop computer, you'll need a BT-type phone socket near to the computer or a long phone extension lead to connect the modem to the phone line. Kits are available that enable individuals to add a socket to an existing phone installation without having to open the existing phone sockets.

When you are connected to the Internet (online) you are being charged for the call. If you've selected a good Internet Service Provider it will be a local call, but there will be a charge for the call time unless your phone company makes special provisions for going online. The other point to note is that whilst you're online, the phone is in use. This means that nobody can make a call from the phone, and anyone calling you will find the line is engaged.

The cheapest solution to part of this problem is to ask your phone company to provide you with an ansaphone service that enables callers to leave messages if your line is engaged. But to really overcome this problem (if indeed it is a problem) a second phone line is required. Many phone companies offer very attractive deals for second lines.

Most phone lines are analogue but digital lines are becoming more common in homes. The price for installing and maintaining an ISDN (Integrated Services Digital Network) line is now much more affordable, and is getting cheaper. The advantage of a digital line is very much faster Internet access, as well as being able to handle more than one call at a time.

You can of course connect portable computers to a landline in exactly the same way as for a desktop computer, but you can also buy kits which will connect to a mobile phone. Strictly these are not modems but adapters (a modem converts digital signals to analogue but a mobile phone, being digital, does not require an analogue signal).

Satellite connection

If you really want to set the world on fire, or you consider ISDN too slow or too out-dated, then why not try using a satellite connection? Kits to connect to a satellite are becoming much more affordable. Basically they comprise a card to plug into your computer which costs about 3 times that of a good quality modem and a monthly subscription charge of about 3 times that of an Internet account. But, you get a connection claimed to be up to 5 times faster than ISDN. For more details, including checking if a satellite footprint covers your area, visit *http://www.satweb.co.uk/*.

The Internet account

To get to the Internet, you must have an account with an Internet Service Provider (ISP).

A few years ago there were relatively few providers and all of them charged their clients per month and some imposed monthly time limitations. Today there are many more ISPs from some very unlikely sources. Many are free.

When choosing an Internet Service provider you should consider eight points...

How much does the connection cost per month?

It varies, but can cost as little as nothing. Don't write off a provider who charges just because they charge. Not all free services offer the quality of those providers who do make a monthly charge. Different providers offer different deals at different prices. You get more or less what you pay for.

How much online time are you allowed before the price goes up?

You should have an account with unlimited access. If the one you're considering doesn't have this feature, leave it and go for another.

Do you connect via a local phone number?

If the connection to the ISP is not via a local phone call (e.g. an 0845 number) you're heading for some very large telephone bills. Discard any ISP which does not use local call connection. A new generation of providers actually give you free phone calls. For really heavy Internet use, this might be beneficial. To sign up with one of these, you'll be charged a registration fee equivalent to between UK£30 and UK£50 plus a flat rate charge per month. If you choose a service of this type, check what other restrictions they impose like times during which you may not use the service.

How many people can the ISP support at any one time?

It is sometimes quite tricky to get hold of this information. Beware of some of the new free services as they often do not have the infrastructure to support huge numbers of people. One famous case occurred quite recently when it came to light that a particular free ISP could only support 1500 people online at a time. No wonder the system was always busy and nobody could get connected!

How fast is the connection?

Like the previous point, it's not always easy to get the answer and when you do (unlike the previous point) the answer doesn't always mean much. Free ISPs often don't run very fast systems. The result will be slow connections, slow download times, but high phone bills.

Are you charged for online Technical support? If so, how much?

This is the downside of many free ISPs. Technical support is usually via a very expensive premium rate call. You only need two 10 minute calls per month (which isn't difficult) and you could have spent as much as the most expensive ISP. On the other hand, if you don't call their helpline ever again, you're in profit. (But then, presumably, you wouldn't be reading this book!)

Does the ISP agreement include email? If so, how many addresses?

Most do include email, but check on the speed of the email delivery as well. Many ISPs provide more than one email address at no extra charge which means you can have a different address for each member of the family. Be aware though, like the letter box on your front door, all emails fall onto the same 'doormat' regardless of who it is for. Emails don't come in envelopes though, so there's no privacy.

Do you get space on the ISP's server to publish your own website? If so, how much space and how much will it cost?

Most ISPs offer space to publish your own website. Some of the free services charge for this, whilst the services that charge per month throw this in as part of the deal. Don't be fooled into going for a huge amount of webspace. Most ISPs offer 5MBytes which is more than enough to publish even the most comprehensive family website.

These eight points are, to a large extent, intertwined, but it is worth investigating very carefully.

Where do I start looking?

Some of the leading subscription ISPs are...

Alta Vista	*http://www.altavista,com/*
AOL	*http://www.aol.com/*
BT Internet	*http://www.btinternet.com/*
Cable & Wireless	*http://www.cwnet.com/*
Demon	*http://www.demon.net/*
Direct Connection	*http://www.dircon.net/*
Easy Net	*http://www.easynet.co.uk/*
Global Internet	*http://www.global.net.uk/*
MSN	*http://www.msn.com/*
Onyx	*http://www.onyxnet.co.uk/*
Virgin net	*http://www.virgin.com/*

The free ISPs are provided on CD ROMs which can be freely picked up in many stores including...

Freeserve	*Dixons, The Link, PC World*
In 2 Home	*Electronics Boutique*
Zoom	*Burtons, Dorothy Perkins, Evans, Topshop, Racing Green*
Breathe net	*Toys 'R' Us*
Currant Bun	*Comet*
btclick.com	*British Telecom*
freebeeb.net	*BBC TV*

Other free Internet services are available from Virgin, Woolworths, Nationwide and WH Smith, to name but a few.

Once you've selected an ISP and got the installation disc (which will usually be on CD ROM, although many offer a choice of floppy disc installation), follow the instructions carefully.

Free Calls

Some ISPs are now offering totally free Internet connection, including the cost of the phone call. In the USA, this is not new but it is quite a revolution in some parts of the world.

Many of these sites will rely heavily on advertising so be aware that you may not always be able to work uninterrupted.

Look out for deals by the cable TV/telephone operators. There are several options in the pipeline.

Alta Vista   http://www.altavista.com/

In the UK, Alta Vista set the ball rolling by offering free calls and a free Internet service, apart from registration.

Phones 4 U   http://4unet.co.uk/

The mobile phone company are offering UK residents totally free Internet access for a small connection/registration fee. Log on to the site, click on the 'Join' button at the top of the screen and complete the online registration form. There is a registration fee and you will be supplied with an adaptor that fits into your phone socket. All your calls will then be at a reduced rate and calls to an Internet number will be free.

The browser

This is the program that essentially does two things. First it is the software which enables the user to commute to different websites throughout the world. The second is to display the pages of information from the websites.

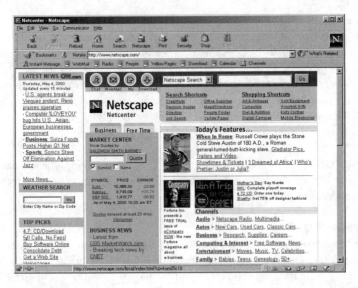

Netscape Navigator (displaying its Home Page)

In simple terms, the browser decodes documents written in a special language called HTML (Hypertext Markup Language). There was a stage when websites featured phrases like 'best viewed with Netscape Navigator', because the different browsers handled documents in very slightly different ways causing slight differences in detail.

Of all the browsers produced since the Internet first became widely used, two have established themselves as supreme: Internet Explorer and Netscape Navigator (latterly tied up in the total Internet package called Communicator). Microsoft's Internet Explorer is now just about ahead of Netscape, largely because (some would say) it is supplied free with all versions of Windows. If you've got Windows, you've got Internet Explorer. Further, if you receive a free Internet start-up kit, the chances are it is supplied with Internet Explorer, not Netscape Navigator.

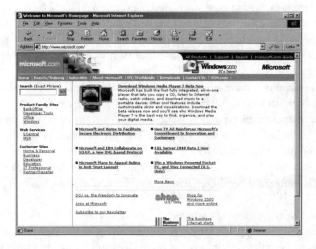

Internet Explorer (displaying Microsoft's Home Page)

New versions of both programs come from Microsoft and Netscape at regular intervals. It's usually worth getting the latest version which will invariably contain the latest gizmos.

Unless you have decided that you want a particular browser, then it'll probably be best if you stick to the one provided by your chosen Internet Service Provider. Of the discs provided by ISPs for free Internet access, most include Internet Explorer and that will be the browser that will automatically install.

Some 'experts' will try to persuade you that one is better than another, but when challenged to provide reasons for their choice, the arguments frequently don't hold water. In fact, in most cases, the explanations provided are based on blind prejudice rather than any logical reasoning.

Views along the lines of 'Anything to do with Bill Gates can't be good' are typical of the explanations forwarded by Netscape followers, whilst Explorer fans will say that there is less chance of their browser conflicting with other Microsoft products.

The reality is that there isn't much to pick between either of them. Each time a new version of either package is released it leap-frogs the opposition. So at the moment Explorer may be technically more advanced in some small area, Netscape will then bring out an upgrade that will overtake Explorer, then a new version of Explorer will overtake that and so on.

There are three pieces of advice worth noting when choosing a browser which, amongst other things, will be used for online shopping:

1. Whichever browser you choose, make it either Netscape or Explorer unless you really know what you're doing and don't mind being in a minority with a browser that will almost certainly not have had the significant investment of time and money (over a substantial period of time) for its development.

2. Stick with your choice. It's not worth swapping back and forth between them. You can just about run both side by side, but it is not recommended.

3. If using your browser for shopping or banking or any service that requires you to enter sensitive details like your credit card number, ensure that it can support a secure line. Several browsers do, some don't. If you stick to Explorer or Netscape you won't go wrong.

Using the browser

Throughout this book you'll find Internet addresses like *http://www.tesco.com/* This is the location of the website and you'll need to enter the address (sometimes called a URL) into the panel at the top of the browser. When you open the browser, there will probably already be some text there – the URL of the currently displayed page. Click the left mouse button on the text and it will highlight. Press the delete key to remove it. Now enter the address of the site you wish to visit and press Enter.

You may find that after you've pressed Enter the address changes. That's fine, sometimes it will do, but you should still get to the place you want to go. At the time of writing, all the URLs published in this book work. If the address can't be found, and you've entered it correctly, it could be because the site has moved and has another address, or the site has closed down – just like a high street shop might move or close down.

You don't have to type in http://, but everything after that must be entered exactly as given.

What else do you need?

In order to pay for any item you have purchased, you'll need some form of plastic money. There are sites which will ask for funds transfer, but this is such a pain my advice is to ignore those sites and shop elsewhere.

You can use four types of plastic money on the Internet. Some companies accept all of them, but many offer just one or two.

Credit cards

If you've got a credit card which carries the name Visa or Mastercard, you'll be able to buy from the vast majority of online shopping sites. In general, this is the best method as, if you make a purchase over UK£100, you'll get some insurance if the goods arrive damaged or don't arrive at all. On the downside, some companies charge a handling fee of anything up to 2% for Visa or Mastercard transactions.

Charge cards

For all practical purposes, as far as online shopping is concerned, a charge card is more or less the same as a credit card. Fewer sites seem to offer the option of payment with a charge card (American Express) than with a credit card.

Store cards

Some stores that operate their own store card allow you to use it online. Typical are Marks & Spencer and John Lewis Partnership.

Debit cards

More and more sites are offering the facility to pay using a debit card which actually takes the money directly out of your current bank account.

Introduction to Shopping

Contrary to what you might read in the newspapers and see on the television, Internet Shopping is not yet widespread.

More than mail order

Mail order shopping is older than many people might imagine. For years we have posted orders for a huge range of goods which have been advertised in catalogues, magazines or even the morning newspaper. Anything from nails to underwear, from saucepans to armchairs have at some stage been offered by mail order. In most cases an order form was printed with the advertisement and, when completed by the bargain-hungry customer, was placed in an envelope together with payment (usually a cheque or money order) and sent to the supplier who in return despatched the goods.

The stock phrase of the day, "Please allow 21 days for delivery", was because the time taken for the order to arrive by post, the supplier to process it, the cheque to be sent to the bank and then cleared, often took that long. Remember, in some cases these orders arrived at the supplier in their thousands. No wonder perishable foods didn't figure very highly in the mail order market.

The advent of credit cards has, to a very large extent, contributed to the more recent popularity of telephone mail ordering. From the retailer's viewpoint, it immediately eliminated the 4 or 5 days' wait for cheque clearance. For the customer, quoting a credit card number meant that it was no longer necessary to send a letter, as the primary reason for the letter was to deliver payment, which the credit card replaced.

It became unnecessary to fill out a form, write a cheque or go to the post box. All the customer needed to do was pick up the phone, dial a number (often a freephone number), place the order and pay by quoting a credit card number. You don't even need to leave your armchair – let alone your home.

And now, you don't need to read either because there are countless shopping channels on television, so all you need is the TV remote control in one hand and the phone in the other. Armchair TV shopping is hugely popular but has one significant drawback – you can't yet shop for a specific item. The items offered for sale are those selected by the TV channel and they are offered one at a time in sequence. It's rather like sitting in front of a conveyer belt watching the goods come past and waiting until something appears that might be of use to you. You choose to either buy or not buy, and then wait for the next item to be offered for sale.

You can't go TV shopping with a specific list of items as all the products displayed are pre-determined by the TV channel.

New technology, as ever, has brought together all of the best features of the other selling methods, wrapped it up in the hi-tech Internet and hatched e-commerce.

Shopping using the Internet opens up a whole new world of home shopping which is going to become far more widespread.

Numerous companies around the world have been selling via the Internet for years. Some have branched out and now offer online shopping as an alternative to their conventional retail outlets, whilst some companies set themselves up as online-only retailers at the outset. These companies don't have shops, just huge warehouses to dispatch orders.

The idea is simple. Previously, if you wanted a book, you'd go to a bookshop and browse through the stock before buying. Now, if you want a book, you go online to a virtual bookshop and order it from there. You can still browse through the stock and read descriptions of the books just as you would in a real bookshop.

The main disadvantage with mail order shopping using the telephone is that you can't browse through the stock unless you have a printed catalogue provided by the mail order company. Internet Shopping overcomes that drawback.

In the real bookshop you would pay by cash, cheque or credit card, in the virtual bookshop you can't use cash, so you must pay by credit or debit card.

Online shopping

All websites offering online purchasing work in much the same way.

Find the item you want to buy

In most cases, products will be found by either entering a word or phrase into a search engine, or going through an index system. Either way, once you have located the item you wish to buy, there will be a button somewhere nearby carrying the legend 'Add to Basket', 'Add to Trolley', 'Buy this item' or something along those lines. Clicking on the button means you've placed the item in your 'shopping basket' or 'trolley'. It does not mean you've bought it, nor have you paid for it at this stage.

Unlike television shopping, Internet shopping allows you to go to the place which sells the items you want to buy.

Keep an eye on the contents of your trolley: it's very easy to drop lots in there. You can remove items before you get to the checkout.

Shopping trolley

Somewhere on the screen will usually be a logo of a shopping trolley showing either the total number of items you have currently selected, or the total cost of the items you have selected.

At any time you can view your trolley, usually by clicking on it. At this stage it should be possible to alter the quantity of a particular item, or even remove it from your trolley altogether.

Checkout

Just like a real store, when you've finished browsing round an Internet store, you go to the checkout where you can alter the number of items you have in your trolley. In most cases, this means deleting the number '1' in the 'Quantity' column and replacing it with a '0'. Once you're happy with the contents of your trolley, click on the 'Pay' button and your order will be confirmed. If it is correct, click on the 'Proceed' button. If you haven't already done so, you'll need to complete an online form entering your details including your name, delivery address, email address and credit card details. Once this has been completed, your order will be processed and the money will be taken from your account when the goods are shipped, not before.

The funds should not be taken from your account until the goods have been shipped.

Feedback

Good companies will follow up your order with an email confirming what you've bought, how much it cost and how you paid. But your credit card details should not be included. If any company confirms your credit card details by email, tear them off a strip and don't use them again.

Returns Policy

For whatever reason, you may have to return items that you have bought. Good sites will have a strategy in place for handling returned goods and their policy on returned items should be available for customers to read. If the goods have been sent in error (e.g. you ordered size 10 and they sent size 16) then all of the costs incurred returning the goods should be met by the vendor. If you ordered a size 10 and you find it doesn't fit and you want to change it for a size 12, then you will usually have to bear the cost of returning the item. But read the Returns Policy: some companies provide a freepost returns service and will change any goods (as long as they are in resaleable condition) without any cost to the customer.

Variations on the theme

Most sites work in much the same way, but sometimes you'll come across slight variations:

Registration

You may be asked to register before actually entering the shop. Usually you'll just have to enter your name and email address, but sometimes you'll be asked to enter your intended payment details. This is not unacceptable, but if you prefer to do it later, then you should be able to.

Cookies

A cookie is a small text file that gets placed on your computer's hard disc by a site you are visiting. It contains settings and preferences so that you don't have to go through the same setting up process every time you return to that particular website.

You can set your system to either accept cookies without question, reject cookies without question or, when a cookie is about to be sent, to prompt you whether to accept it or not.

In Internet Explorer, go to 'Tools' and choose 'Internet options' from the drop down menu. Click the Security tab and then click on the 'Custom Level...' button. About a third of the way down the dialog will be the heading 'Cookies' and the settings you choose should be marked by clicking the radio button on the left.

In Netscape, go to 'Edit' and choose 'Preferences…' from the drop down menu. From the Preferences dialog, click on 'Advanced'. On the bottom right will be the heading Cookies, and underneath the options, one of which should be selected.

Security

Internet shopping can only work if you have a credit card, debit card or charge card, or some sort of arrangement whereby vendors can be paid electronically. But people are reluctant to give away their credit card details to a machine that will transmit the details halfway round the world.

And can you blame them? Contrary to what some might have you believe, the Internet is not a bomb-proof fortress. There have been numerous examples of fraud carried out on the Internet, and as quickly as one hole is plugged, another seems to gape open.

But let's get it in perspective. Users of credit cards are notoriously lax in their everyday 'conventional' (i.e. non-Internet) business. When we buy goods at a shop counter and pay with a credit card, frequently the salesperson doesn't bother to check that the signatures on the card and the receipt are the same.

We can all cite examples when we could have signed the slip 'Donald Duck' and nobody would have noticed. And what do we do with the receipt which contains, amongst other things, our credit card number and expiry date? Walk out of the shop and chuck it on the floor. Wander around any supermarket car park and you're sure to find someone's credit card details on a discarded till receipt. Make sure it's not yours.

Credit card forgery is a huge problem in everyday life. Probably the safest place to use your plastic is on the Net, providing you take sensible precautions.

When eating in a restaurant and paying with a credit card, the waiter takes your card and disappears with it for several minutes. He could be copying the number.

Paying by credit card (not debit card or charge card) usually gives you extra protection, but only on goods currently costing over UK£100. If your credit card is used fraudulently on the Internet, you are not responsible for the bill, neither is your bank – that is the responsibility of the supplier who is required to make adequate checks before supplying goods against a card number.

Some companies apply an excess for using a credit card.

Protection

The number of people making online purchases is increasing steadily, but the clever people feel that many would-be e-shoppers are reluctant to make online purchases because of the risk of fraud.

Here are a few ways to protect yourself:

e-shopsafe   http://www.e-shopsafe.co.uk/

The Partners Group offer a credit/debit card protection plan where up to six
cards can be protected against fraudulent use for a small annual sum. With this
scheme you have complete cover for all frauds made either online or offline as
a result of e-shopping.

At present, many credit card issuers hold the cardholders responsible for
a proportion of the claim. As many purchases are below this threshold, it could
prove expensive for the cardholder. If you are in any doubt, it's well worth
taking a look at this policy.

Web Traders Code of Practice   http://www.which.net/webtrader/
                                                          index.html

A UK trader displaying the Which? Web Trader logo on their website agrees
to follow the Which? Code of Practice which means you can shop online with
confidence. Which? have drawn up a code of practice for online traders to
encourage the highest possible standards and make sure that consumers are
treated fairly. Traders who agree to keep to this code can display the Which?
Web Trader logo.

The Which? Guarantee

The guarantee states, "We believe that giving your
credit card details to one of our traders over the
Internet is completely safe. But if you do lose out
because someone misuses your card, we will
reimburse the first £50 of your loss. Legally, the
credit card issuer must repay the rest."

Escrow service

If you buy from an individual, it is safest to use an escrow service. What happens is that when the buyer and vendor agree to a purchase, the buyer places the cost of the purchase into an escrow account. When the money is there, the service informs the vendor who dispatches the goods. When the buyer receives the goods s/he informs the account holder who releases the money.

There are several companies offering these services, particularly auction sites. For more information about Escrow, visit the Escrow website at *http://www.escrow.com/*

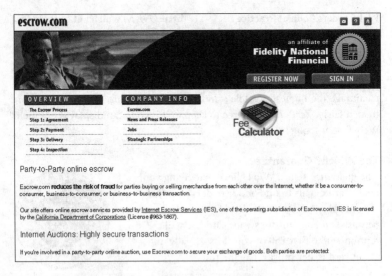

The Escrow home page

What else?
Virus Protection

Whether you're using your computer for online shopping or not, if you access the Internet, you really need a program to protect you against computer viruses. Like a virus caught by a human, a computer virus can spread to other computers and can have devastating effects on your system. A virus can corrupt programs and/or datafiles causing the program to not work properly and the data to become garbled. Some can even erase your hard disc.

I often wonder if the same people who write the anti-virus software are actually responsible for some of the viruses in the first place! Now there's a thought.

It's a great shame that so many intelligent people feel the need to apply their skills in such a negative way. But viruses exist and so you need to be protected against them, especially when downloading files from the Internet.

The Virus Information site will help you sort out what you've got and what you need to get rid of it and stay rid of it.

Apart from the information about the various viruses, there is also free software to download. The website is at *http://www.hitchhikers.net/antivirus/*

Also look at Sophos at *http://www.sophos.com/* for further information about their virus protection software. One of the most recent anti-virus protection solutions is by Panda Software and their website is at *http://www.pandasoftware.co.uk/*.

Precautions

The following precautions should keep you safe:

1. Only give your credit card details over a secure connection. You can check for a secure connection in three ways. First the Internet address will begin *https* rather than *http*. Secondly, a padlock symbol will appear at the bottom of your browser window and finally a message will pop up when you switch between a secure and a non-secure site, although this can be disabled. If the company you're considering buying from has a secure connection, the fact will be emblazoned on the home page of their site.

2. Do not buy from anyone other than a reputable outlet. Giving away your credit card details to a back-street outfit run by a couple of characters of dubious background is asking for trouble. If what you want to buy is legitimate, buy it from a legitimate outlet. This includes buying from a site based on a free web address. A decent company will pay the small fee to set up their own domain. A reputable outlet will also supply their address and telephone number on the website.

3. Avoid buying from overseas companies if possible. They're not dishonest, but if something does go wrong it's much harder to sort it out if they're on the other side of the world and don't even speak the same language.

4. Never send credit card details by email. Email is not a secure service and is easily intercepted. If the company you wish to purchase from is worthwhile purchasing from, they will have a secure service. If they haven't, buy elsewhere. Even sending part of the number with one mailing and the rest with another mailing is not wise.

Your rights

The point to remember when buying over the Internet is that you have exactly the same consumer rights as you would have if you were buying in the high street.

The law in the UK is quite explicit: anything you purchase must be of merchantable quality. In other words is must be safe, free from any defects however caused and sufficiently durable to be able to do the job for which it was designed. Secondly, it must be fit for the purpose for which it was designed. Finally it must be as described.

But remember, this is UK law and it applies to UK companies. In some cases it may also apply to the rest of the EEC, but you should be aware that it doesn't necessarily apply to goods or services purchased from other parts of the world.

Where to complain

If you do have a problem with an Internet purchase, your first course of action is to contact the supplier immediately. Failure to do this may adversely affect your rights to redress at a later stage. If the supplier claims the item must have been damaged in transit, that's fine, but it's the supplier's responsibility to sort that out with the carrier. You still have the right to refuse goods that are not in good condition, regardless of how, where or why the damage occurred. If the goods are faulty, ask for a refund or a replacement. Do not agree to having a repair carried out. Remember, you will not have lost your right to reject the item just because you've signed a form accepting it.

If you do feel a complaint against a supplier is not being followed up appropriately, contact a consumer advice centre.

Office of Fair Trading	*http://www.oft.gov.uk/*
Direct Marketing Association	*http://www.dma.org.uk/*
Mail Order Protection Scheme	*http://www.mops.org.uk/*
Periodical Publishers Association	*http://www.ppa.org.uk/*
Mail Order Traders Association	*malcolmlandau@compuserve.com/*
Ministry of Commerce	*http://www.moc.govt.nz/*
Consumers Institute	*http://www.consumer.org.nz/*

Prevention is better than cure

Nobody wants to fall foul of a fraud, and although there are ways to redress, it's better not to get caught in the first place. You can find out about rogue traders at the Public Eye at *http://www.thepubliceye.com/* and the National Fraud Information Centre at *http://www.fraud.org/*. You could try BizRate at *http://www.bizrate.com/* which features reviews by consumers about businesses.

Tax

Most countries have yet to haul their taxation requirements into the 21st Century to fully take into account international online purchasing. There are basically three types of tax that you should be aware of. The names given to the taxes and the rates, as well as the products to which they apply, vary from country to country.

Product Tax

When you buy goods you will usually be required to pay some form of tax based on the product's value. In the UK this is called VAT, in the US it's State Tax. If you bring goods into a country the chances are you'll have to pay the tax on their value. Be aware of this and calculate the cost of the item before you buy. The tax will normally be paid on receipt of the goods.

In the UK, books, food and children's clothes are not subject to VAT.

Excise Duty

This is an additional tax payable on goods such as tobacco, alcohol and perfume. When you buy these goods abroad you will be charged at the local rate and payment will normally be on receipt of the goods.

Customs Duty

When bringing goods into a country you'll normally have to pay Customs Duty on it. How much will depend on the products and the country.

In many cases, the shopper can ignore the whole issue because it's already taken care of by the powers that be.

Goods bought within the EEC and imported into another EEC country are not subject to Customs Duty.

The whole system seems to break down when it comes to buying software online, and this includes both programs and files that are paid for. Because the item doesn't go through customs, nobody knows you've imported it and so it's left to the individual to declare it. As software is regarded as a service there is no Customs Duty payable, but you should pay VAT on it. I wonder how many calls the VATman gets during a typical week?

The future

In this business, crystal ball gazing is not to be recommended. Not only is the technology moving very rapidly, it also changes direction very rapidly. A concept which may be on the horizon today, may never come to fruition because something else has rendered it obsolete whilst still unborn.

Ordering the weekly food on the Internet can save a considerable amount of time, but it is not always easy to find what you're looking for and then the time you would have spent going to the shop is spent instead sitting in front of a computer. When I visit my local supermarket personally, I always pick up a couple of cartons of fresh juice. I always buy the same and I recognise it from the size of the container, its weight (by 'feel' rather than a known quantity) and colour. I have a vague notion of what it might cost, but that's about it. Trying to pick that particular product online from a written list of 20 other similar products was so difficult that I resorted to raiding the dustbin to retrieve the old carton so that I could copy the description.

The major development will be in the quality of software that we will use to shop. Picking products from a list is not satisfactory, but virtual reality 3D shopping is already available and just around the corner. Once online, you push your virtual shopping trolley up and down virtual aisles and pick products from virtual shelves. It's much easier, far more friendly and when that technology becomes widespread, then e-commerce will really take off.

But to download that type of software so that it will run at a sensible speed needs faster lines of communication. In other words, you're not going to get real-time virtual reality down a conventional telephone line.

The day is fast approaching when we will all need digital phone lines.

Shopping Around

Just as it pays to shop around in the high street, so you should look at different Internet shopping sites to secure the best price. Interestingly, shopping around for high street prices can actually cost you more than you save. Comparing paint prices, for example, might involve driving to three or four stores which could be several miles apart. Phoning the stores is an alternative but that too can be time consuming and costly. You could find that it would have been cheaper to have simply bought the paint at the first shop you visited. The cost of the petrol used to drive around (not to mention time), or the cost of telephone calls could work out far more than the small saving made.

Internet shopping is different. It almost always pays to shop around and it doesn't take long. The only cost incurred is going to be a slightly longer Internet call whilst you're online to the various websites which stock the product you want to buy.

Best buys

Some sites make online window shopping even easier as they compare prices on different websites for a huge number of products. These sites offer users the chance to find vendors selling given products at the most competitive prices. Most are US sites, some are UK sites and some cover both.

Bottom Dollar   **http://www.bottomdollar.com/**
Bottom Dollar is one of the best examples of a site which will compare prices. This US site will get you the best price for computer hardware and software,

electronics, games, office equipment, gifts and household items. There's also a section called 'lifestyle' and information about online auctions.

Once you're into the site, choose the category you want and enter the product into the search engine. You'll soon get a list of the products you requested with prices and locations. There is a link to the online stores, giving full descriptions of the products.

Buy   http://www.buy.co.uk/

This UK site is divided into 'Personal' and 'Business'. The Personal site features the best deals for utilities including dual-fuel, electricity, gas, water and mobile phones.

e-lephant is a clever feature that will remind you when certain stores have their sales as well as supplying personal reminders about birthdays. Choose the information you want to be reminded about and you'll be emailed at appropriate times. Other e-lephant emails include newspaper offers.

The Business side of the site offers big-business discounts for small businesses. You'll need to register, but large discounts are available.

Buy Buddy   http://www.buybuddy.com/

The main feature of this US site is computers, in the broadest sense of the word. Anything and everything which is even remotely associated with computers is covered and includes pre-built systems, components, upgrades and software, but also extends to laptops, palmtops and organisers.

Use this site for technical comparisons between products.

Apart from comparing prices, and giving the lowest for your chosen product, Buy Buddy can also provide technical comparisons between rival products.

Computer Prices   **http://www.computerprices.co.uk/**
This UK site offers pricing comparisons for pre-built PCs and components. You can customise how the results will be displayed in several ways, including choosing to have the prices displayed with or without VAT, and to show mail

Use this site to find the best deals for a particular product.

order and/or online retailers. Products can also be shown in alphabetical order by distributor, or according to price.

A particularly useful section is the discussion area which shows the best deals for particular types of product, and also outlines what you should look for when choosing a product of that type.

Even Better   **http://www.evenbetter.com/**
This site was formerly known as Deal Pilot and it can still be accessed at *http://www.dealpilot.com/*. You can search out the best prices for books, music and movies, but even better is Even Better Express: a program that takes about a minute to download and performs the searches even faster.

Once downloaded and installed, Even Better Express will save you time and money when you shop online. It can be accessed from your desktop and lets you start price comparisons instantly whilst you are browsing any leading online shop.

My Simon   **http://www.mysimon.com/**

Another US site that doesn't actually sell anything but has links to hundreds of online stores which do. Simon will provide you with the best prices for books, music and films, computer hardware and software, hobbies (which includes a link to 'cigars'!) holidays, home & garden, office supplies, sports and toys. It also finds the best financial deals.

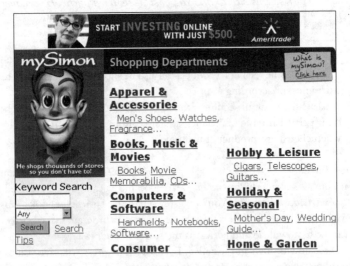

This colourful cartoon character could save you time and money

Price Offers   **http://www.priceoffers.co.uk/**

Even if you don't want to actually shop on the Internet, this site will arm you with all the current money saving offers at your high street stores. There are links to all the top UK supermarkets and stores including ASDA, Boots, Co-op, HMV, Iceland, Morrisons, Safeway, Sainsbury, Somerfield, Superdrug, Tesco, Waitrose, Wickes and Woolworths. You can get latest prices and special deals with deadlines. One area lists all of the current BOGOF (Buy One Get One Free) deals with prices and expiry dates. There is also the 'Our choice current best deals' page which features even more money saving bargains in the high street.

Price Scan   **http://www.pricescan.com/**

Once you're into this US site, enter the type of product you want to get the best price for. Categories include books, computers, consumer electronics, video movies, music, office equipment, sports equipment, video games and watches. You'll get a list of the best prices for the product you chose and links to the dealers who are offering it at those prices.

Robo Shopper   **http://www.roboshopper.com/**

This site lists the suppliers of given products and provides links to take you directly to the supplier's website. Categories include books (by author, title or keyword), music (by artist or song title), movies/video, computer hardware and software, electronics (including cameras) and toys and games.

Scoot   **http://www.scoot.co.uk/**

Scoot is a general-purpose search tool which can be used to locate, amongst other things, UK cinemas and theatres. Once you've located a venue near to you, you can find out what's on and book tickets online.

All of these sites can save you a great deal of time as well as money.

Shop Genie   http://www.shopgenie.com/

This superb UK site will search out the best prices for books, music, films, games and computer hardware and software. Begin by entering the manufacturer and/or the product name and you'll get a list of the best prices with links to the online store and further information about the product.

Shopsmart   http://www.shopsmart.com/

Shopsmart has recently transferred from *http://www.shopguide.co.uk/* and has added more shops and more functions. You can compare prices of books, magazines, clothes, computer hardware and software, electronics, food and drink, home and garden, music, videos, DVDs and video games in seconds. There are also links to over 1400 secure UK shops.

Smartshop   http://www.smartshop.com/

Not to be confused with Shopsmart, this US site provides you with a shopping engine to compare prices of books, music, video, photographic equipment, baby bits, computer hardware and software, consumer electronics, toys, watches, flowers and gifts.

You can search for and sort products by multiple criteria – a feature unmatched by any other comparison-shopping site.

Home Shopping Channel   **http://www.shop-i.co.uk/**

This shopping site which can also be accessed by entering *http://www.shop-tv.co.uk/* in the address bar, is a UK only TV and online shopping service.

> *You can also find this service on ON Digital, Cable and Satellite TV.*

To browse through the extensive range of products available, choose from the shops listed or select a category from the index on the left of the screen.

If you're in a real hurry, use the product search at the top of the page, enter the name of the product you're interested in and the search engine will find it for you.

Shop indexes

Some of these sites give prices, but most connect you to other websites that sell the product or products you want to buy. The best indexes are in three or more levels. For example, the first page might give general categories like 'Home'. The next level will give types of products for the home (furniture, kitchen utensils etc.) and then in the next level you are given a range of shops that stock that type of product. Some indexes go further and break down the categories yet further before giving you a final list. Most of these sites also offer a search feature as well as an index. This enables you to enter a word or phrase, and the system will search for stores that stock that particular item.

British Shopping   http://www.british-shopping.com/

With links to over 2000 UK stores, British Shopping is a good starting point for UK and Western European shoppers. There are about 80 categories in the index so when you choose the category you want, you're not bogged down with thousands of irrelevant results.

Buyer's Index   http://www.buyersindex.com/

The Buyer's Index has links to both US and UK websites. The search engine is effective and it returns a list that contains a lot of useful information like where the company ships from and to, what languages are spoken by the staff and any returns policy used by the company.

Internet Shopper   http://www.internetshopper.com/

This US site lists suppliers of a range of products including books, music, films, computer software and hardware, financial services, toys and games, collectibles and gifts (including flowers and chocolates).

My Taxi   http://www.mytaxi.co.uk/

My Taxi has a good finder in which you can search for products, but if you fail, there is an email link to help.

The 'Departments' link takes you to a long list of categories in which you can search for accessories, auctions & art, auto, business, books & press, fashion & clothes, finance & property, food & drink, games, gifts, health & beauty, high-tech, home & garden, ice & snow, jewels & watches, jobs & training, kids, babies & toys, music & film, pets, phones & cameras, sport & fitness, tickets and travel.

The search engine is very fast and it provides a sensible list of sites to choose from.

Shop Now   http://www.shopnow.com/

This site has links to over 15,000 stores in over 30 categories. There are additional links to shops currently promoting free offers and hot deals. You can also compare prices and search for a particular store.

Shopping Sites   http://www.shopping-sites.com/

This site reads like a magazine in parts and links to both UK and US sites. The index looks rather like a hierarchical file structure, but works well.

Shopping Zone   http://shopping.lineone.net/

This is probably the definitive site for information about Web shopping. The Shopping Zone lists most shops that offer online shopping and rates them according to which services they offer. Details about secure payments are listed and other services are given a star rating.

The information about online services is thoughtfully divided into categories such as banks, bookshops, computers, department stores, music, fashion and videos.

Shops on the Net   http://www.shopsonthenet.com/

This huge site has links to well over 6,500 online stores mainly US and UK which have been carefully divided into categories, which include accessories (jewellery, jags, sunglasses), arts & crafts, antiques, auctions, automotive, books, cards, children (clothes, toys, education), chocolate, classified ads, clothes & shoes, collectibles, computing, drinks & tobacco, electrical goods, employment, films (DVDs, videos), flowers, food, home, insurance, jewellery, gifts, health & beauty, media (news, magazines), music, paintings, pensions, personal communications (mobile phones, pagers, radios), pets & animals, property, special events (weddings, Christmas), sports and toys & games.

Clicking on one of the links takes you to the appropriate store, but you can also search for shops selling particular products. All of the shops featured on Shops on the Net carry a description telling whether they have a secure connection, what country they work from and where they are prepared to deliver to. You're free to browse around this site, but it's best to sign up. This site can also be accessed at *http://www.sotn.co.uk/*.

Yell   **http://www.yell.com/**
This shopping site run by Yellow Pages lists UK stores under categories including books, clothing, office, software, finance, flowers, food, games, health, home & garden, sport and transport. Clicking on the link of your choice takes you to a page listing the shops in that category.

You can also get to Shop Yell by visiting *http://www.shopyell.co.uk/* and clicking on the shopping link.

Searching for shops

Search engines tend to be general purpose tools, but many have indexes which can steer you to a particular area, before searching for a particular product.

If you're going to use a search engine to find a product, learn how to refine your search. If you just enter the name of a product, say 'shoes', you're going to get endless pages of results about buying shoes but intermingled with that will be sites about where they're made, how they're made and very likely who make them. In addition you'll find the search engine will return sites about mountain shoes, walking shoes and evening shoes. You name it, it'll be there. Clearly there will be more information than you can possibly manage and most of it won't be of any interest to you. Refining the search by being more specific about what you want will provide you with a more manageable amount of information to plough through.

The theory behind refining a search is the same for all search engines, but they each have their own way of doing it, which is often peculiar to that search engine alone.

 There are some really good help pages on this site.

The following sites are all well known for their searching abilities, and have links to shopping sites.

All the Web   **http://www.alltheweb.com/**

This site claims access to a staggering 300,000,000 web pages. I wonder who counted them? There are links to over 1 million MP3 files (see the section on Music) but there is also a very powerful and fast search facility where you can enter the name of a product.

I searched for 'coffee', but to ensure I didn't get a lot of sites about how coffee is grown and who transports it, I entered 'online shopping' and 'must include' in the filter section. The result was a list of online coffee shops which can be visited by clicking on the appropriate links.

It's worth spending some time carefully entering your query into the search engine as you can quickly locate a large number of stores stocking the items you want to buy, without also having to wade through countless references to sites that don't.

Alta Vista
http://www.altavista.com/

The home page of the Alta Vista website has several links, including one labelled 'Shopping'. Clicking on this link takes you to a page listing various shop types and products. Clicking on one of these links then takes you to a further page offering specific products. There are links to enable you to compare prices and to compare rival products.

Ask Jeeves
http://www.ask.co.uk/

Jeeves is the name of the butler and you can ask him questions in English. 'Where can I buy a bow-tie?' resulted in a list of three UK online shops. A useful feature of this fun site is the information about safe shopping. The main feature of this site is its search engine, but you can also click on a category before starting a search to narrow down the search area.

Jeeves should be able to provide you with the answer

Excite   **http://www.excite.com/**

This website has a variety of links to take you to various topics, including shopping. Once you're in the shopping area, you can either follow further links or enter a keyword to perform a search.

Fish 4   **http://www.fish4.co.uk/**

This UK site can be tediously slow at times, but it's well presented. Click on the 'Fish4shopping' link or click on the drop-down-menu and choose 'Shopping' to get an index with about 20 categories. Clicking on a category gives a list of company logos which will take you directly to the stores.

There are also links to cheap flights and car hire.

Google   **http://www.google.com/**

When you open this site, you are immediately presented with a panel in which to enter your search word, without any advertising clutter around it that is so familiar with other sites. When you've entered your word or phrase you can click on one of two buttons. 'Google Search' takes you to a page of results listing mainly UK and US online stores, although there are a few European ones amongst them. The list of shops includes a brief description and a link to take you to the store's home page.

Clicking on the alternative 'I Feel Lucky' button takes you directly to a site which hopefully stocks the product you are searching for. I entered 'trousers' and was taken to a gentlemen's outfitters.

If you prefer, you can click on the 'Browse Web Pages' link to take you to the index of 15 categories, each with 3 associated links. Clicking on one of these takes you to further categories until eventually you reach the online store which stocks the item you're looking for.

Hot Bot   http://www.hotbot.com/

The Home & Family link in the Hot Bot directory takes you to a page of links which includes one entitled 'Shopping'. Clicking on this takes you to an index which points to over 32,000 online shops, including over 2,000 clothing stores.

Look Smart   http://www.looksmart.com/

Clicking on the 'Shopping' link takes you to a list of links including major stores & malls, books & art, cards & gifts, clothes & accessories, computers/ electronics, food & wine, health & beauty, home, garden & auto, music & film, sporting goods, toys & hobbies, weddings & bridal and services. There are also buying guides, consumer advice and a classified ads section.

Lycos   http://www.lycos.com/

When you get to the Lycos Home Page, the Shopping link takes you to an index of thousands of categorised shops which you can work through to track down the products you want to buy. Other features include a useful section where prices are compared and products and stores are reviewed.

Northern Light   http://www.northernlight.com/

This site has a very powerful and fast search engine. Choose either 'Power Search' or 'Business Search', enter a word or a phrase and select the category. I entered 'coffee' in the search panel and selected 'Food & Beverage'. The resulting list of mainly US online stores includes a brief description of the store and a link to take you to the shop of your choice.

Searchalot   http://www.searchalot.com/

This is an excellent site for beginning a shopping spree. Searchalot has links to over 11,000 online stores including over 270 shopping malls. Once you've clicked on the Shopping link, click on the type of product (category) you wish to search for and a list of stores, each with a brief but adequate description, will be displayed. Click on the shop and begin. Brilliantly simple.

Shopfind   http://www.shopfind.com/

Part of Yahoo's website, Shopfind can also be accessed by going to *http://www.yahoo.com/* and clicking on the link to Shopping. Once you're in this site, you can make a search or go to the index which includes apparel, accessories & shoes, arts & collectibles, automotive parts & accessories, baby care, bath & beauty, books, computers, electronics, flowers, gifts & occasions, food & beverages, health & wellness, home & garden, jewellery & watches, movies & video, music, office supplies, sports & recreation, toys, games & hobbies and travel.

UK Plus   http://www.ukplus.co.uk/

This is a good website to access hundreds of UK stores. The index links to major shops including arts & crafts, auctions, books & catalogues, Brits abroad, classified, clothes & footwear, computer games, computers, electrical goods, fitness & health, food & drink, gifts, home & DIY, kids, mobile phones & accessories, motoring & cycling, music, personal care, pets, services, sports & leisure, stores & malls, videos & DVD, white goods and work & office.

Yahoo   **http://www.yahoo.com/**

When you enter Yahoo's site, click on the Shopping link to take you to Shopfind, which can also be accessed through *http://www.shopfind.com/.*

Under one roof

Some stores specialise in selling a fairly narrow range of goods, and then there are those that sell just about everything. Like real-life department stores, having everything under one roof can be a mixed blessing. You don't have so far to travel, but you don't always get the choices within a given category.

Big Save   **http://www.bigsave.com**

You can get up to 70% off a big range of branded goods and services. Products include electronics, computers, sports and outdoors, jewellery & gifts, home & garden, toys & games and insurance. From time to time there are special offers like a free top 50 CD when you spend over £20.

Browser Buys   **http://www.browserbuys.co.nz/**

This New Zealand site has an equivalent US site, with Australia and UK coming online soon. This is just like a department store except you can visit all of it without leaving your home. It's all here - arts & crafts, automotive & marine, banking, finance & insurance, books, newspapers & magazines, children, collectibles, computers & software, education & training, electronics, entertainment & leisure, farming & horticulture, fashion & jewellery, food & drink, garden & outdoor, gifts & hobbies, health & beauty, home improvement, home living, office supplies, pets & pet care, real estate, sport, toys & games and travel & tourism.

Fashionbot   http://www.fashionbot.com/

This shopping bot will search through all of the stores in the Arcadia Group. These include Burtons, Dorothy Perkins, Evans, Hawkshead, Principles, Principles for Men, Top Man and Top Shop.

It's quite friendly as it lets you enter a real phrase like *a red shirt for a man*. Enter the phrase and press Enter and the bot will search through all of the stores and display a list of likely results. Click on one of the results and it will take you to the appropriate page of the shop selling that product. If you like it you can then buy it online.

Fubu   http://www.fubu.com/

This US site is one of the newest and largest shopping sites which has just about everything under one roof. The site has lots of flashing lights and funky sounds which tends to make it quite slow to use.

IQVC   http://www.iqvc.com/

This is the Internet branch of the TV shopping channel. The Quality, Value and Convenience store carries a large range of items which can either be searched for or found via an index system. All products carry a picture and description and when you place an item in your shopping basket, the picture is displayed there too, so you know exactly what you've got when you get to the checkout.

UK shoppers should access this site at *http://www.qvc.co.uk/*.

Loot

http://www.loot.com/

The online version of the advertising paper, this site sells many used items from individuals under these headings: transport, computers & business, household, accommodation & property, hobbies & sport, sound & vision, travel, jobs and personal.

Loot is mainly small adverts from individuals rather than companies.

Netmarket

http://www.netmarket.com/

This store offers a good search facility where you can look for either a particular item, a brand name or a model number. You can also track down your purchase via an index system. Netmarket stocks over 800,000 products.

Priceline

http://www.priceline.com/

Visit this US site and name your price on Airline Tickets, Hotel Rooms, Rental Cars, New Cars and Home Financing. When you've decided what you want and how much you want to pay, Priceline will attempt to secure the deal with another company.

Ready to Shop

http://www.ready2shop.co.uk/

This online store is mainly for women's clothes, but also includes beauty and health products, accessories and clothes for children. The site opens with a brilliant graphic menu dividing the products first into rough categories (e.g. Women's Clothes) but within that category are further divisions (e.g. skirts, tops, trousers etc.).

This site is specifically aimed at women and includes some clever features which women should enjoy. Of particular note is the Match2Me feature. You need to register (free) and you'll be asked to enter details about yourself (height, build, skin type etc.), as well as personal likes and dislikes. When you begin shopping, you can ask the system to offer you clothes or beauty products that would or should be suited to you.

Shoppers Universe   http://www.shoppersuniverse.com/

To find a product from the huge stock, type in a keyword and you'll get a list of products available. You can preview one or more of the items listed and you'll get a small photograph with a title and a price. Clicking on the title will provide you with more details and a better picture. If size or colour is an issue, then you'll get the chance to choose what you want before opting to buy online.

Virtual Shopping Malls

Rather like shopping malls, virtual malls have a number of shops under a common umbrella. Virtual malls also have another feature in common with real malls – some are better than others.

Barclay Square   http://www.barclaysquare.com/

This shopping mall is operated by Barclays Bank in the UK and has direct links to a select group of shops including The Book People, Gamez Zone, ChocExpress, The NME CD Store, 2001 Appliances, Interflora, What Video & TV, On Line Hi-Fi Store, Francis Frith Classic Prints and T3 Go!Gadget.

Easy Shopping Mall   http://www.easyshoppingmall.com/

When you enter this US Mall, clicking on the category you wish to track (art, automotive, business, children, clothing/accessories, computer/Internet, electronics, food, gifts, health, home & garden, magazines/newspapers/cards, movies/music/books, pets, smoking/accessories, sports, telecommunications, toys, travel, freebies, games, contests) will take you to an index of associated shops. Each shop has a brief description, and clicking on the link takes you to the shop's home page.

Fashionmall   http://www.fashionmall.com/

This huge virtual shopping mall links to several hundred shops which specialise in fashion clothes and accessories for men, women, teenagers and young children. There are many top high street names like Esprit as well as many who may not be so familiar.

As well as the stores listed as stocking fashion clothes for men, women and children, there are also departments listed as Jewellery, Hosiery and Bridal.

All stores have secure online shopping, preferably using a Visa card.

Home Town   http://www.hometown.co.uk/

Don't miss the special offers from almost 600 merchants. You can join an emailing list by registering and get up-to-the-minute news of the latest bargains. With 567 sites available here already, it will be surprising if you don't find something which takes your fancy!

iMall   http://www.imall.com/

There are over 1000 online shops within the online mall which can also be accessed at *http://www.excitestores.com/*, and the list of products covered is as extensive as you would expect from an actual shopping mall. Products include:

art, antiques, appliances, audio, automotive audio, books, business equipment, camping, clothing, computers, dolls, electronics, entertainment, fashion, food & beverages, fitness, furniture, gifts, health & beauty, hobbies, home & family, music, personal care, pets, restaurants, sports, sweets, toys, travel and video. All of the stores provide online shopping.

Mother Mall   http://www.mothermall.com/
This US site has links to over 10,000 online stores. Products can be entered into the search engine or you can go through an index system which takes you through various levels until you get to the type of shop you want. A useful feature on this site is comparing prices of books, toys, music and movies.

Safestreet   http://www.safestreet.co.uk/
When you arrive at the Safestreet Mall, you can either enter the name of a shop, or enter a keyword or a location into the search engine to find the product you're looking for. Alternatively, you can click on one of the nine categories (audio/visual, business, children, fashion, health & beauty, food, home & gifts, motoring, sport & leisure) and work your way through an index system until you get to the store or product you want. Stores are mainly UK based.

Scottish Bargains   http://www.shopping.scotland.net/
This Scottish website has a wide selection of goods which can be bought online. The products are divided into music & videos, sport, travel, food & drink, finance, flowers & gifts, books, games and clothing. Oh yes, there's also a section called Scottish Shops which has links to shops like The Rabbie Burns Shop, The Loch Ness Shop, The Tartan Shop and Chaude Shetland Knitwear.

Shop Now   http://www.shopnow.com/

Formerly known as the Internet Mall, Shop Now has links to well over 10,000 stores covering just about every type of product you can imagine. Once you've entered the Mall, choose your category (clothes, cars, health etc.) and then choose either the stores with the best goods, those with the lowest prices or local stores. Each store has a brief description and a link to take you to the store's website. Online shopping is available and all stores carry a link to get you back to the Mall.

Shopping Centre   http://www.shoppingcentre.net/

You'll need to register on your first visit and log on for future visits to the Shopping Centre. You should also enter your location (either UK, Europe or World) to get stores near(ish) to where you live. The site is laid out rather like a department store with sections for health & beauty, gifts, audio/visual, toys & games, books and home & garden.

Spree   http://www.spree.com/

You'll need to register on this site, but once you have, you'll get a list of some of the top names in the high street, with more coming online regularly. Many of the stores offer discounts or cashback for shopping online through Spree, and the amount of discount is thoughtfully shown in the index.

Tradezone   http://w3.tradezone.co.uk/

This UK website sells thousands of different products in hundreds of categories from scores of companies. You can search for a specific item or browse through the stock list which is laid out rather like a disc directory structure. The microscopic print and poor contrast between text and background make it a little difficult to follow at times, but the site is worth visiting.

UK Shops **http://www.ukshops.co.uk/**

This online mall is even laid out like a mall with stores on several floors. You enter the store on the ground floor and get a plan of the mall showing where each store is located. You need to take the virtual lift to the other floors to be able to visit the other stores. There are some big names here including Marks & Spencer.

The huge number of graphics means the site is very attractive and user-friendly, but is sometimes a little slow. It's also a little irksome having to go up and down the lift, but there are links to other areas such as travel and property.

Zercon **http://www.zercon.com/**

The simple but effective search engine enables you to easily locate clothes for both women and men by either type (shirt, skirt, etc.) or label. When the search

is complete, you'll get a list of items. Click on the one you're interested in for more details including a picture. If you still like it, choose the size and colour and pay for it online using any of the usual credit/debit cards.

Online department stores

Many high street department stores have their own online store which offers customers the chance to buy the same goods, but without leaving their home. Arrangements for payment at the online stores are normally the same as for the real store. If the real shop provides a store card it will usually be accepted by the online store.

Bloomingdales   http://www.bloomingdales.com/

The online branch of this huge US store features all the usual departments with online ordering for all products. You can freely move between departments adding to your virtual trolley. When you've had enough, go to the checkout and pay with any of the usual plastic cards.

There are also competitions and special features like ideas for wedding presents.

Debenhams   http://www.debenhams.co.uk/

Debenhams regularly feature special offers to coincide with special occasions. To see other items, click on the 'Gifts' button, and a drop-down menu gives you the choice of gifts for men, women, children or home. When you've selected the category, an index of suitable types of product will be displayed and from that you can choose the exact gift. Each item has a small written description and a good size and clear photograph of it. More detail can be obtained by clicking on the image before deciding to buy.

> *When you get to the checkout, you can remove items before you pay.*

J C Penny   http://www.jcpenny.com/
If you've got the catalogue, you can enter the stock number and order and pay for the product online. If you haven't, then you can search through the stock online. Items placed in the shopping trolley are taken to the checkout and can be paid for using a credit or debit card. There are also special weekly features to look out for.

John Lewis Partnership   http://www.johnlewis.co.uk/
This is the online version of the UK store that claims to have never knowingly undersold in 60 years. At present there are only a few products that can be purchased online and these are small gifts which usually featured at a particular time or for a particular occasion like Mother's Day. You can wander around the rest of the departments and decide what you want to buy before actually visiting the shop in person. If you want to buy online you must register and payment can be made with either a JLP Storecard, Visa, MasterCard or American Express.

The site also includes links to Waitrose (the food branch of the Partnership) and to an area outlining the business achievements of the company.

Macy's   http://www.macys.com/

Everything you'd expect to find at Macy's in the US is also at Macy's online. The store index lists At home, Men's, Women's and Children's Young Attitude, as well as jewellery, lingerie, cosmetics, fragrance and accessories. Each category links to further categories, so that by the time you get to the products you want, there are only a dozen or so examples because all the items you don't want have been removed, leaving the few that you could consider. You can also search for a particular brand of product or type of product, with the option of choosing a price range. You'll get a list of those available, all with pictures, and clicking on the picture will give further details about it.

Cleverly, when you ask for more details about a product, another product is often displayed as well. I was looking at a dress watch and found a couple that I liked so clicked for further details. When the larger picture and fuller description of one of the watches were displayed, alongside was a pair of matching earrings which were offered for sale. How's that for marketing!

Marks & Spencer   http://www.marks-and-spencer.co.uk/

The first time you visit the site you should register and on subsequent visits you'll be required to log-in. You can shop online for gifts, clothes and for the home. The site is well organised with good pictures and descriptions of the products. If you select an item that is not in stock, you'll be informed immediately.

Payment can be made using a credit card , or you can use Switch or Delta debit cards and, of course, their own storecard.

Wal-Mart Online   **http://www.wal-mart.com**

This huge US store stocks just about everything you could possibly want for your home, car, holiday, family or your person. All the products are categorised into one of 25 main themes. The prices are well below high street store prices.

Zoom   **http://www.zoom.co.uk/**

This 'all-in-one' website features some of the top names in High Street fashion including Racing Green, Top Shop, Principles and Hawkshead.

The index provides links to music, gizmos, fashion shop, cars, gifts, household, mobile phones, auctions and wine.

Collective buying

This method of buying is already in use in the US and in Sweden, but is now becoming available in other big Internet markets such Europe and Australasia. The theory is simple: a single person buying a single item will have to pay a premium for it. But if several people can collectively make a bulk-purchase, the price will be forced down. This is also called co-buying.

Adabra   **http://www.adabra.com/**

This is the UK's first Community Shopping site. The site opens with a sort of menu pointing you to the various types of product available. These are mostly electrical or electronic products such as refrigerators, cameras, TVs, computers and phones. Once you've gone through the menus and through to the range of products and then to the final product you wish to purchase, you'll see five pieces of information about it.

The first is the normal retail price, the second in the current price, followed by its lowest possible price and finally the two dates between which the product is available – called the sell-spell. You make an offer for the product based on its current price, but hopefully the price will fall to the lower level by the time you actually pay for it.

LetsBuyIt   **http://www.letsbuyit.com/**

LetsBuyIt offers everything from kitchen appliances to home entertainment systems to holidays.

You begin by registering and then choosing a category from motor accessories, computer & IT, fragrances & accessories, home & garden, home electronics, kids & toys, sports & leisure and domestic appliances. When you find something you like, you can choose it at the current price and you effectively agree to buy at that price. But if more people also buy that item, the price could come down.

For example, I chose a Car Navigation kit, the recommended retail price of which was UK£850. When I first saw it, 1 person had already agreed to buy one and the price had come down to UK£800, which was the price I agreed to buy it for. When I bought it there was a message on the screen saying that only two more people (after me) were needed to buy it to take the price down to the next level which was UK£780. Evidently two others did agree to buy one because the price did drop to the promised amount. Had nobody else bought one after those two customers, the price I would have paid would have been UK£780 not the UK£800 I had agreed to. But more people did buy (in this case a further three more) and I ended up paying UK£750 (as had the person who originally agreed to buy it for UK£850). Had more people bought it, the price I finally paid could have come down still further. LetsBuyIt can only deliver co-buy products within the UK.

Freebies

You don't have to pay for everything you see on the 'Net. There are thousands of free gifts out there and registering with Club Freeshop at *http://www.freeshop.com/* will provide you with regular emails pointing out the best free gifts and trial offers.

Food Shopping

I can spend any amount of time browsing around music shops, computer shops and car showrooms, but top of my list of undesirable activities is food shopping. Followed closely by clothes shopping.

If, like me, you don't enjoy trundling round a supermarket with a shopping trolley that refuses to go where you want it to, being pushed and trodden on

Whenever I go to a supermarket and collect a trolley, I always wish I'd bought a can of oil with me.

by scores of other shoppers who are also fighting to keep their trolleys in order, Internet shopping may be for you.

Online supermarkets

In many countries there has been a gradual disappearance of the familiar high street supermarkets in favour of the so-called out-of-town shops. These large, bright stores with wide aisles and a much greater selection of products are far more pleasurable to shop in. Unfortunately, if you haven't got a car it's difficult to use them effectively. Many out-of-town stores have a bus service but it's not always easy to get on the bus if you've got four large bags of shopping and two children. Rather than visiting a store in person, Internet shopping lets you choose your weekly groceries from your home and have them delivered at your convenience.

Tesco   **http://www.tesco.co.uk/**

Whatever is available at a UK Tesco store can also be purchased over the Internet and will be delivered for a small fee. Tesco introduced online shopping in 1997 and provided customers who held a Tesco loyalty card with a free CD ROM which was used to set up their computer with a sort of inventory of items. Today, you can even order the CD online and register by visiting the website and clicking on 'Check to see if we deliver in your area'.

If there is a delivery service, you can register immediately by entering your name and any Tesco Club Card number. As by this stage you will have entered your postcode, the computer at Tesco will know which road you live in and will offer you all the possible houses, from which you pick your house.

You will also need to choose a password and enter it twice. The system will then generate a customer ID number which you will use for future logins.

Iceland   http://www.iceland.co.uk/

Not only can you order the weekly groceries online, but you can also buy a freezer to put it all in.

You'll need to check if Iceland deliver in your area and then register with them. Once you've registered you can start shopping.

When online shopping at Iceland, the contents of your shopping basket must total at least UK£40.

All the products are indexed so it's fairly easy to navigate around the store. Many products will carry one or more of about a dozen symbols which denote special offer, suitable for vegetarians, 3 for 2 etc.

Safeway   http://www.safeway.co.uk/

Although you can't actually shop online, you can search for meal ideas and generate a shopping list which you can take to a store.

You begin by choosing the main ingredient and/or type of meal (dinner, supper) and/or cuisine and/or cooking time. Click on the 'Meal Ideas' button on the right and you'll get a list of suitable meals. Clicking on the one you like the look of provides you with a recipe which can be printed out. Alongside each recipe is a button labelled 'Add to Shopping List'. Clicking on this adds the ingredients to a shopping list which can then be printed out and taken to the store.

Sainsbury's   **http://orderline.sainsburys.co.uk/**

With an emphasis on quality at reassuringly low prices, Sainbury's has been a feature of high streets for as long as I can remember.

One of my earliest memories was waiting outside Sainsbury's whilst Mum was shopping. At that time, Sainsbury's was a shop rather than a supermarket and they frequently had goods on marble tables in the window. Eggs were most common and they were arranged according to quality. A big sign spelt it out, 'Best English New-Laid Eggs'. Next to that, 'English New-Laid Eggs'. On the next table, 'New Laid Eggs', and right at the end it simply read, 'Eggs'.

The Sainsbury website offers customers the chance to order online but also gives other value-added features such as recipes and information about the Sainsbury reward card scheme.

This site can also be accessed at *http://www.sainsburystoyou.co.uk/.*

Somerfield   **http://www.somerfield.co.uk/**

Online shopping is only available in some parts of the UK, but even if you don't fall in one of their delivery areas, it's still worth visiting this site to find the latest bargains. There are also some great recipe ideas.

Waitrose   **http://www.waitrose.com/**

Waitrose is part of the John Lewis Partnership and their website carefully
follows the corporate image of quality goods and sensible prices. You can't do
your complete grocery shop at Waitrose but you can order and pay for some
goods like wine and flowers.

Find the best deals

Shopping is not just about actually buying goods. It's also about searching to
find the best products and the best prices. The Internet is a perfect tool for
research as it enables you to compare prices between several shops without
actually having to visit the shops in person.

Price Offers   **http://www.priceoffers.co.uk/**

Even if you don't want to actually shop on the Internet, this site will arm you
with all the current money saving offers at your high street stores. There are
links to all the top UK supermarkets and stores including ASDA, Boots, Co-
op, HMV, Iceland, Morrisons, Safeway, Sainsbury, Somerfield, Superdrug,
Tesco, Waitrose, Wickes and Woolworths. You can get latest prices and special
deals with deadlines. One area lists all of the current BOGOF (Buy One Get
One Free) deals with prices and expiry dates. There is also the 'Our choice
current best deals' page which features even more money saving bargains in the
high street.

Internet stores

There are a growing number of stores that are best known for their Internet presence. These all offer online shopping which is delivered either by their own staff or by courier.

Food   http://www.food.com/

This US site sells beverages, cookbooks, kitchenware and table wear, as well as a wide range of gourmet foods, speciality foods, meat and poultry, seafood and sweets. Look out for the recipes and tips like things to look for when buying certain foods.

Online Food Shopping   http://www.onlinefoodshopping.co.uk/

This is the UK's first website dedicated to Online Food Shopping. When you get into the site, choose the type of food you wish to buy by clicking on the appropriate button in the index and you'll get a selection of online stores specialising in that type of product. Clicking on the name of the store will take you to that store's website where you can place your order.

There's also a list of UK supermarkets.

Specialists

For me, shopping on the Internet means that rather than visiting one enormous store to buy everything, you can visit several specialist shops and buy a small number of products from each. It actually takes no longer than going to a single shop and you will find that in many cases you'll have a better selection of a particular product than you will find in a supermarket.

If you want to buy from lots of different stores, it's often better to buy larger quantities to make any carriage charges more cost-effective.

Bettys   **http://www.bettysbypost.com/**

This old Yorkshire based company sells tea, coffee, chocolates, cakes and seasonal specialities, including hampers.

Items bought from Betty's can also be sent as gifts. To make it easier, you can have up to three shopping baskets — two for you and another for gifts.

The selection is not huge, but it is very special and can be ordered online.

Fifth Sense   **http://www.fifthsense.com/**

This US company sells whole bean coffees, olives, nuts & snacks, chips, salsa, & dips, oils & vinegars, marinades, chutneys, pastas & sauces, hot sauces, spices & seasonings and condiments.

Everything can be ordered online and sent to almost anywhere.

Fresh Food Company   **http://www.freshfood.co.uk/**

If like me you find that the packaging tastes better than the contents of some supermarket products, take a trip to this site and buy fresh food that actually tastes of something. You can order fresh fish, fresh meat, fresh bread and organic pizzas from this online store.

There's an excellent online recipe section on the Fresh Food Company website.

Items can be searched for by entering a word into the search engine or browsing through the indexed list of products for sale.

Lobster   **http://www.lobster.co.uk/**

When a lobster was served to a well-known guest in a restaurant, he asked the waiter why it had only one claw. The waiter replied, "I believe it was in a fight, Sir". "Take it away", said the diner, "and bring me the winner".

Actually this site sells more than lobsters, but if it is a lobster you want you can buy online and get it delivered the following day if you live in London, or the day after that for anywhere else in the UK.

Carefully count the number of claws. (There should be two.)

The list of foods for sale include caviar and foie gras, champagne and fine wines, jams, marmalade and honey.

But lobsters seem to be the main item on sale and 'Lobster.co.uk' reflects this fact by including lobster recipes, lobster promotions, lobster questions and answers and lobster links (links to other sites that presumably also rank lobster high on their list of culinary favourites).

Morel   **http://www.morel.co.uk/**

Lewis Morel and Arthur Cobbett founded this company in the early nineteenth century. The late twentieth century website draws on a tradition of supplying quality groceries.

Wherever in the world you may be, you can order fine foods from this UK online store.

Oregon Pasta   **http://www.oregonsites.com/pasta/**

If you like pasta dishes, you'll love this US site which specialises in selling top quality pasta and prepared pasta meals. All pastas are egg-free and oil-free, and are naturally dried. They contain no sugar, salt, preservatives or artificial colours, yet they have a shelf life of 12 months when stored in a cool place away from direct sunlight.

Simply Organic   **http://www.simplyorganic.net/**

If you think organic food is just obscure vegetables with a strange colour, visit this site. The Simply Organic Food website is one of the UK's largest one-stop, online organic food shops.

For a totally healthy diet, you don't have to visit half-a-dozen shops, just one. This one. There are over 1,000 healthy organic products on offer so you can do your entire weekly grocery shop in one place and in a few minutes.

This company only delivers in the UK, but it can be anywhere and on the day of your choice.

Click on the aisle heading on the right hand side of the screen to begin your shopping or click on the 'The Shop' tab at the top of the screen to see all the aisles in the organic supermarket.

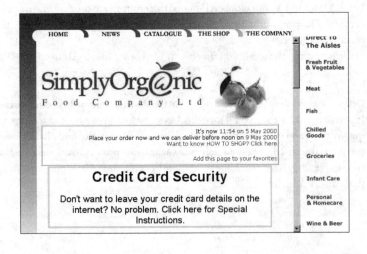

Drinks

The British in particular are noted for being a nation of tea drinkers. Others prefer coffee. Whichever you prefer, and wherever you are in the world, there is plenty of scope on the Internet to buy either. Or both.

Coffee World   http://www.realcoffee.co.uk/

We seem to take so much for granted. A cup of coffee arrives at our desk and we swill it down without a second thought. Yet the route from the bean to the cup is a long and fascinating one. The Coffee World website offers an insight into the production of coffee and includes a huge number of facts about it. The map shows where most of the world's coffee is grown and gives an explanation of the different types and blends available. The Coffee World website has an online ordering service.

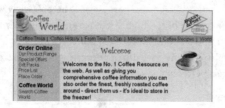

Gourmet Coffee & Espresso Shop   http://www.concentric.net/~Nancyj/

For the owners of this US store, coffee is not only their business, it's their hobby.

The site features a description of every type of coffee they sell. You choose your coffee, decide whether you want it as beans or ready ground and pay online. You can even buy some of the paraphernalia used to make coffee.

Roast and Post   http://www.roastandpost.co.uk/

As the name implies, you choose the coffee you want and it's despatched to you which guarantees that it's absolutely fresh. But this site is more than just an online shop. It contains a huge amount of information about coffee growing, the types of coffee and the different types of roast. This means you can choose the coffee that's exactly right for your palate.

If you're a coffee lover, visit this site for some mouth-watering coffee-based recipes.

You can also access this site at *http://www.realcoffee.co.uk/.*

Whittard   http://www.whittard.com/

This is the online branch of the high street tea and coffee merchant. You can choose from over 150 teas and 20 types of coffee.

The website also contains a wealth of interesting and/or useful information like how to make a perfect cup of tea.

You can download a catalogue and choose off-line.

Harder drinks

Lemonade is fine, but to really get the party going, it's often desirable to have something with a little more kick.

> *You must observe local laws when buying alcohol over the web.*

Drinks Direct   **http://www.drinks-direct.co.uk/**
Visit this site to send bottles of drink to friends as gifts. Some of the more popular gifts are bottles of champagne, assorted bottles of speciality beers and cases of wine.

Enjoyment.co.uk   **http://www.enjoyment.co.uk/**
You'll need to register if you want to buy from this UK site which specialises in wines for drinking, rather than for collecting. The site is divided into: Champagne & Sparkling Wines, Red Wines and White & Rosé Wines. Once you've selected the type of wine, you get a map of the world and clicking over a country gives you a list of wines from that country. You can click on the 'Eye' to get more information about the wine before choosing to purchase either a bottle or a case.

Some of the descriptions are quite incredible. A French Aile d'Argent white wine was described as "...superbly crafted honeysuckle and toffee apple white..." whilst the description of South African red began "...bitter chocolate and cream with a smoky richness...". Whether this is a strong selling point is unclear.

Oddbins   http://www.oddbins.co.uk/

The site opens with the statement, "We are building the World's oddest website…". You can buy some really good wine at bargain prices. There are frequent special offers which are worth looking out for.

Now 365   http://www.now365.com/

This UK site has a huge stock of beers, wines and spirits which you can order online and will be delivered anywhere in the UK.

The name of this site should not be construed as the number of days in a year that you should partake in a little tipple.

All of the drinks are indexed under the headings Wine (Red, White, Champagne, Sparkling), Spirits (Whiskey, Gin, Brandy, Rum, Vodka, Liqueurs) and Packaged (Bottles, Cans, Alcopops, Soft Drinks). All the major brands are there at below high street prices.

Sunday Times Wine Club   http://www.sundaytimeswineclub.co.uk/

This club which was formed in the early 1970's is now on the Web. You can get advice and buy some great wines online. Look out for the 'bin end cases' which are end-of-the-line bottles mixed up in a single case.

All wines carry a guarantee.

The Whisky Shop   http://www.whiskyshop.com/

This is Scotland's leading specialist whisky retailer. Here at the Whisky Shop the objective is to offer customers the most extensive selection of whiskies on the Web. The virtual shelves are organised by regions for Malt Whiskies and by category for the others.

Do not specify a high quality Malt and then flood it with ginger ale.

It's a simple task to locate and buy a wide range of Malts, Blended, Classic and Liqueur in a variety of sizes including miniature.

MALT WHISKY
RARE WHISKIES
BLENDED WHISKY
LIQUEURS
WORLD WHISKIES
HALF BOTTLES
MINIATURES
MONTHLY SPECIALS
MILLENNIUM

Welcome to Scotland's leading specialist whisky retailer. Here at the Whisky Shop our objective is to offer you the most extensive selection of whiskies on the Web. We have organised our shelves by category and Malt Whiskies by regions, we hope this helps you to find your way around.

If you are looking for particular whiskies which you can't find here, don't worry - just contact us and we'll match your request against our full stock list, or we can source individual bottlings, if they are available through our contacts in the industry.

All bottles on this site are 70cl unless otherwise stated.

If you have any questions about how to purchase

The Wine Corporation   http://www.thewinecorporation.com/

You'll need the Flash 4 plug-in (see the section on software) to run this site properly. You can choose from an extensive range of wines which you can either buy by the bottle or by the case. The search engine allows you to search for a wine by occasion and/or country and/or price and/or colour.

You can save money by buying a mixed case of wines rather than odd bottles. The carriage also works out much cheaper.

Once you've chosen your wine(s), you can add it to your basket and then proceed to the checkout to pay using most credit and debit cards.

The Home

When we leave work at the end of yet another gruelling day, what could be better than going to a smart home. But a home is not just the building, it's all the creature comforts that we choose personally that makes it a home. If you prefer to spend more time in it than searching the shops for things to put in it, then read on.

Buying and selling property

Estate agents seem to occupy a special place in the hearts of the buying public. There is a perception they do little or nothing for their percentage and generate enormous delays by not acting as promptly as they should. If you feel this is the case, then you could have a go at selling your home yourself.

Easier   **http://www.easier.co.uk/**

Easier is not an estate agent. This company basically put buyers in touch with sellers and makes it possible for you to buy and sell your home, as the name implies, a lot more easily. As well as providing buyers and sellers with the chance to buy and sell, they also offer some excellent advice on this website which should make the task of moving house less daunting.

They are at great pains to point out that the advice offered is there for you to accept or not, but should not be construed as professional advice. Based on that premise, Easier will not accept liability for any loss suffered as a result of following the suggestions.

If you've every tried finding a house by trooping around estate agent after estate agent, then you'll appreciate what a great idea this is.

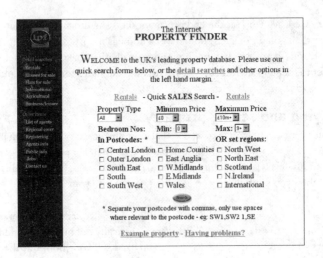

This site features properties from the books of some of the UK's top estate agents. You can search for a specific type of property within a particular area and within a specified price range. A list of suitable properties will be displayed with a brief description, thumbnail picture and price. A button is provided by each property description which provides fuller details and a decent size picture. There are links to take you to the website of the estate agent handling that particular property.

Always seek out professional advice whenever you consider it necessary.

Right Move   **http://www.rightmove.co.uk/**

Another newcomer to the house buying and selling arena is Rightmove. Using the site is brilliantly simple. First choose the area you wish to move to and click the 'Go' button. An order form will then be displayed on which you must refine the area. In other words, if you chose North London in the first section, you will be presented with a list of places within North London. Next enter the type of property and the amount you wish to pay. A list of suitable properties will be displayed giving a thumbnail picture of the property and some brief text. Clicking on the picture provides a much fuller description and a photograph you can actually see.

The site also includes links to conveyancing solicitors and to surveyors. Each property you're interested in can be added to your personal file and can be referred to later. There's also a section for lettings.

Selecting a house on the Internet is an excellent way to save shoe leather.

Judy McCutchin   **http://www.dallashomes.com/**

There are countless real estate websites covering the US. Typically, the sites cover fairly large chunks of individual states, like the Judy McCutchin site which deals in properties in and around Dallas.

The site opens with some music presumably intended to help you buy a home. You can choose properties based on price and/or location.

A Property4U
http://www.aproperty4u.com/

With over 23,000 properties across the UK worth an estimated UK£3,500 million, this is claimed to be the leading independent property resource within the UK.

When you visit this site, register your details and your requirements for your new property and you will be sent details of properties as soon as the Estate Agents make them available.

This website contains a very useful and easy to follow guide for the home buyer called 'Tips for Buyers'.

UK Property Shop
http://www.ukpropertyshop.co.uk/

Use the online form to send your requirements instantly to all selected agents in your chosen area. Then follow the links to over 4,000 websites and over 350,000 houses and flats for sale or to let.

Advice

When you're buying a house it seems there's a plentiful supply of people willing to give you unsolicited advice. Making the decision to buy a home is a huge leap and not one to be taken lightly. It's best to get advice from the experts.

FT Your Money
http://www.ftyourmoney.com/

The FT site has a huge amount of help and advice about buying a home. Once you're into the site, click on the 'Home Buying' link to get to a range of useful advice about the whole buying process. There's even a Home Buying Checklist to browse through.

New homes

The idea of a brand new home (as opposed to a home that has previously been lived in by another family) is, it seems, a mixed blessing. On one hand everything is new and shiny, on the other hand you sometimes have to be content with small rooms and doubtful building quality. At the very least, many of the features common in older homes such as panelled doors, dado rails, cornices and ceiling roses will almost certainly be missing, but then so will the draughts, the leaks and the constant need for maintenance. Not to mention the problems associated with imperial measurements that were used to build the house, and the metric fixtures and fittings available now.

Print out the Home Buying Checklist and refer to it frequently.

Ashwood Homes   http://www.ashwoodhomes.co.uk/

Ashwood Homes was founded in 1986, and has built up a reputation for building quality homes in the picturesque county of Lincolnshire. You can't buy a home directly from this site, but you can complete the online registration form and receive a brochure about the new developments.

Bryant Homes   http://www.bryant.co.uk/

When you enter this site, choose the 'Homefinder' link and complete the online form to find the home of your dreams. You'll need to enter details about the type of home you want, including the location, and Homefinder will offer some possibilities.

David Wilson Homes   http://www.dwh.co.uk/

This UK website features 'Home Search' which will help you locate a new home. Choose the number of bedrooms you want and the location and you'll be provided with a list of possible homes, in which you take a virtual tour around.

To view this site at its best, you'll need to download the iPIX® plugin, which can be accessed from this site. (Full details are in the chapter on software downloading.) Once the plugin is installed you can stroll around your dream home.

Doll's House Emporium   http://www.dollshouseemporium.com/

If you feel you don't want to be troubled with running a full-size second home, or you can't afford that mansion in the country you promised yourself, you could try a miniature house. The Doll's House Emporium not only stock a selection of houses, but also all the decorations and furniture, and even people. All items can be purchased and paid for online, with no estate agents' fees.

You can also access this site by entering *http://www.dollshouse.co.uk/*.

Things for the home

Everyone wants a nice home, but not everyone wants to stand queuing for hours to buy all the bits you need to make it nice. Try some of these Internet sites to collect all the furniture and accessories you need for your home. They feature a complete range of products for the home and garden, all in one place. Many have paper catalogues which can also be ordered from the website.

Argos Online   http://www.argos.co.uk/

The online spin-off from the famous catalogue store benefits from no queuing, although delivery can take up to 3 working days. When you get onto the site, you'll need to choose the section that you wish to visit, which is roughly equivalent to turning to the appropriate chapter in the paper catalogue. You can then select the product or products you wish to purchase and add them to your shopping basket.

If you have a catalogue, shopping can be even quicker because you can simply enter the product code and immediately get full details about the product.

To ensure a high level of security, all card details are automatically encrypted, and the cardholder's details will be verified with the appropriate bank. Orders will only be processed when full authorisation of payment has been obtained.

Ordering an item from Argos is a lot faster if you've got a catalogue. Enter the catalogue number and it will immediately recognise the product you're trying to buy.

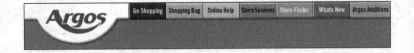

eshop   **http://www.eshop.co.nz/**

This huge online store is based in New Zealand. The store is divided into departments with easy access between them. There's a good online shopping service and prices are very keen.

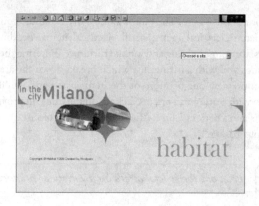

Habitat   http://www.habitat.co.uk/

Although, at the time of writing, you can't order online from Habitat, (apart from ordering a catalogue) I'm sure it's only a matter of time before you will be able to. For the time being, this is effectively an electronic version of their catalogue with a few other bits thrown in for good measure. Like a screensaver. Full details of all of Habitat's products are given in a clear friendly style. To get the full effect, you need to download Shockwave. (See the chapter on downloading software.)

It's worth visiting the section entitled 20th Century Legends which gives a brief introduction to some of the designers like Lucienne Day, Alan Fletcher and Pierre Paulin.

Home Zone   http://www.shoppersuniverse.com/

After entering the Shoppers Universe address, click on the Home Zone link on the right hand side of the screen. Just about everything you could possibly want for your home is here. The Home Zone is divided into about 20 sections including large electrical items, small electrical items, bedding, bedroom furniture, bathrooms, lighting and lounge furniture. Entering the section you want provides you with a further list which breaks down the area further.

You can preview one or more of the items listed and you'll get a small photograph with a title and a price. Clicking on the title will provide you with more details and a better picture. After choosing any colours or sizes, you can add it to your basket.

Look out for special offers on a variety of products.

House Mail Order   **http://www.housemailorder.co.uk/**
House is about simple, uncluttered interiors. Simple products, very stylish, reasonably priced. Online shopping is available, but even if you don't shop here, it's well worth seeing what they have to offer.

The Ideal Home Show   **http://www.idealhomeshow.co.uk/**
Although you can't actually buy anything at the website for the Ideal Home Show, you can create an itinerary so that when you visit the exhibition you can be sure you visit all the stands that you want to, without missing anything. Enter your email address and then search through the site. You can search through the various sections and get brief information about the exhibitors and what they will be exhibiting. When you see something you like, click on the 'add to itinerary' button. When you've added all the stands you want to see,

click on the 'email my itinerary' button and within seconds you will receive your itinerary.

> *Print out your itinerary and don't forget to take it with you to the show.*

Interior Internet   **http://www.interiorinternet.com/**

If you want a really well designed home that will be the envy of all your friends, spend some time on this site. You can choose a category or room, or a look and get thousands of ideas and products to help you realise your dream. The site is fully indexed, but there is also a search engine to get you to the right place quickly. The section headed 'features' contains an article or a study of a particular aspect of interior design.

All products can be bought online and can be sent to most parts of the world. (Look our for the Editor's Choice – a few extra special items.)

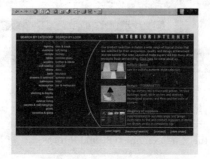

Rather than queuing at a cashdesk and then queuing to collect your purchase, you can now buy online from this famous catalogue shop. Index Online offers you over 7000 products to buy over the Internet 24 hours a day and 365 days a year, with the option of a 3 month interest-free flexible account. Most items can be delivered within 48 hours.

The site also features a handy gift finder so that if you're stumped for something to buy for someone, this should be able to give you a few possibilities. Some items carry a price reward logo which have an additional saving. There are also special Web promotions worth looking out for.

You can search for a product by entering the name, or catalogue number. Searching for a product is simplicity itself. Enter the type of product you're looking for and the search engine will find it for you.

Index offers secure online shopping, so all your payment details are safe. More details on secure transactions are available from the Customer Service area.

If you've got an Index catalogue, it's quickest to get the product codes from there and order online.

Ikea   http://www.ikea.com/

Is there anyone who hasn't heard of Ikea? You can't shop online yet, but you can view all the products and collect all the information so that you can place an order with your nearest store – which can be found with the online store locator. Online shopping, I'm sure, will be just around the corner.

Marks & Spencer   http://www.marks-and-spencer.co.uk/

Although apparently going through a sticky patch, Marks & Spencer is still a by-word for quality at realistic prices. You can shop online for gifts, clothes and for the home.

Marks & Spencer are probably more famous for clothes which you can also buy online at the same website.

The first time you visit the site you should register and on subsequent visits you'll be required to log-in. The site is well organised with good pictures and descriptions of the products. If you select an item that is not in stock, you'll be informed immediately.

Selected items are placed in your shopping trolley and a running total is kept, together with carriage charges. Payment is not available by credit card, but you can use Switch or Delta debit cards and, of course, their own storecard.

Terence Conran   http://www.conran.co.uk/

The Conran website is as stylish as one would expect from one of the foremost names in modern design. When you get to the site, you can choose to 'visit' any of his restaurants or his shop. The Conran Shop website is no more than an online catalogue which clearly outlines the products available in the shop. Regrettably you won't be able to buy any of these items online. At present, the only things available over the Internet are a selection of ashtrays, gift vouchers, food hampers and books, many of which are authored solely or in part by a certain T Conran.

Furniture

Aeromail   http://www.aero-furniture.com/

Apart from quality furniture for the home, Aeromail also offer a huge selection of quality contract furniture, lighting and accessories for businesses. The site is thoughtfully divided into Contract and Home furniture, with the latter being divided into bedroom, kitchen, living room, kids, bathroom and office.

Alma   http://www.almahome.co.uk/

The Alma home collection is a stunning range of furniture, furnishings and accessories in leather and Almara, the real washable suede. Alma also offers a manufacturing service for any new leather or suede product.

Country Desks   **http://www.countrydesks.co.uk/**

Elegant reproduction furniture for home and office, all of which can be bought online, if you can afford the carriage. Despatching heavy chairs and cupboards is not cheap, but buying them couldn't be simpler. Choose the section you want, view the products available within that section and click the products you wish to order. Once at the checkout you can amend the contents of your shopping basket, including deleting and altering the quantity. Payment by Visa, Mastercard and American Express.

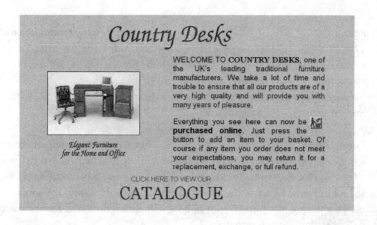

Blue Deco   **http://www.craftdesign-london.com/**

This site features very stylish, but rather pricey items including chairs, metalwork and ceramics. All products are available to buy online with prices quoted in UK£, US$ and Euros.

The interesting feature of this site is that each item displayed includes a link to a page containing information about the designer. This page in turn has links to other items by the same designer, enabling you to easily find all of that designer's work.

> *Blue Deco offers a 14 day refund and the gift picker is a great way of choosing gifts.*

Found   **http://www.foundat.co.uk/**

This small site features original, distinctive and well made products for the home. Amongst the 100-odd products available through this site are luxury silk cushions, fine linen bedding and children's toys.

All of the products have been chosen for their quality, style and price – they really do represent excellent value.

Futon Direct   **http://www.futondirect.co.uk/**

If you suffer from vertigo and don't like climbing up to get into bed, try a futon which is only slightly higher than the floor. You can't buy online from this shop, but you can choose the design of frame and fabric easily. Drawings are used to preview the futons, with photographs being displayed for the items you're particularly interested in.

There is a good selection of fabrics available and pictures of all of them can be displayed, although they can take a while to download. They also sell bunk beds for students with a working or sitting area under the bed.

There are frequently discounts of up to 15% on futons from Futon Direct.

Furniture Online   **http://www.furniture-on-line.co.uk/**

You can browse through the virtual showroom which is divided into the usual categories – dining room, lounge, bedroom etc. Alternatively you can search for a specific piece of furniture using the search engine.

The prices seem good, although it's not easy to judge the quality of the items being offered. This, of course, is the case with all items bought over the

The colours and the fabrics are not always easy to see on-screen and so this site offers free samples of fabrics.

Internet that do not carry a known brand label. All furniture ordered from this site has free delivery in mainland UK.

Iron Bed Company   **http://www.ironbed.co.uk/**

No wood or plastic here, just beds made from iron and occasionally, brass. They also sell mattresses and a variety of bed linen and pillows. If you feel you like your own bed too much, you can buy a surround which make it look like an iron bed, but still maintains all the lumps and bumps you're used to and have spent years developing.

Online ordering is available and goods can be shipped to Austria, Belgium, Denmark, France, Holland, Italy, Spain, UK, USA, and Switzerland.

McCord

http://www.mccord.uk.com/

McCord sell furniture and accessories, but for UK residents only. This is a huge operation and so the prices can be kept down. Items are divided into categories for easy hunting and there is a good online ordering service.

Metal Maniacs

http://www.wrought-iron-furniture.com/

This company offer a fine range of wrought iron furniture suitable for the garden, but also conservatory and even the kitchen/diner. Products include beds (including headboards for beds), chairs and tables. Online ordering is not available but you can email your order.

Oakridge   **http://www.oakridgedirect.co.uk/**

Oakridge supply a range of good quality settees and sofabeds delivered directly to your door. Online ordering is not available, but you can request a catalogue online.

Sofa Beds   **http://www.sofabeds.co.uk/**

Although you cannot actually pay online, you can place your order online as well as look at their entire range of sofabeds.

Sofas Direct   **http://www.classicchoice.co.uk/**

Classic Choice manufactures quality upholstered furniture which it sells direct to the public in the UK and Europe. This site shows the range of sofas and chairs in both leather and fabric. Fabric samples and furniture can be ordered using the online email form.

Stompa   **http://www.stompa.co.uk/**

This site has a good range of furniture for children and teenagers. You can't buy online at present, but you can contact the company using the online enquiry form.

Thistle Joinery   **http://www.thistlejoinery.co.uk/**

This company specialise in custom made joinery for home use. To get the sound effects you'll need to run Quicktime 4 (which can be downloaded from the site). Online ordering is not available but there is an email link for more information. There is an interesting section about the materials they use to create libraries, bookcases, wardrobes and home offices.

Vermont Fitness   **http://www.vermontfitness.com**

Many of us eat too much and exercise too little. Visiting the local gym is not an option open to everyone so why not bring a gym into your home?

You don't have to set up a complete gymnasium in your home if you haven't got the space.

Vermont fitness have everything you need from a simple rowing machine or exercise bike to weights machines and treadmills. They even have heart monitors.

Ordering is via email to *vermontfitness@vermonthouse.co.uk* but don't send your card details.

Accessories for the home

It's often the little bits and pieces that make a home seem like home and so here is a selection of websites which don't really sell very much that you need, but lots that you'd like.

Appeal   **http://www.appeal-blinds.co.uk/**

It seems a shame to block out the sun, especially in the UK where we seem to get so little of it. But it can be a nuisance and if this is the case, some sort of blind is probably in order. With the current popularity in conservatories, the blind manufacturing business appears to be booming.

These superb handmade blinds for conservatories are available in "National Trust" colours.

Click Deco   http://www.clickdeco.com/

The Click Deco site features a range of lights, candles and cushions, and some other home accessories like picture frames. You can browse through the site and buy online. Look out for the special offers.

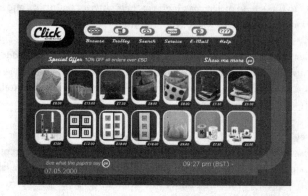

Battle Orders   http://www.battleorders.co.uk/

You don't have to live in a castle to own a suit of armour. Now, even the man arriving home from the office can open the door of his semi in suburbia to be greeted by a medieval knight ready for battle. Online ordering is available on most items but check the postal charges - I imagine armour is quite heavy.

The Bottle Rack   http://www.thebottlerack.com/

If you want a wine rack that's a little bit different from the usual, buy one from this site and all of your friends will be asking you where it came from. The racks come in three unique designs, all very stylish.

Carpet Right   http://www.carpetright.co.uk

You can't buy carpet on the web, but you can get 10% discount by visiting this website.

CP Hart   http://www.cphart.co.uk/

Log-on to this site to order a catalogue of their range of bathroom and kitchen fittings and accessories.

Chadder and Co   http://www.chadder.com/

The current trend for Victorian bathrooms has provided work for countless stores. Chadder & Co can supply all the antique fittings for baths, toilets and showers. Ordering is by email.

Chesney's   http://www.antiquefireplace.co.uk/

Chesney's offer a range of bespoke, antique and reproduction fireplaces in Georgian, Regency and Victorian styles. Online ordering is not available but you can request a brochure online. The site features some good pictures and a comprehensive pricelist.

Dyson   http://www.dyson.com/

How did we manage before the vacuum cleaner? This simple piece of 19th Century technology has enabled us to keep our homes a lot cleaner with a great deal less effort.

Vacuum cleaners have hardly changed since they were invented. That was until James Dyson applied his brilliant mind to the problem of dust bags. The Dyson vacuum cleaners don't have bags that need to be changed but have a cyclone system which ensures that the cleaner retains its efficiency.

You can order any of the Dyson vacuum cleaners from the website, and whilst you're there you can find out more about James Dyson and the technology behind his amazing products.

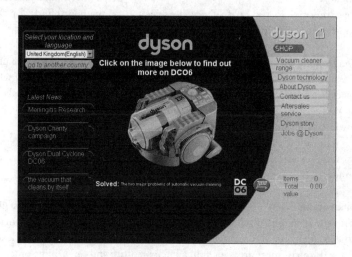

Flames   **http://flames.estreet.co.uk/**
This UK manufacturer of reproduction Victorian fireplaces has a good range of styles to add a certain touch of homeliness to your living room. There are tips to help you choose the right fireplace for your hearth, online ordering and online fitting instructions. The site regularly features offers and there is a selection of fireplace-related accessories, like clocks. There's a full description of each item with pictures and prices.

It's particularly pleasing to see a section covering the environmental issues associated with installing and using one of these fires.

Hillarys
http://www.hillarys.co.uk/

Visit this site to get hold of a wide selection of window blinds for the conservatory, or anywhere else around the home.

The Holding Company
http://www.theholdingcompany.co.uk/

If you want something to hold something, visit the Holding Company who specialise in providing storage for just about anything and everything. Baskets, racks, shelving and fancy pots to keep your desk a little tidier are all here, but my favourite is the hanging shoe holder.

The online catalogue is clear, with enough information to enable the user to make an informed choice. All products are available online via a secure connection using most credit or debit cards.

Innovations
http://www.innovations.co.uk/

This site is crammed full with clever gadgets and gizmos that invariably make you wonder how you managed for so long without them. Items are indexed into a dozen or more areas including kitchen, office and car. Online ordering and fast delivery are a key feature of this site.

Liberty
http://www.liberty-of-london.com/

The famous London house of sophisticated style has this website where you can buy gifts for the home, for him and for her. You can also order Liberty print material.

Mathmos   http://www.mathmos.co.uk/
This wacky site, which looks like a child's comic, is available in English,
German and Japanese. The main product is lamps – Astro lamps or Lava lamps
as they've become known. Also available are fibre-optic lamps and disco-type
projectors which will beam psychedelic patterns onto your walls. If you are
hankering after a taste of the 1960's, then visit Mathmos. Online ordering is
available.

Maelstrom   http://www.maelstrom.co.uk/
The site is summed up by the opening phrase – 'Contemporary designs for
modern lifestyles'. There are some superb designer items on sale here for the
kitchen, bathroom or office. There's also a lighting and a gifts section. You can
order online and/or order a free catalogue.

Mr Resistor   http://www.mr-resistor.co.uk/
Lighting can transform a room and it's as important to carefully consider the
lighting as it is to consider the rest of your decorations. Mr Resistor has a range
of lighting systems including low voltage downlighters, non-glare lights and
security lights. You can't order online, but you can email for advice and order
a catalogue.

Nauticalia   http://www.nauticalia.co.uk/
If you'd like to add a nautical flavour to your home, or you want to buy some
bits and pieces for your yacht, Nauticalia is the place to go. They stock a curious
range of products from quite expensive jewellery, to cheap trinkets like the cup
holder fashioned as a pair of hands. Not everything has an overtly nautical
theme, but they do include items which would prove useful on the high seas.
But being a nautical company, lighthouses are quite prominent and you can

have a lighthouse doorstop or tablelamp depending on your taste, or lack of it. There is also a good range of Global Positioning gear and some superb replicas of sextants.

Nauticalia's online ordering is actually run in conjunction with their Mail Order catalogue, and you'll need the catalogue to be able to place your order.

To order a product, click on the 'Go to Order Form' button, enter your name and address, order requirement, card payment information and catalogue code number which is in the bottom left hand corner of the catalogue. Finally, click the 'Order' button. UK orders are usually despatched within 24 hours but any personalisation may take a little longer. Overseas orders are welcome.

Plümo   http://www.plumo.com/

There are 32 pages filled with hand-crafted products from all over the world on this site. Plümo are offering pashmina wraps, zebra patterned candles, Moroccan baboosh mules and Egyptian kaftans. Oh yes, and incense sticks.

But more than this, Plümo is promoting the work of young designers whose creations have influenced this collection. Use this site to choose a gift or to treat yourself.

Rabid Home   http://www.rabidhome.com/

Filled with lots of gadgets and gimmicks you don't actually need, but if you're not careful you could find yourself collecting a great deal of bits which are really stylish and fun. Free shipping and free wrapping is one of the best features of online buying from this site.

South Downs Trading Company   http://www.southdowns.co.uk

The catalogue company from the South Downs area of the UK now provides an online ordering service. It sells a diverse range of useful and sometimes stylish accessories for home and garden. Amongst the regular items is a selection of quality bed linen. All products are well described and well illustrated.

Sträad Direct   http://www.straad.co.uk/

A good selection of accessories for the home, and some furniture. You can use this online shopping site to order all manner of goodies from transparent toilet seats with embedded seashells to luggage and executive toys. There's a good section on lighting and an interesting section called Gifts and Gadgets where you can choose a present for a friend who has everything.

Tie Rack   http://www.tierack.com/

The problem with owning a lot of ties is that it's difficult to store them safely and be able to choose one easily without the whole lot going on the floor. This US website has the answer – a system that displays 42 ties and makes it easy to get at the one you want.

Kitchens

There is no shortage of websites catering for the cornerstone of any house.

All-Clad Online   http://www.metrokitchen.com/

This US company is currently offering free shipping, but only within the US. All-Clad features a large selection of quality pots and pans, mostly stainless steel, copper or cast iron, with online ordering.

Appliance Online   http://www.applianceonline.co.uk/

Appliance Online claims to offer the easiest way to buy domestic appliances. They supply the best quality domestic appliance brands with up to 20% discount off typical high street prices. There is free UK Mainland delivery on all items.

With so many products available, you're almost certain to find what you want, but if you can't, there's an online enquiry form which you can use to find out about a product not listed.

Be-Direct   http://www.be-direct.co.uk/

The problem I find with many high street electrical dealers is that, although they have a great range of products, if you want to know anything about a

particular item other than the price, the sales staff are completely lost. Be-Direct not only sell a wide range of products, but they actually know about what is being sold.

Visit this site to find out all the details and then buy at reduced prices over a secure connection using most types of credit and debit card.

Brabantia   http://www.brabantia.com/

Brabantia produce a range of solid utility household items like bins, ironing boards and jar openers.

Chef's Store   http://www.chefs-store.com/

More pots and pans, knives and forks and other kitchen bits, but also cookers and hobs. There are various offers and free gifts with orders. This is a US based company so consider the cost of shipping before ordering sets of cast iron pans from this site which features online ordering.

Cook Craft   http://www.cookcraft.com/

Cook Craft offer quality kitchen utensils from top names at keen prices. The site features a currency converter, special offers and online ordering.

Cooks Kitchen   http://www.kitchenware.co.uk/

This is listed as the one-stop-kitchenware-shop in the UK but is much more than the usual selling machine as it features tips and even recipes. The site operates in a different way from most of the others where you have to wade through a sort of index system. In the Cook's Kitchen you simply enter the brand name or type of product you're looking for and a list will be displayed. Those items you're interested in can be investigated more fully and ordered online if you want them.

Cucina Direct   http://www.cucinadirect.co.uk/

Cooking equipment, drinks and glasses, electrical appliances, household, knives, linen, mixing and measuring, outdoor entertaining, storage, tableware and utensils are just some of the items on sale from Cucina. There is also online ordering and low prices.

Discounts Online   http:/www.discounts.co.nz/

This New Zealand store stocks a huge range of kitchen appliances.

Empire Direct   http://www.empiredirect.co.uk/

This is one of the UK's largest online electrical superstores . At Empire Direct
you will find the latest products from the top names at the lowest prices. You
can choose from a wide selection of televisions, video recorders, DVD players,
camcorders, hi-fi systems, hi-fi separates, portable audio, in-car entertainment,
and major domestic appliances. Once you've chosen, you can buy online over
a secure connection.

Helpful Home Shopping Co   http://www.helpful.co.uk/

This new UK company sells a wide range of domestic appliances with free
delivery, 3 year warranty and 15% discount.

The products on sale include home laundry, dishwashers, refrigeration
and built-in cookers and some home entertainment like TV, video and hi-fi.
In addition to the excellent prices, the site offers some technical comparisons
between different models

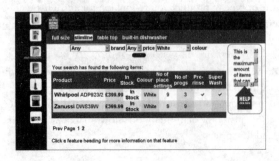

When you place an order, you'll be given a choice of whether you want confirmation by letter, fax or email, or any combination. Products are delivered and installed within 5 working days, although in practice it's frequently less.

When comparing prices, don't forget to include delivery charges and the cost of any additional warranty you may require.

Home Electrical Direct   http://www.hed.co.uk/

This UK firm offers free delivery within the UK on a huge range of electrical products for the home including hi-fi, TV, vacuum cleaners and white goods. There is no search engine on this site, but all of the products have been carefully indexed. You place your order using an online order form and you will be invoiced later.

Home Creations   http://www.myinternet.co.uk/home

No kitchen is complete without a cooker, and this company will sell you either a cooker, or hob/oven separates from top names like AEG, Bosch, Creda, Hotpoint, Miele, Neff, Smeg, Stoves and Zanussi. Also, lots of kitchen utensils from all the top manufacturers at ridiculously low prices.

Kitchenware   http://www.kitchenware.co.uk/

This site not only sells a huge range of kitchenware, but also features some really good recipes.

Pots and Pans   http://www.pots-and-pans.co.uk/

This Scottish company has four shops North of the border and their website
includes many of their shop-based products with special offers. The products
are described with good pictures and adequate description, and can be located
by entering a keyword in the search engine. Once you've found what you're
looking for, you can either order online or email the order form.

Small Island Trader   http://www.smallislandtrader.com/

This US company is offering free shipping with orders over US$300, but only
within the US. This site features the very best names in kitchenware like
Sabatier, Le Creuset and Aga. There is also a good selection of quality china and
crystal from companies like Portmeirion, Waterford and Royal Doulton. The
prices are low, and orders can be placed online.

Smeg   http://www.smeguk.com/

High quality cookers and hobs can be viewed but not ordered via this website.
Brochures can be ordered and there is an email service for queries.

Watershed   **http://www.watershedonline.com/**

This UK company offers a small range of quality products for the kitchen and bathroom. The kitchen section is dominated by Ariston cookers and hobs, with a few coffee pots and some of the largest freezers I've ever seen.

Online ordering is not available, but orders can be emailed or faxed.

China

Eating from paper plates is fine if you don't like washing up, but china is better.

Edwards China   **http://www.edwardschina.co.uk/**

Top names like Denby and Wedgwood, as well as quality crystal from Waterford and other famous names, at hard to beat prices. This online shop is divided into giftware and tableware, but there is also a section for collectors. Online ordering is simple and items can easily be added and removed from your shopping trolley without fear of breaking them.

Missing china

Everyone seems to have odd plates, often due to marital disputes, I'm told. So if you're short of two dinner plates, a soup dish and a saucer, and two of your cups don't have handles, you can match them up.

China Search   **http://www.chinasearch.co.uk/**

China Search can match up your oddments to make full sets. They specialise in Wedgwood, Doulton, Marks & Spencer, Worcester, Denby, Villeroy & Boch and Hornsea to name but a few. They will also buy old China from you.

Replacements   **http://www.replacements.com/**

This US company have over 100,00 patterns of china and crystal in stock.

Tablewhere?   http://www.tablewhere.co.uk/

Another chance to match up your broken pieces of crockery. Wedgwood, Doulton, Spode, Aynsley, Coalport, Minton, Royal Albert, Denby, Hornsea, Paragon RC Derby and Poole are the specialities here. Odd pieces of china are also bought.

The garden

I really do like to see a well-managed and maintained garden. My father-in-law loves his garden, and it's a joy to be there. I just can't stand gardening myself.

Garden.com   http://www.garden.com/

This site contains everything under the sun, but the highlights are the personalised plant encyclopaedia and access to garden planner software, which theoretically will make your gardening dreams come true.

You'll need to register, (which is free) but doing so allows you to access all the areas of this site. The kids can visit the gardening camp, learn how to plant a terrarium and grow their own jungle. Regular tips are published on the website covering topics like lawn care and improving your planting technique.

This is the definitive Internet garden resource with more than 20,000 products for sale.

British Gardening Online   http://www.oxalis.co.uk/

Continuing the theme of the great British Gardener this superb website has got it all. You can buy seeds, plants and even gardening tools online. If you're not sure what you need or what you want, or indeed what is available, go to the plant selector to help you make up your mind.

Technology is moving very rapidly in this area, but regrettably nobody has yet come up with online planting or online grass-cutting.

Crocus   **http://www.crocus.co.uk/**

This is a great site for people who love gardens but hate gardening. Buy some crocuses at Crocus, and not only will they deliver them, they'll send someone round to plant them and even keep you informed about their development with emails. They also sell a huge range of plants and tools for gardeners.

eSeeds.com   **http://www.eseeds.com/**

This Canadian site offers a huge selection of bulbs and seeds which can be delivered anywhere in the world. They also sell trees but I'm not sure it's a practical proposition to post these.

Pictured above (l-r), pretty in pink are Petunia 'Carpet Pink', Papaver (Poppy) 'Mayne Island Mix', and Pelargonium (Geranium) 'Orbit - Rose'

Exhibition Seeds   http://www.exhibition-seeds.co.uk/

If you fancy growing a huge marrow, or you'd like one of those pumpkins that two people have to push in a wheelbarrow, Exhibition Seeds is the place to come. You can also buy online quality vegetable, herb, grass and flower seeds.

Suppliers of high quality seeds. Seeds for growers, to the trade and gardeners around the world. We supply vegetable seeds, herb and amenity grass seeds, including wild flower seeds.

Garden Shop   http://www.thegardenshop.co.uk/

This site specialises in furniture and accessories for the garden. This includes chairs of all descriptions, hammocks and the compulsory patio table with parasol. Orders can be emailed, postage is a little pricey but they can, for a small fee, install your purchase, provided you don't live too far away.

Garden World   http://www.gardenworld.co.uk/

Registration to this site is recommended, but not compulsory. Apart from online orders, there are countless tips for gardeners and growers. Sections include gifts for gardeners, water gardening, plants and shrubs, conservatory gardening and garden furniture.

International Bulb Society   http://www.bulbsociety.com/

You must register (for which there is a fee) before you can take advantage of what this US site has to offer. Amongst the numerous benefits is the seed exchange programme.

Nicky's Nursery   http://www.nickys-nursery.co.uk/seeds

This simple but effective site provides everything needed for seed sowing. You can download the seed catalogue before emailing your order. Nicky's Nursery supplies seed from world leading producers who run tests on germinating in their nurseries and laboratories to ensure seed quality.

Pelco   http://www.pelcogarden.com/

This site opens with the claim, "Where Gardening becomes easier and more rewarding". I can't vouch for that, but the online ordering is simple enough.

Seed Potatoes   http://www.seed-potatoes-international.co.uk/

Kids find it hard to believe, but this is what chips start out as. Several varieties of potato can be bought from this site and the amount you need can be calculated online according to your acreage.

Shrubs Direct   http://www.shrubsdirect.com/

This site features some lovely plants from Cheshire, NW England. You can search for a plant and when you've found what you want, order and pay for it online.

Woolmans   http://www.woolman.co.uk/

This UK nursery supplies a wide variety of plants online. They will deliver anywhere in the EU.

DIY

With the cost of labour being so high, it often makes sense to do-it-yourself. The advent of mass DIY has had two spin-offs. First it has provided a thriving cottage industry with an inexhaustible supply of jokes and anecdotes about DIY failures. The second is that it has provided hospital casualty departments with an ever-increasing supply of patients suffering from one or more of a whole range of DIY-related injuries including severely cut limbs, missing fingers, and foreign bodies in eyes. Easter weekend is the time hospitals brace themselves for the rush of patients who've come a cropper with their once-a-year DIY session.

The trick is not to take on anything you're not absolutely confident about especially if it is anything to do with heights (roof), foundations, structural walls, electricity supply, water supply or a project bringing you into contact with both water and electricity. It's also important to follow safety rules regarding all hand tools, but especially power tools.

B&Q   http://www.diy.com/

The B&Q website offers advice on a wide range of DIY ventures and provides you with an easy way to create a shopping list to take round to your local B&Q branch to purchase.

Cookson's Tools   http://www.cooksons.com/

Every hand and power tool you can think of, plus a great many more you probably didn't even know existed, can be purchased online from Cookson's Tools. Whether you are a professional or a DIY enthusiast, you're likely to find what you want here, and at very low prices. There's also a security and ironmongery section.

Look out for special offers on a wide range of power tools at Cookson's Tools.

Dulux Paints   **http://www.dulux.com/**

This is a well organised site with some really good features. First, you can choose the type of room you want to paint and select the general style and layout before displaying it in a choice of colours. In the decorating help section, you can choose the type of surface you wish to paint, choose the colour from the appropriate palette and then enter the dimensions of the items you wish to paint. Clicking on the 'calculate' icon will tell you how much paint you'll need and, if you wish it, can be added to your online order. Very clever.

Homebase   **http://www.homebase.co.uk/**

Homebase is Sainsbury's 'do-it-yourself' shop. Although you can't actually shop at this site at present, you can wander around and get some ideas for improvements for both house and garden. There are details about the Homebase 'Spend and Save Card' as well as seasonal tips to brighten up your home and garden.

The section on choosing gifts is a particularly interesting and useful one aimed at people who, like me, never quite know what to buy for a birthday present.

Screwfix   http://www.screwfix.com/

The most expensive way to buy screws is to go down to the local DIY superstore and buy a little packet containing about half-a-dozen. Apart from the cost of the packaging and the high cost of the screws, you always have to buy two packs because each pack is designed to hold one less screw than you actually need.

Screwfix can supply every size screw for every purpose, and at sensible prices. They also carry a wide range of handles, hinges, bolts and brackets.

Home insurance

You can't afford not to have insurance on the building/contents of your home.

CGU   http://www.cgudirect.co.uk/

There is an online quote calculator where you can work out your monthly premium for home insurance.

Rapid Care Insurance   http://www.domgen.com/

This company offers insurance cover on your appliances to protect yourself from the cost of unexpected repair bills in the event of a breakdown. They also offer pet healthcare policies to cover you for unexpected vet fees.

Take an inventory of your contents. It'll take a while and with any luck you'll never need it.

Things to Wear

We all like to look good, but for some it's easier than others. Clothes can make or break the effect, and so we've got into the habit of trekking down to our high street for a tour of the clothes shops looking for the latest trend and/or the best price.

For some people, shopping for clothes is like an extended holiday and the ultimate retail therapy. Personally, I can't think of anything worse than queuing up at changing rooms, being badgered by commission-hungry sales assistants and then having to haul several heavy bags home on an overcrowded train. If you feel the same, online clothes shopping may be the answer.

But first, a word of caution. The main drawback with online clothes shopping is that you can't try anything on. You may know your size, but different manufacturers seem to follow different rules when it comes to

As with all mail order shopping, someone has got to be at home to receive the goods..

cutting the cloth. Therefore a size 12 from one shop may fit perfectly, whereas a similar garment from another outlet may not. Similarly, a colour that appears on your computer screen may not look quite so good when you actually wear it.

Some companies allow for this and provide free return carriage for unwanted items, but many do not. If you're not careful you may find that what you save in the cost of the garment is spent on postal charges.

Online clothes shops for women

There are a huge number of mail order companies that offer a small selection of specialised clothes for women. Many of these have now added online ordering to the traditional printed catalogue-based ordering. There are also companies who have set themselves up to sell only on the Internet. The advantage is clear: the cost of designing and printing the catalogue and then distributing it is removed. Some of the savings then have to go into maintaining the website, but there will be an overall saving and the website will potentially be delivered to many more customers. Assuming people actually use the Internet.

Take note of the postal charges when ordering goods via the Internet.

Artigiano   **http://www.artigiano.com/**
When this Italian site is entered, you must choose to view either the Artigiano collection for sizes 10-20 or the Spirito collection for sizes 18-26. Once you're into the chosen collection you can then select the type of garment which includes blouses, trousers, knitwear and tailoring.

When you've located the item you want to buy you are provided with an online form in which you must enter details about the size and, if appropriate, the style. The pictures accompanying the order form help you decide on the colour. When you've selected all the garments you want you may proceed to the checkout where you can adjust your order and pay using any of the usual credit or debit cards.

The Cashmere Company   http://www.cashmerecompany.com/
The Cashmere Company is the world's largest direct seller of cashmere and pashmina with prices between 30% and 50% less than shops selling similar quality. Online ordering is available and you can request a catalogue from the ite.

CXD

http://www.cxdlondon.com/

More sumptuous cashmere for women from this London store. Online orders are via a secure server and orders will be confirmed by e-mail within 24 hours of the order being placed. Although despatch is quoted as 28 days, it will be less than 48 hours in most cases, with free postage and packing for UK orders. Orders outside the UK will incur a small postage charge.

There is an excellent sizing guide which is worth visiting before you attempt to make an order.

CXD have a no-quibble returns policy and they even include a pre-paid envelope with each purchase.

Dorothy Perkins

http://www.dorothyperkins.co.uk/

Now part of the Arcadia Group, Dorothy Perkins has changed a great deal since the 1960's when all of the shops were decked out like cottages complete with a tiled pitched roof over the shop window. The online department has most of the features common to other Arcadia online stores – you can browse through the stock, use the index to locate a particular product or, if you have a catalogue, use the fastrack ordering by entering the product code.

The fashion clothes also include maternity wear and clothes for the petite figure.

Other features of this website include requesting a catalogue and regular competitions.

Esprit   http://www.esprit-intl.com/

The opening titles and fancy effects are very clever, but sometimes you just want to get in, buy and get out. Esprit have considerately provided a 'Click to skip intro' button to enable you to do just that. On the downside, I found the minuscule dark red writing on a black background almost impossible to read. You can buy online by clicking on the 'e★shop' link.

All descriptions of Esprit clothes include cleaning/washing instructions.

Evans   http://www.evans.ltd.uk/

Once known as the Outsize shop, now it's part of the Arcadia Group it's referred to as the affordable fashion store for women's wear size 16+.

The fast find feature generates a handy text listing of all the styles and products available to purchase online. The items are grouped according to department and clicking on your selection will provide a picture of the item. If you like it, choose the size and colour and add it to your shopping basket.

To order via fastrack you'll need a printed catalogue or to have seen the products in an advertisement. You can then use fastrack to place your order by entering the catalogue number.

Fat Face   http://www.fatface.co.uk/

Not the most flattering title for this website which includes women's and unisex clothes and clothes for the kids under the heading 'bratface'. The pictures and descriptions of the clothes are clear and there is an online ordering service.

FCUK   http://www.frenchconnection.com/

French Connection United Kingdom has produced a variety of fashionable clothes, many with suggestive slogans such as "Don't fancy yours much" and "Too busy to fcuk". Their website follows the same trend.

Ghost   http://www.ghost.co.uk/

Ghost offers a range of women's clothes with one distinguishing feature. Everything on sale is either black or white, or sometimes black and white. At present the online ordering service is available to UK/US customers only.

Kays   http://www.kaysnet.com/

The Kays website features mainly women's clothes which are divided and then sub-divided into categories which includes everything you could possibly need for every occasion at any time of the year, day or night. The prices are keen and you can choose to pay over a number of weeks if you prefer.

A clever feature is 'choose a gift' where you can get some ideas for gifts for friends and relatives who seem to have everything.

Kingshill   http://www.kingshill.co.uk/

Kingshill sell women's clothes from several top fashion names which you can browse through from the comfort of your own armchair. It's not dissimilar to strolling through a shop. Just click on a fashion name and look through the collection. You don't have to be a member to view the site, but you do need to register to make a purchase.

You can order a catalogue for £3.00 and once registered you can shop without leaving your home. You can wander through several top design names and place items in your virtual shopping basket. If you haven't registered, go to the site and browse through the stock.

The Leotard Company   http://www.tlcsport.co.uk

Although there is a small selection of products for men, this site features mainly women's wear, including lingerie and sports wear. You can't buy online at present, but you can order a brochure and contact the company by email.

The Peruvian Connection   http://www.peruvianconnection.com/

A small and very exclusive catalogue of Peruvian inspired clothes for women. The knitted tops are beautiful, but expensive. You can choose and buy online and your order will be shipped to most parts of the world.

Principles   http://www.principles.co.uk/

The Principles website has much the same features as other online stores which are part of the Arcadia Group. Fast Find gives a plain text listing with no pictures. Select what you like from the list to get a better description and the option of choosing size and colour. The fastrack ordering system requires a printed catalogue (which can be ordered from this site) so that you can enter the product codes.

If you're not in a hurry, you can browse through the store which is indexed by both department and item. The pictures of the clothes are clear and give you a good idea of what they'll look like 'in the flesh', so to speak.

It's worth visiting the sizing guide as it could help prevent you ordering the wrong size.

Selective   http://www.selective.co.uk/

If you've got a printed catalogue you can find the products you want to buy by entering the product code in the search engine. Alternatively you can search through the stock of pashminas, silk and cashmere.

All garments are shown with a brief but clear description which also lists any colour options. Clicking on the thumbnail picture gives a larger picture to help you choose. Once you've selected the items you like, you can order and pay for them online.

There's a useful size guide to help you order the size most suited to you and a section giving tips to help you care for your clothes once you've bought them.

Shop at Anna   http://www.shopatanna.com/

Anna Park opened her first shop in Norfolk six years ago, and two years later, a second shop in London. She specialises in selling labels not normally available in the UK, but also has her own label which concentrates on special fabrics.

Top Shop   **http://www.tops.co.uk/**

If you want the latest fashion clothes, this is the place to come (I'm reliably informed). You can get a rundown on the hottest trends, latest looks and the best buys.

If you place an order before 3pm Monday to Friday, you'll normally get next day delivery for most of the UK mainland. This, coupled with a no-nonsense refund and exchange policy, makes this a popular online store.

When you receive an order, returns details will be included – you can even make returns to any of the high street stores.

If you're short of a little inspiration, you can look at the new looks created every week.

Clothes for men

Unlike many printed catalogues of clothes which seem to contain 90% clothes for women with men's clothes shoved in at the end to fill up the space, the Internet has a really good selection of sites that deal exclusively with men's clothes.

America's Shirt Catalogue   http://www.hugestore.com/

Claiming to be the world's largest Internet warehouse with over 20,000 customers worldwide, this company certainly justifies its Web address. It *is* huge. The prices are low, as are the carriage charges, and the company aim to pack products within 5 minutes of you placing an order.

These prices are astonishingly low, but you can get even better value if you order several at a time.

Apart from shirts, they also sell a range of suits, trousers and accessories like ties and belts. All of the products are indexed and once you've chosen the category you can search for a particular item by price, size or type. All items are described with a good picture and some text.

Burton   http://www.burtonmenswear.co.uk/

This UK high street men's store is now part of the Arcadia Group. This online store sells just about everything for men including shoes, underwear, formal wear and smart casual clothes. You can request a store card from this site.

Charles Tyrwhitt　　　　　　　　　　　　　　　**http://www.ctshirts.co.uk/**

This maker of fine shirts from Jermyn Street, London now sells on the Web.
You can choose men's shirts by colour, collar style or material, or ladies' shirts
by colour or style.

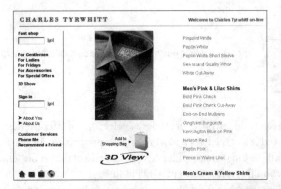

To help you choose the shirt you want, you can
see a picture of it complete with complementing tie.
If you're still not convinced you can get a 3D picture
which you can zoom in and out, and rotate with
your mouse so that you see the shirt from every
angle. (To see the 3D view you'll need to install a
plug-in, which is available from this site.) There's
also a range of accessories like ties and cufflinks.

Edward Teach   **http://www.edward-teach.com/**

This very classy website befits a very classy establishment. Edward Teach offers a fine range of classic tailoring, including hand-made shirts and shoes. Of course, as with much of this type of product, you need to be properly measured and so online ordering is not always appropriate, but you can order a made-to-measure shirt online.

If you've never worn a handmade bespoke shirt, you should try it.

You can choose from over 50 cloths, select one of 10 collar designs, six cuff designs and select the back and front of your preference. All you need to do is enter your personal measurements, with the help of the online guide. In about 3 weeks you'll receive your tailor-made shirt.

Orders are taken from almost anywhere and postage is reasonable.

Harvie and Hudson   **http://www.harvieandhudson.com/**

This family-owned UK shirt maker and Gentlemen's outfitter is based in Jermyn Street, St James's and Knightsbridge, London. They supply a range of stock shirts in hand-cut 100% cotton, with mother-of-pearl buttons and silk ties as well as a full range of luxury clothing.

You can buy online from the ready-to-wear collection and enjoy a 5% discount for online purchases.

Highland Dress Online   http://www.highland-dress.co.uk/

This online store offers top-quality kilts in a massive range of over 1200 Clan
and Family tartans.

The HIGHLAND DRESS Store

At the Highland Dress Store you can be assured of both top-quality products and excellent
customer service. We offer kilts in a massive range of Clan and Family tartans. Our suppliers
carry over 1200 patterns in stock at any one time, the world's largest collection! We are
delighted to be able to bring you this expertise, choice and quality coupled to our
commitment to customer service giving you an unbeatable opportunity to buy your kilts and
Highland Dress with total confidence.

**ON-LINE
SHOPPING**
Enjoy secure on-line
shopping for kilts,
highland dress and
regalia. To enter our
store,
CLICK HERE

MORE ABOUT US
We offer a secure,
exciting shopping
environment. To find
out more about us
before you shop,
CLICK HERE

**ASSOCIATE
RETAILERS**
If you have your own
web site and would like
to earn generous
commission fees
CLICK HERE

Hilditch & Key   http://www.hilditch.co.uk/

Hilditch & Key of Jermyn Street make what are widely regarded as the finest
men's shirts in the world. If, like me, you find that high street shirts are cut
rather too short so they are always pulling out of your trousers, or the sleeves
finish halfway up you arms, a quality shirt from a company like this will be a
welcome change. Rather than trekking off to London, you can buy a Hilditch
& Key shirt by visiting their website.

Kelsey Tailors   http://www.kelseytailors.co.uk/

Describing themselves as England's funkiest tailor, Kelsey Tailors have some very famous clients including Paul Weller and Noel Gallagher. You can buy jackets and trousers, shirts, ties and various accessories online.

> When you first enter this site, you'll think it's going to be really expensive. It is.

The Shirt Press   http://www.shirt-press.co.uk/

If there's anybody still ironing and wishes they didn't have to, take a look at this UK website. The Shirt Press supplies shirts which require no ironing whatsoever. You can choose from a huge range of styles including, classic collar, button-down collar and cutaway collar, double cuffs and dress shirts.

Sax Design   http://www.saxdesign.com/

Sax Design sells quality ties and neckwear. All ties are priced at either UK£8.99 or UK£12.99 with discounts on more than one tie. The designs are grouped with titles like City Gent, Sports Fanatic and Novelty range. Some are very smart, others are best worn in the privacy of your own home so as not to offend those of a nervous disposition.

Top Man   http://www.topman.co.uk/

This trendy men's clothes shop is part of the Arcadia Group. Apart from the usual Arcadia features, you can apply for credit online and browse the interactive magazine, 'Up for It'.

You can browse through the store or search for a particular item and buy it online.

If you click on 'Daily' there's a new joke everyday.

US Cavalry   http://www.uscav.com/

This US store sells everything you need to look, feel and act like a soldier. Apart from Army fatigues and the biggest boots I've ever seen, you can get billy cans, camp stoves and canteens.

Children's clothes

Buying children's clothes is probably easier than buying clothes for men or women as the children haven't yet had the chance to grow into 'non-standard' shapes.

Anteater-Togs   http://www.anteater-togs.com/

This is not the most inspired site I've visited, but it works well enough if you're patient and you've got a good memory. It features lots of fun clothes for kids divided into 12 categories. Click on the category you want and locate the item you want. It's at this point you need a good memory or a pencil and a piece of paper. You need to write down the details of all of the items you want to buy before going to the online order form. You then have to copy the details of all of the products you want to buy before submitting it.

You have to enter all the goods you want to buy in one go. You also have to add up the costs yourself.

   Online ordering is on a secure site with payment by the usual credit/debit cards.

Dragonfly Children's Clothes   http://www.dragonflys.co.uk/

Although you can't order online yet, you can see the entire range of clothes for children. Details are also provided of how to order by fax.

   The clothes have been inspired by the vivid colours and shapes seen in the exotic travels of the designer. Coral reefs next to rain forests and a pure blue sea next to white sand is, as the designer admits, what inspired him to create the colourful styles. All of the prints are exclusive to Dragonfly.

Children will want to wear the animal and floral patterns.

All the clothes are made from 100% cotton and are machine washable. Each piece of fabric has been hand printed using the age-old tradition of batik which ensures that no two pieces of fabric are identical.

Kids Clothes   http://www.urchin.co.uk/
This site features everything for babies and young children including food, nappies, bedding, furniture and clothes. There is a search engine to help you locate the items you want and everything can be bought online.

More than one

Just as real shops sell different combinations of clothes, so do online stores. The following sell clothes for men and women, women and children, or men, women and children.

Abercrombie & Finch   **http://www.abercrombie.com/**

This site features simple but classy looking work wear, lifestyle, casual and outdoor clothes. There's even a section entitled paratrooper.

Ameea   **http://www.ameea.com/**

Like their printed catalogue, the Ameea website features quality fashion clothes for men and women by some of the most exclusive names like Alfred Dunhill, Drake's, Keys and Loewe, with Porsche, Mont Blanc and Links heading the list of high quality jewellery and accessories.

APC   **http://www.apc.fr/**

This French fashion brand for men and women is distributed throughout the world through its own shops and its international mail order catalogue, and now online.

You can use the powerful search engine to find an item by a keyword. Alternatively you can select a catalogue page from a sliding bar arrangement which is the equivalent of turning the pages in a book. When you've found something that takes your fancy, click on the picture to get a better description. You can then choose your size and colour before adding to your shopping basket prior to purchasing online.

Apart from fashion clothes, you can also buy accessories like leather bags online.

Aquascutum   http://www.aquascutum.co.uk/

Former British Prime Minister, Baroness Thatcher was (and I believe still is) a frequent visitor to Aquascutum. Here you will find quality tailored clothes for both men and women. The site doesn't really do justice to the clothes, although the photos of the clothes are clear with good descriptions.

Bluefly   http://www.bluefly.com/

Visit Bluefly and you can buy fashion clothes including Gucci, Donna Karen, Tommy Hilfiger and Calvin Klein for all the family. When you enter this US site, first choose Men's, Women's, Teenagers' and Kids' clothes, then choose the designer you want and/or the garment you require. Each item comes with a good description including washing requirements and a photo that can be enlarged if you wish. When you've made your choice, you are then asked to enter size, colour etc.

You can have your purchases sent to a different address if you wish and there's a 90 day return policy.

Once all the items have been collected, go to the checkout where, if you haven't already done so, you'll need to create an account. Once you have your account set-up, in future you'll only need to enter your email address and a password to place an order. Delivery charges are clearly laid out, payment is made by the usual range of plastic and orders are confirmed by email.

Boden
http://www.boden.co.uk/

This UK site has a good range of quality clothes for men, women and children at reasonable prices. One of the strengths is that suits can be ordered as separates so if you've got an oddly shaped body you can buy trousers in one size and the jacket in another size. All items can be ordered online and international orders are taken.

There's an interesting section about cashmere on this site.

Brora
http://www.brora.co.uk/

This UK site sells the very finest Scottish cashmere for men, women and children at very affordable prices. The ladies section has been divided up into seven categories (eclectic mix, ruffle edged, silk/cashmere, fitted collection, classic cut, textured knits and stoles & pashminas). The range isn't huge so it's a simple job to choose the garment, select the size and colour and add to your basket.

The checkout section is much the same as many other secure payment systems.

Browns Fashion
http://www.brownsfashion.com/

You'll find fashion clothes for women and men, kids clothes and things for the home at this fashionable online store. Clothes are categorised as Soft & Sensual, Soothing & Spiritual, Delicate & Detailed, Fun & Fantastic, Precious & Provocative, Eclectic & Ethnic and Comforting and Collectable.

Christian Scott   http://www.christianscott.com/system

Founded by the daughter of a Scottish woollen manufacturer, Christian Scott has been selling quality clothes and accessories for over ten years. The online branch clearly describes the products with clear photos and when you've found something you like (which isn't difficult – it's all superb) you can choose the size and colour and buy online.

Clothing Connection   http://www.clothingconnection.co.uk/

When the site opens you must first decide whether you want fashion clothes for him or her. The Men's section includes suits, jeans wear, fashion and casual clothes and sportswear from many top brands such as Ralph Lauren, Kickers, Rockport and Ben Sherman. With a selection of underwear, shoes and accessories, you can get completely kitted out from top to bottom.

The women's section includes evening wear and suits, high fashion and casual clothes in a full range of sizes. There's also maternity wear and shoes. You can search for items or just browse through. Once you've filled your basket, you can pay online with most credit and debit cards.

The Clothes Store   http://www.the-clothes-store.com/

Billed as the ultimate online clothing collection, The Clothes Store sells a fairly small range of smart casual clothes, shoes and miscellaneous accessories from names like Kangol, Fred Perry, Lee Cooper and Kickers.

The Cross Catalogue   http://www.thecrosscatalogue.com/

When this site opens, if you cannot see the flower changing colour, then you will need to download Shockwave if you want to see the clever bits on this website. (There is a link to freely download Shockwave. For more information about downloading, see the chapter on software.)

This site features fashion wear for children as well as women, and there are some items for the home. You can search for items by description or by the product code from the catalogue.

You can have your purchases gift-wrapped and, if you wish, include a personal message.

Online purchasing is over a secure system and payment can be made with most cards.

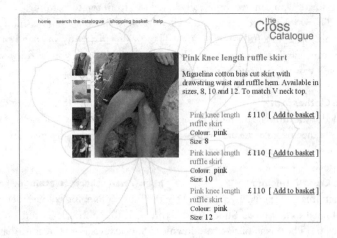

Debenhams Direct   http://www.debenhams.com/

This is the online branch of the high street store which sells mainly clothes, but a few other bits as well. The clothes are divided into men's, women's and children's and there's a good selection spanning a wide price range.

Designers Direct   http://www.designersdirect.com/

You can search for clothes by type or label, or browse through the indexed clothes. Many of the top designers are here and Designers Direct ship to over 150 countries and offer language support to six, plus English.

Diesel   http://www.diesel.co.uk/

When you visit the website of the famous designer label you have a choice of selecting the Shockwave version or the non-Shockwave version. If you're short of time, pick the latter. (For more information about Shockwave, see the chapter on software.) You can browse through the stock which is clearly described with good photographs. When you find something you like, you choose the size and colour and optionally send it to the 'changing room'.

Unlike a real store, you're not limited to three or four items in the changing room.

When you've selected enough clothes, you can visit the changing room where you'll be shown the items you've selected which will include a sample of the fabric showing the weave and colour. You can alter your choices, including removing any of the items, before proceeding to the checkout to pay for them.

At present, Diesel can only be used for purchases made within the UK.

Fade Fashion   http://www.fade-fashion.com/

A curious name which hopefully bears no relation to the way the colours survive during washing. Fade Fashions offer a range of golf wear, sports wear and lifestyle for both men and women. There is a search engine to locate the item you're after and when you've tracked it down you can buy online.

Freemans   http://www.freemans.com/

This site can take a little time to open if you want to browse the online catalogue. If, on the other hand, you have a Freeman's catalogue then it's a simple task to enter the product numbers from the catalogue to place an online order.

The personalised gift reminder prompts you to buy a gift for friends' birthdays or other special occasions.

Gap   http://www.gap.com/

Click on a category to choose from a wide range of stylish smart casual clothes for men and women. It's best to register on this site and sign in on each visit. Registration is free and provides email updates on the latest promotions, personalised address list and gift reminders, a chance to win prizes in online contests and stored billing information so you don't have to re-enter your mailing details every time you visit the checkout.

IC3D Jeans   http://www.ic3d.com/

You can buy jeans online from IC3D in almost any material you like. There's leather, suede, velvet, rubber and even denim. If you're not sure of the properties of each, you can get a full description including a close-up of the fabric.

The online measuring guide helps you select the right size for men and women, and you can choose various details including belt-loops and zip or button fly.

Joe Browns   http://www.joebrowns.co.uk/

This is one of those sites which is difficult to place. They describe themselves as a true lifestyle company which sells adrenaline-based activities, motorbikes, Mexican jewellery, American accessories, books and interesting clothing.

There's a handy section on sizing which helps you decode the sizing terms such as small, medium and large.

The interesting clothing includes jeans, leather, fleeces and T-shirts. Online ordering is available for all items and you can pay using most of the credit and debit cards. There's a returns policy: if you change your mind you can return it (unworn) within 21 days for a full refund. Unlike many other companies, this one takes the trouble to remind you that the goods are your responsibility until they are delivered back to the supplier. Make sure they are adequately packed and insured.

Jojo Maman Bebe   http://www.jojomamanbebe.co.uk/

The UK site with an almost unpronounceable name was founded by Laura Tenison in the early 90's after discovering the difference in attitudes to pregnancy between English and Continental women. As a result she has a range of quality maternity wear which doesn't hide the growing bump, but actually flatters. In her own words, to celebrate pregnancy. The clothes are cleverly tailored to fit throughout the nine months, and beyond. There's also a range of fashionable clothes for babies.

Everything on view can be ordered via a secure connection and paid for with the usual range of credit and debit cards.

Liberty of London   http://www.liberty-of-london.com/

The famous London store has a small online shopping section where you can buy a limited number of items in Liberty print for men and women. For men it's mainly ties, shorts and holiday shirts, whilst women have to choose from blouses and scarves. Expensive, but exclusive.

La Redoute   http://www.redoute.co.uk/

You don't have to go to France to shop in Paris if you visit this online fashion store with clothes for la femme, l'homme and l'enfant. You can pay immediately using Visa, Mastercard, Delta or Switch, or opt to be billed each month.

Lands End   http://www.landsend.com/

A good selection of clothes for men, women and children categorised in Tops, Polos & T-shirts, Cotton Sweaters, Cashmere, Woven Tops, Pants & Jeans, Dresses & Skirts, Collections, Swimwear, Shorts, Sleepwear, Outerwear, Winter Accessories, Wool Sweaters, Slippers, Activewear, Accessories and Footwear.

The Swim Finder will help choose the best-fitting and most flattering swimsuit from almost 100 available. You either choose your body shape from the list of eight, highlight any areas of anxiety (those bits you'd like to hide) or select a swimsuit according to any of your attributes. You'll then be shown an assortment of swimsuits which theoretically should be perfect for you.

L L Bean

http://www.llbean.com/

A large range of casual, outdoor and sporting clothes for men, women and children. If you have their latest catalogue, you can 'quickshop' by just entering the stock number. There's also a good range of travel goods.

London Wide

http://www.londonwide.co.uk/

Designer streetwear for young men and women at affordable prices is the staple diet of this UK website.

Marks & Spencer

http://www.marks-and-spencer.co.uk/

Is there anyone who hasn't at some stage worn M&S underwear? Although many people think of knickers, pants and vests when M&S or St Michael are mentioned, this store has a great deal more on offer. High quality but reasonably priced clothes for men and women are not always the last word in fashion, but they are nevertheless very stylish.

The first time you visit the site you should register and on subsequent visits you'll be required to log-in. You can shop online for clothes and for items for the home. The site is well organised with good pictures and descriptions of the products. If you select an item that is not in stock, you'll be informed immediately. Payment is not available by credit card, but you can use Switch or Delta debit cards and, of course, their own storecard.

Metropolis Clothing   http://www.metropolis-clothing.com/

This massive US designer store sells top fashion names like Armani, Boss, Cabourn, Calvin Klein, Diesel, DKNY, Dolce & Gabbana, Iceberg, Katherine Hamnett, Lacoste, Newbury Street, Ralph Lauren, Red Or Dead, Stone Island, Timberland, Tommy Hilfiger, Valentino, Versace and Vivienne Westwood.

If you get bored shopping you can always take in the scenery by choosing one of three New York Web cameras which broadcast pictures from either the Rockefeller Building, 5th Avenue or the inside of a New York cab.

Monsoon   http://www.monsoon.co.uk/

This is the online branch of the UK store selling women's and children's fashionable clothes at sensible prices.

Next   http://www.next.co.uk/

The Next website offers the user an online catalogue showing many of the Next products. Originally men's and women's fashion clothes for those who no longer qualify for a Club 18-30 holiday, Next now sell accessories and a range of stylish household products and children's clothes.

Although online shopping is not yet available, you can order a catalogue by completing the online form. You'll be invoiced for UK£3.00.

N Peal   **http://www.npeal.com/**

From London to New York and San Francisco, more quality cashmere for men and women. Orders will be taken from most parts of the world.

N.PEAL
CASHMERE

LONDON · GLENEAGLES · NEW YORK · SAN FRANCISCO ·
BEAVER CREEK

Beautiful cashmere available online.
Click your region for the store nearest you.

Outlet Direct   **http://www.outletdirect.co.uk/**

You can get huge discounts on sports and designer wear at Outlet Direct. You'll find amazing bargains from many of the popular names like Adidas, Ralph Lauren, Puma and Gant. You can search by type or brand, and request emailed details of the current offers.

All items can be purchased online and most major credit/debit cards are accepted.

Paul Smith   http://www.paulsmith.co.uk/

Another site requiring the Flash plug-in (see the chapter on software for more details). If you want a T-shirt, this is the website to visit.

Racing Green   http://www.racinggreen.co.uk/

Racing Green is part of the Arcadia Group which includes Burton and Dorothy Perkins. Their website shows all of their products available through mail order and also includes online ordering. Once an order is started, each page gives you an opportunity to add to your virtual shopping basket. The bill is totalled for you and secure credit card payment is available.

Scotia   http://www.scotia.uk.com/

A selection of some of the best names in British clothing including Barbour, Tilley and Musto is available online from this UK website. Not everything in the various ranges is available online, but there is an efficient email help line should you have any queries about products you can't find.

Skinzwear   http://www.skinzwear.com/

Skinzwear supply a wide assortment of men's and women's sportswear, beachwear, swimwear and underwear. It's all very mouth-watering with clothes that look as though they've either been painted directly onto the model, or the model has somehow been poured into the garment.

Sui Generis   http://www.fabric8.com/sg/

Sui Generis custom-makes quality clothing for men and women. The collection of jackets, shirts and trousers looks good; even better (you'll be glad to know) it feels good, too. The garments are hand-made in San Francisco from top quality materials.

The first job is to go to the fitting room to take your measurements. The website provides full instructions of how to do this and stores them all so that when you come to order, you'll get the correct size.

Traidcraft   http://www.traidcraft.co.uk/

Traidcraft is an organisation which trades with workers in developing countries and imports their products for sale in this country. What makes Traidcraft stand out is that it deals fairly with the workers and pays them a sensible wage for the work they have done.

In short, the people of Third World countries are not being exploited to provide goods, so that we in the developed world can buy more of the products at lower prices.

There is a small, but exclusive range of clothes for men, women and children. You can now order online from Traidcraft.

T-shirt King   **http://www.t-shirtking.com/**

The claim that this is the largest T-shirt shop in the world must be true. You can buy a T-shirt from this US store with virtually anything you want printed on the front. Or the back. Every tenth customer gets a free T-shirt.

Zoom   **http://www.zoom.co.uk/**

This 'all-in-one' website features some of the top names in High Street fashion – Racing Green, Top Shop, Principles and Hawkshead. You also get loyalty points which you can 'spend' on future purchases.

Accessories

Many of the clothes stores also stock accessories like scarves and shoes, but there are also thousand of smaller retailers with online stores that specialise is a particular garment or accessory.

Accessorize   **http://www.accessorize.co.uk/**

Bags, bracelets, earrings, flip-flops, hair accessories, necklaces, purses and sunglasses are among the wide range of female accessories on this UK website.

Action Fit   **http://www.actionfit.com/**

You can design your own swimsuits and aerobics wear using the selection of backs and fronts provided. When you've designed your swim suit, you can complete the online order form to email your order.

Billy Bag   **http://www.billybag.com/**

If you need a bag to carry home your shopping, or to keep your makeup safe, Billy Bag will probably have it in stock. Their selection includes satin bags, beaded bags, denim bags, straw bags, canvas bags and paper bags.

Café Coton   http://www.cafecoton.co.uk/

Visit the Café Coton website and you will find a fabulous selection of 100% cotton shirts. All of the shirts are available in four different collar styles and are made using the finest cotton. All products can be purchased online.

Global Caps   http://www.globalcaps.com/

Personally I cannot abide baseball caps but some people seem to need surgery to have them removed. If you feel the need to make a statement at your next job interview, visit this company who sell nothing else.

Intofashion   http://www.intofashion.com

A designer accessory store specialising in, well, designer accessories like silver chains and plastic chokers, but also separates like tops and bottoms.

Shopline   http://www.shopline.co.uk/

This online stores sells a wide range of ties, braces, cufflinks and other miscellaneous items usually emblazoned with a cartoon character. Some of these fun items are actually more classy than you might at first imagine, but still not recommended attire for a job interview or court appearance.

Tie Rack   http://www.tierack.co.uk/

The shop that sells nothing but ties (and a few scarves) has this website from which you can see the entire range and buy online.

Lingerie and underwear

If you're too embarrassed to go into a shop to buy some of these goods, the Internet is more anonymous.

Aaargh Fashions   http://www.aaargh.co.uk/

This UK site features underwear in rubber and leather, and a selection of raunchy items for all tastes and pockets. There's a range of classic lace lingerie and an assortment of items you might want to think twice about before hanging on the washing line for all to see. They now cater for full-figured ladies.

Agent Provocateur   http://www.agentprovocateur.com/

A very provocative site, but one to visit if you're longing to get your hands on some sexy underwear. The site is divided into five self-explanatory sections entitled Revelation, Exhibition, Temptation, Provocation and Domination. Most items carry pictures clearly showing all views.

Ample Bosom   http://www.bras-online.co.uk/

Continuing to keep fully abreast of the lingerie scene, this UK company sells top makes of brassiere for the fuller figure.

WELCOME to

AMPLE ♥ BOSOM

—— bras-online ——

Prices inc UK VAT and there is free UK postage on orders over UK£30.

Ann Summers
http://www.annsummers.com/

"Prepare to be elevated through our sensual world", the opening title begins. Items from Ann Summers' catalogue of sexy undies for men and women can be viewed and purchased online.

Don't visit this shop if you're likely to be offended.

Billet Doux
http://www.billetdoux.co.uk/

For those not fluent in French, it's pronounced "bia-do", which translates as "love letter". This is an apt name for a store that sells lingerie and an assortment of gifts, which are described as "tokens of affection".

Bras Direct
http://www.brasdirect.co.uk/

This UK online store has a good selection of bras at less than usual high street store prices.

City Boxers
http://www.cityboxers.com/

If you love boxer shorts this is the place to come because that's about all they sell. If you're considering buying boxer shorts for the first time, this site should get you off on the right foot.

Easy Shop
http://www.easyshop.co.uk/

This UK site is billed as 'Virtually the greatest underwear store in the world'. In the women's section there are three 'quick finders' to help you find a particular item to suit you. Legs Finder is a five step guide to buying the right hosiery. Choose the make (if applicable), the type (stockings, tights, footsies etc.), the occasion, any other important features relating to price, quality and quantity and the denier rating and you'll get a list of items that either match or nearly match your requirements. Briefs finder and Bra finder work in a similar way. Items in the lists can be added to your shopping basket for later online purchase. The men's section includes shorts, briefs, T-shirts, socks, bathrobes and thermals.

Henry & June   http://www.henryandjune.com/

This US store promises same-day shipping and free carriage (over US$50) on a huge range of lingerie. You'll be told how long it is likely to take to deliver (which will depend on stock) before you place your order and there is a no-questions-asked 90-day returns service.

Although this is primarily for women, there is a good range of men's underwear.

Janet Reger Direct   http://www.janetreger.com/

Although you can't actually buy directly from this site, it does describe all of the very expensive lingerie on show and details how to place an order by phone or fax.

Kiniki
http://www.kiniki.com/

Kiniki is described as being the Internet's premier men's underwear shop. Everything for the nether regions is available online including boxers, briefs, thongs and swim wear.

This site features a 'freebie' section where you can download some screensavers and wallpaper for your desktop. Why anyone would want underwear on their desktop is unclear, but it's there should you want it.

My Tights
http://www.mytights.com/

You'll need to register when you first visit this site and log-in on subsequent visits. You can search for tights and stockings by either type or by make, which includes Aristoc, Charnos, Christian Dior, Levante, Marque de Maternite and Pretty Polly.

Men need not bother to visit this site unless they're planning to rob a bank in pairs.

Full descriptions of the products are supplied and online shopping is available over a secure connection. The shopping basket keeps you informed as to how much you've spent as you go along and when you get to the checkout you'll be told if the parcel will fit through the letter box. There is a small postage charge.

Rigby and Peller
http://www.rigbyandpeller.com/

This London based company carrying two Royal Warrants will supply you with a made-to-measure bra, although this is not an Internet service as fitting is crucial. But you can buy online from a range of bras to suit all sizes and pockets.

Rigby and Peller claim that about 85% of customers who visit their shop for the first time are wearing the wrong size bra. Top of the list of problems

There's a particularly good advice section to help you choose the right bra for you. The way to a good fitting bra, R&P claim, is to not know you are wearing one at all.

are the band at the back of the bra riding up, underwire digging in under the armpit, chafing of the skin, indents on the shoulder where the straps have dug in and breasts falling out of the underwire.

The 'Fitting Room' offers help and advice about choosing a bra.

Shortsite   **http://www.shortsite.com/**

With the opening punch-line 'underwear with pulling power', this UK website stocks quality men's underwear by Paul Smith, Hom and Converse All Star at attractive prices.

Smart Bras   **http://www.smartbras.com/**

This UK online store offers 'off-the-peg' bras from about a dozen manufacturers at less than usual high street store prices.

Victoria's Secret

http://www.victoriassecret.com/

This well-presented website has a range of lingerie, hosiery and swimwear available to buy online. If you don't want to browse through the 'store', you can enter a product code from their printed catalogue, which can also be ordered from the site.

Check to see the returns policy on shoes bought via the Internet.

Shoes

I think buying shoes on the Internet is probably the hardest thing to do. If you buy, say, a jacket and find it doesn't fit exactly, you can put up with it. If you buy a pair of shoes that don't fit perfectly, they're crippling. But retailers know this and many try to provide you with as much information as possible to ensure you get a good fit. Many make special arrangements for returns.

There is a good section to help you with sizing.

Birkenstock

http://www.footwise.com/

This US site sells sandals, clogs, shoes and boots. The foot finder feature helps you to choose the right type of shoe – enter the style, price range and material and you'll get a list of possibilities with thumbnail pictures. Click on the ones you like and you'll get more details, including a better picture and a couple of other similar shoes to help you decide. The descriptions also tell you if the sole is repairable.

Celtic Sheepskin Co.   http://www.celtic-sheepskin.co.uk/
You can purchase high quality sheepskin hats, gloves and mitts as well as boots, slippers, foot and hand muffs and moccasins. All of the sheepskin products are hand made by craftsmen in Cornwall, UK.

Cow Town Boots   http://www.cowtownboots.com/
If you want something a little different to put on your feet when in the office, try a pair of cowboy boots from this US site. These high quality boots for men and women are made in the traditional way from quality skins.

JJB Sports   http://www.jjb.co.uk/
This is the online branch of the UK high street sports shop. Most of the items which can be purchased in the shops can be bought online including bikes, replica kit, fitness equipment and golf equipment.

Begin by selecting the category you want and then selecting the product type. When you've finally got to the particular item you want to buy, click the 'Buy this Item' button and complete particulars about size and colour before paying at the virtual checkout.

Scholl Sandals   http://www.shoe-shop.com/scholl
The famous manufacturer of foot care products has a range of exercise sandals and mules for men and women available from this online shoe shop.

Shipton & Heneage
http://www.shiphen.com/

This UK site has a selection of good quality shoes, boots and slippers for men and women.

Jones
http://www.jonesthebootmaker.com/

Shoes seem to hold a special place in the hearts of the fashion conscious. This is an excellent site for those who want to buy shoes without wearing out shoe-leather tracking them down,

Shoes.com
http://www.shoes.com/

This US store offers free carriage in the US for thousands of shoes which can be bought online. You can search for shoes by brand name, or if you prefer, shoes for men or women, in which case you'll be able to choose the general type of style before being shown a selection.

It's worth visiting the Sale section which contains lots of trainers at vastly reduced prices.

Sweatshop   http://www.sweatshop.co.uk/

Every type of training shoe is available online from this site. Trainers are divided into cross country, running, aerobics and trail.

Apart from buying trainers, there's a useful advice section which is a sort of electronic notice board carrying hints, tips, advice and Frequently Asked Questions from customers and staff. Anyone can post a tip by clicking on the Post Message button.

Vans   http://www.vans.com/

You can choose from a wide selection of shoes and snow boots from this US site. There's also a selection of T-shirts, headwear and bags to browse through, add to your shopping list and buy online.

Glasses

I find choosing glasses really difficult. You wander around the opticians trying on pair after pair until eventually you're totally confused and you end up not liking any of them.

Dollond & Aitchison
http://www.dollond.co.uk/

This famous UK optician has this excellent website where you can actually 'try-on' glasses.

Do not spend too long in front of a VDU – it's not good for your eyes. D&A have a piece of software called Eyesaver which can be freely downloaded to warn you if you need a break from using your VDU.

PersonalEyes is a unique service, which allows you to 'try on' different spectacle frames across the Internet. To make your own picture available on PersonalEyes, you will need to produce a picture of yourself. This can be done in one of two ways. You either have a picture taken with a digital camera or you can scan an existing photograph. Either way, you must end up with a JPEG file

If you're not sure about the size, compare it to the example shown on the website. Most art programs will provide you with the picture size somewhere in the information section.

(this is a type of file format for pictures) which must be 275x285 pixels. You should be looking straight at the camera and (obviously) not wearing glasses.

You'll then need to complete the online form with your personal details and a username and password, and finally upload your picture to the server. This is not as complicated as it sounds – you simply have to locate your picture on your computer and the rest is done for you. As soon as the picture has been uploaded, you can connect to the site and see how you'll look in a variety of different spectacle frames.

Josephson Opticians   http://www.josephsonopt.com/

This Canadian site features a huge range of frames which are indexed in alphabetical order by make. All models feature some written description and a picture of the frames. You can't actually buy online, but you can get a list of stockists.

Internet Shopping is not always about spending money. The Internet is a great place for research before you buy.

SpecSavers   http://www.specsavers.com/

Although you can't actually buy glasses online, you can choose them and then find the store nearest to you to buy them and have them fitted.

Salcombe Sunglasses   http://www.designer-sunglasses.co.uk/

Buying sunglasses has never been easier. When you enter this site, you can choose from a wide range of sunglasses by most of the top names like Zeiss, Hornet, Gucci, Diesel, Ralph Lauren and Calvin Klein. All of the frames shown on this website have been given a 'fit-to-face' rating which basically gives you an indication of the shape of face they are most suited to and whether they are for men, women or both.

There are often special offers at this site.

Once you've chosen, you can buy online and pay using one of the usual credit/debit cards over a secure connection.

Dollond & Aitchison Sunglasses   http://www.danda.co.uk/sunglasses

For the latest range of designer sunglasses, visit the Dollond & Aitchison website.

Post Optics   **http://www.postoptics.co.uk/**

Providing you know your prescription, you can order all types of contact lenses and solutions at significantly reduced prices, even after you've added postage and packing.

Body products

We spend countless millions of Dollars, Pounds and Marks on potions to make our bodies look and smell better, and also to try to cover up the embarrassment they sometimes cause us.

Avon   **http://www.uk.avon.com/**

One of my earliest recollections of TV advertising was of the Avon commercials when the lady rings the front door bell which gave rise to the immortal catch-phrase – 'ding-dong, Avon calling'.

You too can be an Avon representative. Details are available on the Avon website.

The Body Shop   **http://www.bodyshop.com/**

Using animals for testing medicines that will eventually save lives is one thing, but using animals for testing make-up so that women (and men) can make themselves appear more attractive is something else.

The thousands of people who agree have made the Body Shop the success that it has been.

The name Body Shop has become synonymous with fair trade, natural products and non-animal testing. For lovers of Body Shop products, this site provides a wealth of information about them, about the company itself and its trade links.

The Fragrance Shop
http://www.fragrance-shop.co.uk/

There's lots of smelly stuff here for both men and women. The Fragrance Shop also sells toiletries and gifts. All of the leading brands are here at below high street prices. Watch out for special offers that save you even more.

Island Trading
http://www.island-trading.com/

Free shipping to UK and US makes shopping at this site worth considering. There are perfumes for both men and women as well as cosmetics. The

Perfume is subject to excise duty in many countries.

products are indexed according to brand and most of the top names are available. There is secure online ordering and fast delivery.

Look Fantastic
http://www.lookfantastic.com/

You get up to 60% off many hair care products and access to additional resources when you register. You can securely purchase many 'salon only' hair and beauty products; the advice offered is supplied by industry professionals.

Manpack

Manpak try to make life easier for men by delivering a variety of grooming products direct to your door, anywhere in the UK. Items include shaving gel, shampoo, condoms and contact lens solutions.

If you join the subscription service (UK£15 per month), Manpack will deliver grooming products each month.

Instead of accepting the standard pack of products, you can pick exactly what you want for an extra UK£3.50 per month.

Tisserand

Aromatherapy is claimed to be beneficial and has been used for thousands of years. Tisserand manufacture a wide range of products which can be ordered via email from this site.

Molton Brown
http://www.moltonbrown.com/

For over 25 years, Molton Brown have been satisfying cosmetic needs with formulas that include natural ingredients. There are skin and hair products and sections headed Chinese Remedies, Bathroom Treatments and Travel Companions.

Try their exclusive Gift Wrapping Service. Tick the Gift Service box on the Order Form and your gift will be sent complete with a personalised, hand written card.

Sephora
http://www.sephora.com/

Just about every makeup product currently available is here, online, at this US website. All the top names are on offer including Dior, 4711, Alchemy, Gucci and Yves Saint Laurent. The prices are low with frequent special offers.

Many products can be supplied gift-boxed and you have a choice of shipping methods ranging from free (for surface delivery) to US$20 for overnight delivery.

Sephora currently only ships within the US.

This site also features a superb makeover section which is basically a list of products used to produce a particular effect.

Condoms

Continuing on the general theme of things to wear...

Condomania   http://www.condoms4u.com/

Apart from a wide selection of condoms from names like Durex, Mates, Benetton, CMD, Condomi, MAPA, RFSU and Trojan, Condomania also sell lubricant and other 'personal' products. All items are delivered in a discreet wrapper so you won't see the postman falling about on the drive.

Condoms UK   http://www.condoms.co.uk/

This UK company buys condoms in large quantities direct from the manufacturers, enabling them to negotiate substantial discounts which are then passed on to the customers. There is free delivery to any UK address and they arrive in a discreet plain wrapper.

Condoms help prevent sexually transmitted diseases.

The Condom Shop   http://www.condomshop.co.uk/

With a claimed discount of up to 45%, the Condom Shop is one of the largest Internet retailers of condoms. They stock a huge range which varies in shape, size and feel. In fact, there's almost certainly something that's right for you. The range includes many famous names like Durex, Mates, Benetton, RFSU, Contempo, Billy Boy, Vitalis, Condomis, Boys own, Girls own, Condomi Ticklers and a wide range of personal lubricants.

Durex   http://www.durex.com/

This is the website of what surely must be the most famous condom in the world. You can take a ride through the pages containing essential information to keep fully tuned into safer sex. There's plenty of material on the whole Durex range and tips on how to use condoms as well as up-to-the-minute information on the latest sex trends.

If the site itself doesn't provide enough sexual innuendo, then go to the postcard page where you can send a friend one of the Durex online postcards.

You can buy Durex online, by going to the link labelled 'Condom Store'.

Glyde Products   http://www.kiaorapacific.com.au/

This Austrailian site has a wide range of condoms and other sexual health products, all of which can be purchased online.

ME Mail Order   http://www.memailorder.com/

This UK site offers up to 50% off the usual price of a wide range of condoms and other sexual aids like lubricants.

The Rubber Tree   http://www.rubbertree.org/

The Rubber Tree is a US non-profit making online store. They have the best prices and selection on all brands of condoms, lubricants, safe sex supplies, and information about sexually transmitted diseases.

Safex **http://www.safex.co.uk/**

This popular brand of condoms can be purchased online from this secure site. There is a good range to choose from and the site also offers lots of help and advice about safer sex.

Watches

Like it or not, time dominates the lives of many of us. If we really must keep an eye on the passing seconds, it makes sense to have something that's worth looking at.

Charles Rennie Mackintosh Watches   *http://www.charles-rennie-mackintosh-watches.com/*

Charles Rennie Mackintosh was a designer and architect. As an architect he designed the Glasgow School of Art but also applied his talents to furniture and textiles. Currently enjoying a recent resurgence of popularity, Mackintosh jewellery is simple and uncluttered. You can browse and buy Charles Rennie Mackintosh watches, clocks and jewellery from this UK website. They will ship anywhere in the world.

Jaeger le Coultre
http://www.mjlc.com/

Although you can't buy online from this site, you can get a list of email addresses of retailers throughout the world.

The site features some excellent demonstrations of these fine watches, but some of the graphics are quite large and can take some time to download.

The Swiss Watch Company
http://www.watches.co.uk/

This UK company buy and sell quality watches from top brands like Tag Heuer, Brietling, Omega and Rolex. All watches are described and illustrated with pictures of the actual watch. The prices are amazing.

Watches
http://www.watches.com/

This US site offers quality watches from over 300 world class brands. There is free overnight shipping in the US and free gift packaging if required.

Watch Heaven
http://www.topbrands.net/

You can buy Swatch, Casio, Seiko and Swiss Army watches online from this UK website. The search engine helps you choose a watch by model, type or price range. The prices are considerably lower than in the high street.

Cars and Bikes

Apart from a house, a motor car is likely to be the single most expensive purchase made by a family. The cost doesn't end there, either.

Just before my 17th birthday, my father told me, "If you choose to learn to drive, you'll have your hand in your pocket for ever". How true that was. But the promise of increased personal mobility and the freedom that that provided were too great. On my 17th birthday I started driving lessons and 5 months later I passed my test. Twenty-odd years later, I still haven't stopped spending.

In the 100 years since the first motor car clattered along a cobble-stoned path at little more than walking pace, we have learnt to rely on them.

At the time of writing, very few motor manufacturers will actually sell you a car over the Internet. There is no reason why they shouldn't, but most do not. So why include websites from which you can't shop in an online shopping guide? Quite simply because however you choose to buy your car, the Web will provide you with an excellent reference source for you to look, compare and even dream about what you'd like to be seen driving. Research has shown that in the US, more and more people have armed themselves with facts from the Internet before speaking to a dealer about buying a car.

The manufacturers' websites will provide all the information you need to arm yourself ready for a one-to-one 'discussion' with the man or woman in the garage. Indeed, this is the most important point. It doesn't matter that you can't actually make the purchase online from a manufacturers' site, it's being able to easily collect the information to make a sound and considered choice that's important.

That said, there are many websites at which you can buy a car online, and most of those listed here will at least sell you something – even if it's not a car.

Official car websites

Virtually every motor manufacturer from around the world has at least one website, known as the official website, and in most cases, typing in the make of the car followed by .*com*/ will take you there.

Many people latch onto this and visit the exotic sites of Ferrari or Porsche, but don't forget the sites of some of the more ordinary cars like Renault or Honda.

AC   http://www.accars.com/

Originally based at Thames Ditton, Auto Carriers' (or AC as they are more commonly known) greatest claim to fame was the awesome Cobra. Actually inspired and developed by American racer Carroll Shelby, the Cobra was based on the AC Ace, but fitted with a V8 engine whose size eventually rose to 7 litres. This very new website features an email link for more details.

Alfa Romeo   http://www.alfaromeo.com/

The second most famous Italian car manufacturer has lost its 1970's image of biodegradable cars and now builds quality performance cars which ooze style. The website gives all the specifications of the current models in the virtual showroom, and you can download an Alfa Romeo screensaver, desktop wallpaper and even some film clips from this site.

Aston Martin
http://www.astonmartin.com/

Aston Martin has become synonymous with craftsmanship, performance and individuality, and this is clearly reflected in their website. Although you cannot actually buy cars from this site, you can contact the parts department for spares dating back to 1958. You can also buy a range of Aston Martin merchandise online.

Audi
http://www.audi.com/

The Audi site provides full details of all their current models including the variants, options and accessories. There is also an online contact form for local details – i.e. specification relevant to a particular country. Vorsprung durch Technik, as they say on some parts of the Web.

Bentley
http://www.rolls-royceandbentley.co.uk/

WO Bentley's cars were once described by Ettore Bugatti as 'the fastest lorries in the world'. Today, even though kitted out with half a forest of walnut on the dashboard, a herd of cow hides on the seats and enough wool in the carpet to provide coats for most of the population of Siberia, they are slightly lighter. But not much. Although many models are little more than re-badged Rolls Royces, they are the epitome of opulent performance for a favoured few. You can't buy anything from this site, but you can collect all the information about the current models.

BMW
http://www.bmw.com/

The key feature of this really impressive website is that you can calculate the exact cost of your new BMW including all the extra bits you want that make an already very nice car, even more special. Once you've entered the site, you can choose the language you wish to read, and also find details about the cars for a particular market. So, if you're buying in Australia, you can find the exact specification of the car you want and get it priced. The final quote can then be taken to your dealer. You can also book a test drive on this site, which will be passed to your local BMW agent.

Bristol
http://www.bristolcars.co.uk/

A small, exclusive manufacturer of quality cars that are very traditional and very desirable. Bristol has no agents or dealers and so to buy a Bristol, this is the best place to start. This site provides details of current models and provides a link to their stock of used Bristol motor cars.

Cadillac
http://www.cadillac.com/

Once the manufacturer of luxurious cars boasting V12 and even V16 engines, Cadillac (now owned by General Motors) produces cars of slightly less excess.

Caterham   http://www.caterham.co.uk/

Originally a Lotus dealer, Caterham took the rights to the Lotus 7 to produce the Caterham 7. When describing the Caterham, the word 'minimalist' comes to mind – emphasis is on performance, with scant regard to weather protection, but enormous fun to drive, although sometime a little uncomfortable. If you drive over a coin, you could probably tell if it's heads or tails. Visiting this website will enable you to order genuine Caterham merchandise online, as well as look for pre-owned cars and download a variety of images and information about the cars.

Chevrolet   http://www.chevrolet.com/

Part of the GM Group, Chevrolet produce some very desirable cars, as well as some affordable ones. Full details of all current models are available on this site. Through GM BuyPower you can order a new or used Chevrolet online, arrange a test drive and even get the best purchase price from a dealer. Visit *http://www.gmbuypower* for full details about buying and financing a Chevrolet online.

Chrysler   http://www.chryslerjeep.co.uk/

Once you've arrived at the home page, click on the Chrysler logo to retrieve information about the cars, the people carriers, and the amazing concept cars that are shortly to go into production. The Prowler and the Cruizer look like 1950's hot rods, but are packed with all the modern technology you'd expect from a modern motor car. Once into this site, you can gather all the information you require and even find your nearest dealer. Through this site, you can also place an Internet phone call directly to Chrysler. Even though it may be a long distance or even an international call, you'll only be charged local rate.

Citroën
http://www.citroen.com/

Only the French could produce a Citroën. These refreshingly different cars look like no other and the best way to describe them is, well, French. This very clear and well constructed site provides information on the full range of cars (most of which seem to begin with 'X') and puts you in touch with your nearest dealer.

Daewoo
http://www.dm.co.kr/

You might need to download Korean characters to be able to access parts of this site, although much of it is in English. It shows the full range of cars and I think it describes them too. A website you can't read? That'll be the Daewoo.

Ferrari
http://www.ferrari.it/

Everyone has heard of Enzo Ferrari and his red cars, but you can find out more about the cars on this site. You can't actually buy anything online, but you can send a friend an electronic postcard featuring a picture of, guess what?

Fiat   **http://www.fiat.com/**

Full information about all the current models including the peculiar but highly
practical Multipla. There are links to club sites and the opportunity to
download various gadgets like a screensaver and desktop wallpaper.

Ford   **http://www.ford.com/**

The Ford website provides you with the opportunity to 'configure your own
vehicle' by which they mean select a model, add on all the options and
accessories you like and get the price and delivery time. You can also arrange
finance through the site.

Holden   **http://www.hsv.com.au/**

The website of General Motors' Australian operation provides visitors with
full details of the cars, including options and accessories. One of the most
interesting parts on this site is that you can choose branded merchandise for
a gift for a Holden owner. Go to the online shop and choose 'Gift'. Next enter
the price range and a list of useful everyday objects will be displayed. Select the
one you want, pay for it and arrange for it to be sent directly to the person you
think is most in need of a penknife bearing the Holden logo.

Honda   **http://www.honda.com/**

The Honda site carries detailed descriptions and specifications about their cars
and includes a method of locating your nearest dealer. There's also a vehicle
locator which enables you to choose from a range of Honda approved used cars
from the area in which you live, or beyond if you don't mind travelling. You'll
need to enter some requirements like price and/or model and/or year and a list
is displayed very quickly.

Hyundai   http://www.hyundai-car.co.uk/

The showroom details current models giving ample data and clear descriptions which are well illustrated. There is an approved used car scheme and a variety of fun items like crosswords, a screensaver and desktop wallpaper to download.

Isuzu   http://www.isuzu.com/

The Isuzu site features a 'build your own' section where you can specify a custom-built car and get it priced.

Jaguar   http://www.jaguar.com/

Although now owned by Ford, the official Jaguar website seems to bear no reference to the fact. British Racing Green is a strong feature of the site which carries information about Jaguar's motor racing exploits as well as their road vehicles. All new models are covered in their showroom section and the used car locator can provide details of hundreds of approved pre-owned Jaguar cars.

Jeep   http://www.chryslerjeep.co.uk/

Once described as one of the three keys to American success in the Second World War, the Jeep has come a long way and is now owned by Chrysler. Once you've got into the site, clicking on the Jeep logo takes you to the details of the vehicles which now bear absolutely no resemblance to the cheap utilitarian motors designed by Willys in the late 1930s.

Jenson   http://www.jenson-motors.com/
A classic British car that never achieved the fame of its rivals like Jaguar and Aston Martin. This was probably due to the fact that they never raced cars, which undoubtedly brought rivals a great deal of kudos. (It was Henry Ford who once said 'Race on a Sunday, sell cars on Monday'.) Jenson also didn't build their own engines, preferring to use American V8s. The company went from one crisis to another and finally collapsed. The marque has recently been resurrected and now produces a Jenson sports car. The site includes all the details about Jenson and has email links to the company for orders and enquiries. There are also tips about restoration.

Kia   http://www.kia.com/
Kia began by building bicycles in Korea. When Koreans wanting motorised transport, they started building motorbikes. When there was a market for cars, Kia built cars. It's a pity the industries in some other countries couldn't be as flexible. The Kia website features full details of the current range of Kia cars including pricing.

Land Rover   http://www.landrover.com/
The best '4 x 4 x Far' was the jewel in the crown for BMW when it bought Rover. After entering the website, you can access all the information about the models in the range, locate the nearest dealer, order brochures and even book a test drive.

Lexus   http://www.lexus.com/

The luxury division of Toyota build cars to rival Mercedes Benz and BMW in everything but price. Full details of the models are given, but there is little opportunity to get prices for cars equipped to personal specification. The reason is simple: Lexus cars have few optional extras as virtually everything you want is included as standard. The used car locator is brilliantly simple to use but dealers could be more pro-active in getting pictures of used cars onto the site.

The New IS. It's Sufficiently Radical.

When trying to market the newest and boldest member of the Lexus family, one can get a little carried away. This site features a number of ideas for promoting the IS 300 that were canceled after giving our lawyers massive coronaries.

5 Create Your Own TV Spot And Win An IS.

Lotus   http://www.lotuscars.co.uk/

The website features details about these highly desirable cars whose reliability has very often been suspect. Remember the Lotus acronym: Lots Of Trouble – Usually Serious. This site features the usual diet of model specifications and information about their dealer network. Also available is a range of clothing and other badged merchandise which can be purchased online. Gifts include aluminium pens, shirts and caps.

Marcos   http://www.marcos.co.uk/

The Marcos name came from its two founders Jem Marsh and Frank Costin who built some lovely cars usually on a plywood chassis. The modern cars are very expensive and very desirable being similar in appearance to the cars of the 1960's, but much faster and much more technically advanced. The website features links to other sites, including the unofficial Marcos websites and a list of dealers. All of the current models are outlined with full specifications, but no prices are given. There is an email link to put you in touch with the company.

Maserati   http://www.maserati.it/

Like the site of its Italian rival Ferrari, Maserati has a loyal following of fans. At present, this site features only scant details of the model range which currently stands at one.

Mazda   http://www.mazda.co.uk/

I'm not really sure why one should want to order brochures, when all the information is contained on this website, but that is one of the things you can do. Once here, you can choose the model or models you're interested in and get full details about them including the price. You can also choose an approved used Mazda from this site.

Mercedes Benz   http://www.mercedes-benz.com/

One of the most desirable cars in the world, it has even had a song written about it. This site includes no pricing, but full technical specifications of all current models from the cute little A Class to the luxurious and ultra-safe S Class limousine. Look out for links labelled 'Technical Drawings'. Follow them and you'll get to an amazing collection of cutaway drawings to download.

MG   http://www.mgcars.com/

William Morris used his garage in Oxford to tune-up production cars and so was born MG – Morris Garages. Now owned by Rover who dropped the marque for some years but then resurrected it with the MGF. Full details of the MGF cars are available with information about the nearest distributor. The inevitable merchandising is in evidence here with an assortment of clothes and clutter (including models of the cars) which can be ordered online. You can also download an MGF screensaver and desktop wallpaper and test drive a virtual MGF Steptronic. You'll need to have Shockwave 7 installed (see the chapter on software downloads) and you'll need to be using Internet Explorer for this to work. Steptronic is an automatic transmission which is controlled by buttons on the steering wheel.

Mini   http://www.mini.com/

Along with the E Type Jaguar, Harold Wilson and the Beatles, the Mini was the icon of the 1960's. Designed by Sir Alec Issigonis, it featured a revolutionary front wheel drive layout with the engine mounted across the car instead of inline. Forty years on, the motoring public is being force-fed a diet of front wheel drive cars using a similar configuration. This is a curious site, with links to a section where you can buy a classic Mini and take part in an auction where you pay with 'Bobs' - the site's own currency. You earn Bobs by winning online games and by sending emails. When you've earned enough Bobs, you can visit the auction and bid for items. If you buy it, you're sent it. You can also design a car online and buy a range of Mini merchandise.

Mitsubishi   http://www.mitsubishi-cars.co.uk/

You'll need a fast Internet link and/or lots of patience to use this website, as every screen seems to have a large animation to download. But you get full details about the cars and a list of the nearest dealers. The download section includes the almost obligatory screensaver and a rally game.

Morgan   http://www.morgan-motor.co.uk/

Apart from the odd bulge to enable a larger engine to be planted in, the exterior design of the Morgan sports car hasn't changed since its introduction. If you want a new Morgan, there's a waiting list. This website will feature cameras showing such events as the unveiling of a new model.

Nissan   http://www.nissan-usa.com/

The car company formerly known as Datsun flooded European markets with cheap but reliable cars in the early 1970's. They haven't looked back since. The 'Showroom' link takes you to a list of current cars with full details. You can find your nearest dealer and also search for an approved used Nissan.

UK residents should visit *http://www.nissan.co.uk/*.

Opel   http://www.opel.com/

Opel are part of General Motors and have an identical model line-up to Vauxhall in the UK. In fact, if you enter 'United Kingdom' when you choose your location, you'll be sent to the Vauxhall website. Apart from the dealer links and approved used car list, there's a rather useful route planner.

Peugeot   http://www.peugeot.com/

This site opens in French, but there is a link for English. You can find the specification for new Peugeots and choose from over 8,000 approved used cars. Watch out for special offers including free insurance on some models.

Porsche   http://www.porsche.com/

This site befits one of the most sought-after sports cars in the world. Full model details are available and the search facility enables you to track down approved used cars.

Proton   http://www.proton.co.uk/

Full model details and dealer information is the backbone of this site. Also included are finance options and brochure ordering.

Renault   http://www.renault.com/

You first need to choose your location from the map of the world and you can then access details about the current models available in your market. You can choose the model you're interested in, the body type (saloon, hatchback) if applicable and you'll be given a list of standard and optional features for that model. Tick the options you wish to include and you'll be provided with the price of your car. You can also arrange a test drive through this site.

Rolls Royce   http://www.rolls-royceandbentley.co.uk/

A website as luxurious as the world's most famous motor car. You can't buy anything from this site, but you can collect all the information about the current models, except the price. If you need to know the price, you can't afford it.

Rover   http://www.rovercars.com/

Now in a state of flux after their connection with BMW, the Rover website is clear, if a little brief in some areas. The clever part about this site is that once you have chosen the model you're interested in, you can view it in all of the available colours. You can also choose to have a 360° tour around the inside and outside of the car. All the technical details are available, although they are not always easy to find.

Saab   http://www.saab.com/

The site opens with a very avant garde introductory screen. After selecting your market, you can view the current models and check the technical specifications. The accessories section provides some useful information about some of the extra equipment available such as a tow bar and even includes a plausible justification for a spoiler. You can order brochures and book a standard test drive from this site and also a 24 hour test drive.

SEAT   http://www.seat.com/

Now owned by Volkswagon, the cars have improved significantly and this is emphasised in their website. You can browse through the range of cars which are well illustrated, before ploughing through the technical bits. You can also locate your nearest dealer through this site.

Skoda   http://www.skoda-auto.com/

Which car manufacturer has won more rallying cups than any other. Audi?
Ford? Lancia? No, Skoda. But for all their success on the track, they were not
well liked by the motoring public. The jokes about Skodas came think and fast
and in most cases, were well deserved. But since becoming part of VW, the
jokes no longer count. This classy, well designed website provides the visitor
with clear signposts for the current car line-up which includes ample
information, both of a technical nature as well as some rather poetic lines to
capture the spirit. The photo gallery features a good selection of pictures of
both the interior and exterior features.

Subaru   http://www.subaru.com/

Subaru are clearly very proud of their All-Wheel-Drive cars and have made it
a prominent feature on their website. The theory being that the flat-4 engine,
with a low centre of gravity, provides sufficient… You can find out about it
yourself. Also featured are the cars with all the information about them and lots
of references to their competition successes. The usual dealer search is
available, as are current colours and prices. To get the best from this site you
really need to have Flash 4 installed and a link is provided to download this if
necessary. (More details about Flash 4 can be found in the chapter on software
downloads.)

Suzuki   http://www.suzuki.co.uk/

This is one of the slickest of the motoring sites with some superb graphics and
animations. You can get information about the cars and the bikes here, order
brochures, and choose colours and investigate the various options. Information
about insurance is also included.

Toyota   http://www.toyota.co.uk/

The Toyota site features the usual diet of dealer search, model search, additional equipment and accessories. You can also find a used Toyota from this site.

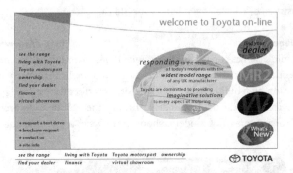

TVR   http://www.tvr-eng.co.uk/

One of the few remaining independent UK car manufacturers left, TVR began just after the war when TreVoR Wilkinson built his first car based on someone else's chassis. By the late 1950's he'd built a car on his own chassis and from there the company grew. This site outlines the history, the racing successes and lists the dealers. The TVR finder is simple but effective: just choose the model you want and you'll get a list of all those available throughout the UK.

Vauxhall   **http://www.vauxhall.co.uk/**

The website of General Motors' UK operation opens with an introduction to BuyPower which is your chance to buy a Vauxhall over the Internet. The rest of the site gives details about the cars including full technical descriptions. You can search for a new or used Vauxhall, locate your nearest dealer and sort out your insurance. You can even have your old car valued.

Volkswagon   **http://www.vw.com/**

The people's car has come a long way since 1938, when Hitler dreamed up the first 'Beetle'. The range now includes some very stylish models with heavy emphasis on high build quality. The website describes the cars and provides a dealer locator. You can book a test drive through the website and search for pre-owned Volkswagons. UK residents should go to *http://www.volkswagon.co.uk/*

Volvo   **http://www.car.volvo.se/**

Volvo were selling safety when other manufacturers were keeping very low-key about the whole issue, fearing that customers did not want to be reminded that the car they were about to buy might be the one they eventually die in. The Volvo website describes some of the safety aspects of their cars, but probably no more so than many of the other manufacturers, who seem to have caught up. You can browse through the virtual showroom, locate selected pre-owned Volvos and find your nearest dealer. There is also information about the accessories, finance and insurance.

Official bike websites

BMW   http://www.bmw.com/

BMW motorbikes are as desirable as their motor cars, and share the same attributes: quality machines with emphasis on performance, but also restrained and responsible driving. The website provides full details of the bikes and gives the visitor the chance to find the nearest dealer.

Ducati   http://www.ducati.com/

Ducati is a name to stir the memories and this site does just that, opening with a picture of Mike Hailwood, former Ducati racer. Visiting the virtual store is just like visiting a real store. You have to go through the doors, report to reception and so on. Once inside, you can view the bikes, find out more about them and find your nearest Ducati dealer.

Harley Davidson   http://www.harley-davidson.com/

If ever the term 'work of art' was applied to a piece of machinery, then it must have been to a Harley Davidson motorcycle. Few machines capture the imagination in quite the same way as the American Harley, which is reckoned to be No1 throughout America, and way beyond. This website contains some of the most stunning pictures of banners and badges that really do look like chrome has been laid on with a trowel. There are lots of pictures of the bikes past and present. Yes, and there are plenty of shots of the Electra Glide.

Honda   http://www.honda.com/

The first screen of the Honda site looks bleak, but click on the motorbike link and the website opens up and looks far more palatable. It contains full details of the current range of bikes with lots of pictures to get the adrenaline flowing.

Moto Guzzi   http://www.motoguzzi.it/

Often referred to as the Ferrari of motorbikes, the Italian Moto Guzzi bikes are very fast and very desirable. Full details of all of the bikes may be found on the website.

Kawasaki   http://www.kawasaki.com/

One of the big four Japanese bikes, Kawasaki has a long racing history and this is clearly shown in the pages of their website. There are lots of pictures of fast bikes (and bikes going fast) with full technical specifications as well as some subjective text to give you the full flavour of what you're looking at. Kawasaki make more than just motorbikes, but if it's motorbikes you want to look at, click the appropriate button on the home page.

Suzuki   **http://www.suzukicycles.com/**

Another great name in motorbike racing, Suzuki's website contains all the important information as well as some details which are perhaps less important. Full technical specifications to make your mouth water and the almost obligatory dealer locator.

Triumph   **http://www.triumph.co.uk/**

This British bike manufacturer has had its share of ups and downs in recent years, (notably during the 1970s) largely due to their inability to fight off the competition from the Japanese. But they're back and their website provides full details of their bikes, together with accessories and all the special clothing you need to go with it. The history has not been overlooked and there is a link to the US site.

Yamaha   **http://www.yamaha-motor.com/**

Full details about Yamaha's competition success are included in this site together with lots of pictures of bikes, with the full technical details.

Importing cars

The current cry in the UK is that cars are overpriced compared to other areas of the EEC. This has led to individuals importing cars themselves which in turn has led to individuals forming companies that specialise in importing cars built to UK standards at significantly less than the 'official' dealers charge.

Parallel import

If you choose to buy a car through one of these companies, make sure you are satisfied that the company will still be operating when they say the car will be delivered. In other words, use a reputable company. Several people have come unstuck by handing over large sums of cash by way of a deposit, only to find the company ceases trading. The scenario usually goes along the lines of "…sorry, we've been experiencing some delays, but your car should be ready next week." Next week comes and goes and further enquiries yield responses like, "…the car is on the boat." The next thing you know is that the company has ceased trading and further enquiries reveal that the order had never been placed with the overseas agent.

With some companies, you have to pay a small sum of money to get the actual quotation, followed by a deposit equivalent to anything between 10% and 25% of the cost of the car. The balance is payable when the car is delivered.

The warranty arrangement will vary from market to market, but as a guide, EEC cars imported into the UK will carry at least a 12 month manufacturer's warranty which will be honoured by the company in the UK. Dealers will be legally obliged to service your car if it was purchased within the EEC, but not if it was purchased elsewhere. You will be the first registered owner of the car and the fact that you have purchased the car from Europe will in no way affect the resale value of it. It will be exactly the same specification as a similar car purchased in the UK.

Autoworld Direct   **http://www.autoworld-direct.demon.co.uk/**
Autoworld Direct will import virtually any make of car into the UK with a substantial discount on the UK list price. There is no registration fee and quotes are usually provided within 24 hours.

Burbank   **http://www.burbankautomotive.com/**
Burbank is one of the largest importers of cars into the UK. They have teamed up with P&O and the full description of this scheme is provided under the P&O heading. Burbank is listed here separately should you wish to contact them directly.

Continent Vehicles   **http://www.continent-vehicles.com/**
The car finder system will ensure you get a very competitive quote for virtually all models. This is a well-constructed site, which includes lots of additional 'value-added' services like finance arrangements and insurance.

P&O   **http://www.posl.com/**
The cross-channel ferry company now offer this service which is actually carried out by one of the largest private car import companies, Burbank. When you enter this site, click on 'Passengers' and then the link to 'Save up to £19000 on a new car'. You'll then be presented with the nine steps you'll need to take to buy a car. You'll need to pay a small deposit to register, but you can get quotes on as many cars as you wish. There are some example discounts but the next step to take is to complete the online form giving details of the car you wish to enquire about, as well as your address and payment details. You'll be asked to pay a deposit of about 15% of the cost of the car you choose.
 As a bonus, registration will also provide you with competitive ferry costs.

Sussex Imports   http://www.sussex-imports.co.uk/

Some cars are available immediately at Sussex Imports and it's worth checking through these in case there's something similar to what you want. Most people will want to specify a car and for this you'll need to move to the online form which requires the usual details about your address and the car you're interested in. Once it's been submitted, you'll get a quote emailed back to you, or if you prefer, posted.

Virgin Cars   http://www.virgincars.com/

This is yet another of Richard Branson's fingers in the Internet pie, and as with all his Internet ventures, it's been well thought out.

To buy a car from this site, you first select the model you want and for this you get the virtual help of Quentin Willson who presents the BBC's Top Gear Motoring programme who has long been an advocate of buying overseas.

You can choose the make and model you want and get the full price (with the percentage saving) and the full technical specification of the car you have chosen. You can then add any options you want, before getting a final price.

Having decided to buy a car this way, you then have the hassle of selling your car. Not so with Virgin because you can get an impartial online valuation of your current car and Virgin may, subject to a certain conditions, buy your old car from you.

Wundercars   **http://www.wundercars.co.uk/**
The new and nearly new car finder service featured on this site is simple and quick to use. Once you've completed and sent the online form (or forms if you want to search for a new or a nearly new car) you'll get a quote emailed to you, or if you prefer, it can be posted. You can also arrange car insurance through the Wundercars website.

Grey import

A grey import is a car that has been built for one market but has been brought into another market either as a new or used car. As far as the manufacturers are concerned, these cars do not exist, so warranties may be an issue in the country to which they are being imported. Cars bought into countries which they were not originally designed for, may have to undergo a type approval test, which may involve making some modifications to the car. Typically, a car bought into a country where the speed is normally set in miles per hour may have to have the speedometer changed if it was originally set up for kilometres per hour. There may also be issues with lights and the petrol filler, not to mention the type of petrol it was designed to use which may not be available in the new country.

Some insurance companies do not look favourably on grey imports, and selling on your grey import may result in a fairly hefty loss. Used cars are usually sourced from rich countries like Japan where they have frequently been saved from the scrap heap after a relatively short life stuck in Tokyo's traffic jams and/or raced round car-parks. They are then sent to poorer countries (like the UK) where they are re-sold. But you can get some super cars at a fraction of the cost you could expect to pay for a genuine (parallel) import.

Blue Chip Motors   **http://www.bluechipmotors.co.uk/**
If you're thinking about a grey import, try Blue Chip Motors who specialise in new and used grey imports. You'll get a good condition car which is UK street legal, although it many have quite a high mileage if it's not new. The website is regularly updated showing the current stock with good descriptions.

Elite Classics   **http://www.elite.co.uk/.**
This site provides photos of cars currently in stock which are mostly new or near-new grey imports. Again, any modifications needed to the cars to make them street-legal will have been carried out before you buy.

SMART   **various – see below**
The SMART is made under licence in France but there are several importers in most countries. To find out more about this amazing car, start off visiting *http://www.wykehams.com/* and then go on to *http://www.ksb.co.uk/* before looking at *http://www.planetmoto.co.uk/* to see how to change the plastic body panels.

Internet retailers

In many ways, these are much more interesting than the manufacturers' sites as they tend to be more impartial. Good deals can be had, as well as finding out a lot more about the car you're interested in. Some car traders have extended their business by selling on the Internet as well as the usual showroom or car lot.

Autobytel

http://www.autobytel.com

Autobytel is one of the largest independent Internet retailers and their website is packed full of information to aid the buyer. Of particular note is the 'Research' section which provides specifications of just about every new car. You can even compare up to three cars side by side so you can really make an informed choice. Once you've made your choice, you can add on all the extras, get an Autobytel quote and buy online.

Autohit

http://www.autohit.com/

Lex Service plc has recently invested heavily in Autohit, making it a major player in Internet car buying. Once you've entered the site, choose the make and model of the car you're interested in. You can add all the extras and accessories you want and you'll then be shown the full specification of the car with a competitive quote. If you prefer a used car, you have a similar form to complete, although you have less opportunity to specify some of the extras. You can, however, choose the transmission type, fuel type and price range.

Autohit can also arrange finance and insurance, find a suitable dealer and provide you with a trade-in value for your old car.

When you begin the six-step buying process, no information is sent until you have completed the last step.

Car Credit   **http://www.yescarcredit.net/**
If you want or need a car but you can't afford one, you can apply for a car loan online from this UK site.

Carshop   **http://www.carshop.co.uk/**
Buying a used car is as easy as 1, 2, 3 here. The first step is to select a used car from the thousands on the site. There is a fast search engine which will locate the car of your choice by make and model and/or price. You will be presented with a list of cars, and clicking on a model will provide you with more details about it. You can then either book a test drive or buy it online there and then.

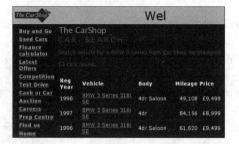

Dixon Motors   http://www.dixonmotors.co.uk/

You can buy new and used cars from this UK dealer. Search for the car you want from the 5,000+ cars available. Dixons will even arrange finance for you. If you want to sell your car, you can get it valued online at this site.

If you don't fancy using a dealership to get your car serviced, try Dixons who offer a flat rate. Choose the service centre nearest to you and then book online.

Motorpoint Cars   http://www.motorpoint.co.uk/

Motorpoint specialise in new or nearly new cars at unbeatable prices. Their search engine enables you to quickly and easily find the car of your dreams, but if you can't find what you want, subscribe to their email service and they will send you up-to-the-minute details of their continually changing stock.

They can arrange finance and you can also buy car-related products like car security and in-car entertainment.

Trade Cars   http://www.trade-sales.co.uk/

Trade Cars specialise in near new cars at dramatically reduced prices. The list is huge, but they are generally mainstream makes like Ford and Vauxhall.

Leasing

You don't have to buy a car, you can lease one. The advantage of not owning a car is that you don't have to worry about servicing costs and you don't have to worry about selling it when you want a new car. You just hand it back. Many people prefer this method of running a car and consider that it works out cheaper. There are lots of leasing companies with websites, these are but a few. NB some of these are for business users only:

AMA	*http://www.vehiclecontracts.co.uk/*
AVC Rent-A-Car	*http://www.all-vehicles.co.uk/*
Brooklands	*http://www.brooklands-group.co.uk/*
Car Myke	*http://www.carmyke.co.uk/*
City Contracts	*http://www.citycontracts.co.uk/*
DVC	*http://www.dvc-contracthire.co.uk/*
Fairway	*http://www.fairway-leasing.com/*
Fleetlease	*http://www.fleetlease.co.uk/*
Fulton	*http://www.fultonnetwork.co.uk/*
West Midlands Vehicles	*http://www.westmidvehicles.co.uk/*

Buying and selling privately

Second-hand car dealers seem to hold a special place in the hearts of the car-buying public. Survey after survey usually places them somewhere between double-glazing salesmen and estate agents. But nobody has to use them. You can buy and sell cars yourself, if you don't mind a little bit of hassle.

Parkers Guide   **http://www.parkers.co.uk/**

When selling your car, you'll first need to find out what it's worth. Parkers Guide is one of the most popular guides to current used car prices and their website is easier to use than their books. To find the value of a car, first select the Make of car from the drop-down menu, and then the model and click on the 'Go' button. You'll next need to choose the derivative (i.e. GSi, SE, GTi etc.) and it is important you get this right because a single letter can mean a significant difference in value. Next you must enter the year of manufacture and the registration letter, and finally the mileage. Click on 'Show me Prices' and you'll get the valuation based on the car being in good condition. Clearly, if it's got bald tyres, dented panels and the engine belches out blue smoke, then the valuation may be a little optimistic.

The Parkers website also contains some valuable information about new and used cars, including best buys. There is a useful section on ways to reduce your insurance premium, which includes buying cars which are relatively cheap to repair. Cars with expensive body parts are therefore expensive to replace and that pushes up insurance premiums. There are several recommended cars and recommended insurers.

There are numerous links to other sites including Auto Trader.

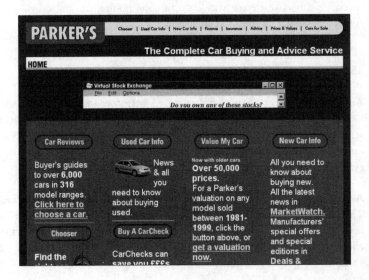

AutoPig   http://www.autopig.com/

Apart from buying used cars, you can sell your car for free.

 This site also features Vehicle Alert which will alert you by email when a car matching your requirements is offered for sale.

When you enter the site, choose the 'Sell' button and choose car, bike or commercial vehicle. Complete the online application form which involves little more than entering the make and model, ticking boxes alongside a list of special features like electric windows, air conditioning etc. and providing a contact telephone number and email address.

If you have a digital picture of your car or bike, (taken with a digital camera or scanned from a conventional photograph) you can send that in to be displayed alongside the description of your pride and joy.

Auto Trader   http://www.autotrader.co.uk/

One way of selling your car is through Auto Trader which offers an Internet service at a reasonable cost. When buying a used car through Auto Trader, you can enter the Make and Model you're interested in and it will list all those cars available.

Autoexchange   http://www.autoexchange.co.uk/

This is Exchange and Mart online. You can search for your dream motor from over 10,000 vehicles advertised by both dealers and private traders. You can, of course, place an advert which will appear both online and in the printed version.

Autohunter   **http://www.autohunter.co.uk/**

Enter the make and model of a new or used car, and Autohunter will try to find
it for you. With approximately a quarter of a million cars for sale on their site,
there's a good chance you'll find what you're looking for. Alongside the car
descriptions is a button labelled 'Test Drive'. Clicking on this will take you to
a description of that type of car, including some of its background. Following
on from that are some problems you're likely (or not likely) to find with that
type of car. There is also some discussion about the prices you could expect to
pay. All in all, some very valuable information for the used and new car buyer.

*There's a lot of information on this site which will be of use to
the buyer and seller like car buying guide, used car price guide
and liabilities.*

Fish 4 Cars   **http://www.fish4cars.co.uk/**

You can also find the Autohunter website at Fish 4 Cars.

What Car   **http://www.whatcar.co.uk/**

When deciding on which car to buy, visit What Car to find out about pros and
cons of just about every model from the last 10 years. It's well worth spending
time finding out what a car is worth, whether it be your car that you want to
sell or a used car you want to buy. To get a car valuation, click on the 'Value
Car' button and choose the make and then the model from the drop down
menus. If the car you want is not in the list, then you've got something either
very old, rare or strange.

After entering the make and model, you'll need to choose the derivative (i.e. GSi, SE, GTi etc.), the fuel type, body type and the year/registration plate. After clicking the 'Submit' button, you'll be given 5 prices – the cost when it was new, the trade price, how much you could expect to get in a part exchange deal with a dealer or trader, how much you could buy or sell the car for privately and how much you could expect to pay if you bought the car from a dealer. The prices are based on the car being in good condition and with average mileage which is usually reckoned to be between 10,000 and 12,000 miles per year. The full list of ifs and buts are also provided on the site. You can advertise your car on the car buying website using a secure payment facility.

Daily Telegraph   **http://www.motoring.ads@telegraph.co.uk/**
If you want to sell your car in the small ads, send details to the Telegraph.

Buying and selling bikes

Many of the online car buying and selling websites also feature bikes for sale or carry adverts for bikes for sale, but these sites specialise in bikes.

Bike Trader   **http://www.biketrader.co.uk/**

Every bike imaginable is for sale on this site – both new and used.

Motorcycle City   **http://www.motorcycle-city.co.uk/**

If four wheels is two too many, then visit Motorcycle City. Here, new and used bikes are categorised by make and type.

Motorcycle City also stock helmets and leathers for all shapes and sizes of rider.

You can't buy bikes online, but you can buy all the clothing and accessories online and pay using the usual range of debit and credit cards. You can also tailor your insurance requirements and get great deals on finance/insurance/recovery packages.

Car clubs

Shopping online is not always about buying. Sometimes it's wise to investigate before buying and if you're in the market for a classic car, a trip around some of the associated sites would be prudent. Owners' Clubs can provide a good source of cheap parts for those whose world revolves around spending Sunday mornings renovating an old wreck, aka a classic motor car. Some even offer cars for sale or at least carry adverts for cars.

There are several club websites for virtually every car ever made and many provide enthusiasts with valuable background information about the love of their life. Some offer a parts buying service through their website, whilst others simply offer other important items like coffee mugs emblazoned with the name of a car, and other useful items like badged string-backed driving gloves.

Yahoo   **http://www.yahoo.com/recreation/automotive**
A good starting point is Yahoo, which lists hundreds of car clubs throughout the world. The quality varies enormously but many have sites which include links to other associated sites.

Old English Car Club   **http://www.islandnet.com/~oecc/oecc.htm**
A good place to begin searching for an Owners' Club for a particular make of UK car is at this website which lists dozens of sites in North America.

Classic Car Owner's Clubs   **http://www.288online.co.uk/classiccars/**
clubs.htm
This UK site lists the major UK car clubs for most world makes. Full details are provided including Web links, email addresses and phone numbers.

Some of the most popular and well-run owners' club sites include:

Auto Classic   **http://www.net.hu/autoclassic/**

This website is actually the online division of Hungary's leading automotive magazine. The site is crammed full of up to date news and views about Hungarian automotive endeavour. There are extracts from past issues of the printed magazine and a useful set of links to other Hungarian Automotive sites. Oh yes, there's also an English translation.

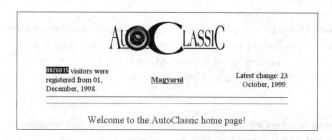

`0026019` visitors were registered from 01, December, 1998.   **Magyarul**   Latest change: 23 October, 1999.

Welcome to the AutoClassic home page!

Team Net   **http://www.team.net**

This website also has links to lots of clubs and motoring organisations. Again, the quality varies enormously, but if you persevere you'll be able to track down classic cars and parts.

Team.Net Automotive Webs

Welcome to the Team Net (the dot is not silent) World Wide Webs.

Aston Martin Owners Club   http://www.amoc.org/

Probably the most famous Aston Martin driver is James Bond who drove a DB5 (with a few modifications) in the third Bond film, Goldfinger. I suppose the second most famous is Prince Charles who has a DB6 Volante. For more information about the cars, rather than the drivers, the Aston Martin Owners Club is the place to go. It's also worth visiting the online store where you can buy a selection of useful everyday items carrying the Aston Martin wings.

Jensen Owners   http://www.british-steel.org/

This site, built and run by enthusiasts, documents the Jensen marque and provides a valuable insight into the company when it was at its height. Lots of pictures and email contacts for help. There is also a good selection of cars for sale.

Norton Owners Club   http://www.noc.co.uk/

Just so the bikers don't feel left out, there are owners clubs for bikes too, and top of the list is the Norton Owners Club. This site is run by a dedicated few and includes a merchandising area where you can buy mugs and pens online, as well as a parts locator. You can even buy a bike from the small ads. If you're thinking of starting an owner's club website, or you run one and want to improve it, take a look at the Norton Owners' Club website to see how it should be done.

Rolls Royce and Bentley   http://www.rrab.com/

Everything you wanted to know about Rolls-Royce and Bentley: all models since 1904, technical data and production figures. You'll find a selection of books on the marques, a detailed description of every model ever built and some answers to some frequently asked questions. Additional highlights are

The Car of the Month, reports about coachbuilders based on in-depth research plus lists of important addresses worldwide, links to other websites etc. You can order books online.

Triumph Owners   **http://www.harding.co.uk/triumph/**
Triumph was part of BMC (British Motor Corporation), which became BLMC (British Leyland Motor Corporation), then British Leyland before becoming Austin Rover and finally Rover, which was bought by BMW who subsequently off-loaded most of it. Somewhere along the way, Triumph got dropped, but the memories live on and the name is now owned by BMW. Owners of a Spitfire, Herald, GT6, TR6 or Dolomite (amongst several others) can visit this site to share news and to get in touch with spare parts, and even whole cars.

Sunbeam Tiger Owner Association   **http://www.engravers.com/tiger/**
The Sunbeam Alpine was a pretty little car of the late 1950's and 60's. Its four cylinder engine was quite good, but it wouldn't really go very fast. So someone had the bright idea of shoehorning an American V8 engine into it, and the Sunbeam Tiger was born. Now very much sought after, this Owner Association website can put you in touch with parts and cars and provide plenty of help with a restoration project.

Registration plates

It's a peculiarly British habit to have special registration plates on cars. Ever since RR1 was sold for a fortune, the British motoring public have been obsessed with registration plates that make up a word or name, preferably relating to the driver (S4LLY (*Sally*), S1MON (*Simon*), S73VEN (*Steven*)) or even to the car on which it is displayed (M3 BMW, V18 MGF). Even the DVLA

(Driver and Vehicle Licensing Agency) has got in on the act by withholding special numbers so they can auction them off at a later date.

If you think you're likely to succumb to this habit, beware that it is an offence to alter the spacing between the characters or deform characters to make them look like something else. This includes strategic positioning of background-coloured rivets. Common examples are '7' made to look like 'T', '4' made to look like 'A' and placing a '1' and a '3' so close together that it looks like 'B'.

Some are quite amusing, like 1 MOK (I'M OK) and ORG 45 M which you can work out for yourself.

DVLA   **http://www.dvla-som.co.uk/**
Visit the DVLA website and you can search for your desired registration mark and get a price on it.

There are countless other websites listing numbers for sale, among the largest are…

Ne-Numbers	*http://www.ne-numbers.co.uk/*
Registration Transfers	*http://www.regtransfers.co.uk/*
Registration Plates	*http://www.regplate.com/*
Speedy Registrations	*http://www.speedyregistrations.co.uk/*

Car insurance

The annual hunt for the cheapest car insurance usually requires numerous telephone calls and several hours waiting around whilst your quote is calculated. An alternative approach is to get a quote online. If you want to give this a try, be aware that the amount of time you're likely to save is negligible – instead of hanging around on the telephone, you'll have to spend about the same amount of time completing online forms.

Once you've completed the online form, many will give an instant response. But in general, you need to be seeking uncomplicated and straightforward cover. If there are any special circumstances, (e.g. you have a high-performance car, two accidents in the last 12 months, three driving convictions and another pending) most instant online insurance quoting software just won't be able to handle it.

Also, if you've previously been refused insurance, had insurance cancelled or special terms imposed, hold a driving licence not issued in the country for which you are applying for insurance, then you will probably not get an instant online quote. Further, if you drive a modified car, a rebuilt car or a kit car, don't be surprised if you can't get instant online cover. In some cases, grey import cars are also excluded from the list of cars available for insurance cover. This is partially due to the possible difficulty in getting parts.

The most important point to note when applying for online insurance, as with any other insurance proposal, is that you must enter correct information. If you make an incorrect or untrue statement, your insurance could be invalid.

AA   **http://www.aainsurance.co.uk/**

The Automobile Association can provide an instant quote, but the form takes quite a time to complete because it's spread across several Web pages each of which contains quite a lot of graphics to download. The good news is that there's a 10% reduction for insurance over the net.

Admiral   http://www.admiral.uk.com/

This insurance company will only quote on cars and insuring drivers within the United Kingdom. Much of the form has to be typed in, but this does mean that any special details can be included. The more detail you can give, the more accurately they can calculate your premium. You do not get an instant quote, but they do contact you, usually within 24 hours.

Bell Direct   http://www.belldirect.co.uk/

Once you've completed the form, Bell Direct will quote, usually within a day.

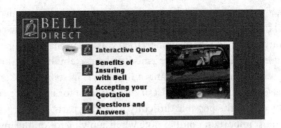

Car Quote   http://www.carquote.co.uk/

This is the one-stop car insurance site that puts you in touch with the best quote on the market. You fill in one form and your enquiry is sent to your choice of some of the biggest names in car insurance. You'll receive your insurance quotes either by email or post. Car Quote sends your proposal to about a dozen insurers including Admiral, CGU Assurance plc, The Direct Insurance Centre, First Rate Direct and Norwich Union Direct.

CGU   **http://www.cgudirect.co.uk/**

For an insurance quote you must complete the online form, print it and post it to CGU and you'll receive a written quote by return.

Direct Line   **http://www.directline.com/**

This site has been very well designed with as much use made of existing information as possible. For example, you only have to enter your postcode and house number and the system knows your address.

Diamond   **http://www.diamond.uk.com/**

Jokes about women drivers have been told ever since women started driving. But the fact is, women have fewer accidents than men. Young men in particular, have a much worse driving record than women of the same age. Sexist it may be, but because of this women attract lower insurance premiums than men and Diamond recognise this by specialising in insuring the fairer, less aggressive and safer sex.

Eagle Star Direct   **http://www.eaglestardirect.co.uk/**

This company offers a well organised online proposal form and a very competitive quote.

Ironsure   **http://www.ironsure.com/**

To insure with Ironsure you must be the main user of your car, keep your car at your home address, have no more than 6 current conviction points on your driving licence and not have been disqualified from driving in the last 10 years. Furthermore, you must not have made more than 2 motor claims in the last 3 years. You must be under age 75 and not employed in the following occupations – professional sportsperson, driving instructor, courier, fast food delivery, entertainer, actor, musician, TV or Radio presenter or any purpose in connection with the motor trade. Your car must be less than 15 years old and must not be left hand drive or have any modification to wheels, body, engine or audio system that are not part of the manufacturer's standard specification. Once you've passed that lot, the form is quite straightforward.

Norwich Union Direct   **http://www.norwichuniondirect.co.uk/**
Provided that your vehicle has not been modified and not valued at more than £35,000, you could get it insured with Norwich Union. But you or the other proposed driver must never have been refused insurance or had a criminal conviction or had terms imposed on previous insurance policies. You and other proposed drivers must not have had any more than one claim/accident in the last four years and not had any motoring convictions in the last five years. Like many others, Norwich Union don't seem to like actors or actresses of film, stage, TV or radio including presenters, professional sportsmen/women including trainers, taxi or minicab drivers, driving instructors, couriers or fast food delivery drivers.

The online motor quotation service is available between 6am to 10pm Monday to Friday and 8am to 6pm Saturday and Sunday.

Quoteline Direct   **http://www.nwnet.co.uk/wilsons/**
The form is quite straight forward and quick to complete, largely aided by the fact that each 'page' of the online form has very few graphics to download. As a result, pages load much faster. Overall, one of the best sites, although it sometimes trips up over your occupation. The quote is calculated quickly and returned to you within a minute.

Sun Alliance   **http:/www.sunalliance.co.uk/**

If all of the drivers you want on a motor insurance policy are between 21 and 74, have driven regularly in the UK on a full EU or UK licence for the past year, are accident, loss and claim-free for the past 5 years, are conviction free for the past 5 years and have no prosecution pending (parking and one SP30 or SP40 speeding conviction per driver can be ignored), the car you wish to insure is not a company car and is a family saloon, estate or hatchback (not a modified or high-performance car), you are the registered owner/keeper and no drivers have been advised by a doctor not to drive or have been refused a driving licence in the past year, you could get a really competitive quote from Sun Alliance. The online form is easy to complete and you get an almost instant quotation.

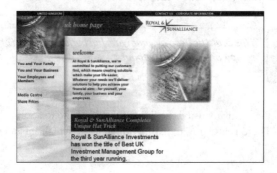

Screentrade   **http://www.screentrade.com/**

Rather than entering your details lots and lots of times, you can find a cheap insurance quote from a large range of leading insurers through Screentrade. Different policy options for cover, excess and drivers are available and you can buy quickly and easily online.

Anti-theft devices

Car crime is big business in virtually every county that uses motor cars. Car alarms are notoriously ineffective. It seems to me that the best time to steal a car is when the alarm is sounding because everyone assumes it's a false alarm. New technology has bought about new methods of detecting crime and recovering the stolen car before it's dismantled and/or exported.

Carbug   http://www.carbug.co.uk/

Carbug uses satellite tracking technology to pinpoint your car anywhere on the planet at any time, day or night. A special unit is fitted into your car and some software supplied for you to install in your PC. If your car is stolen, the program will tell you exactly where it is.

This could be used by your wife, husband, boyfriend or girlfriend to spy on your whereabouts.

Email the company using the link on their website to arrange fitting and payment. There is also a nominal monthly charge which includes software upgrades.

Trackstar   http://www.ractrackstar.co.uk/

RAC's Trackstar is technically similar to Carbug. The main difference is that if your car is stolen, you notify HQ and they track it, inform the Police and arrange collection and return of your vehicle. There are several versions available including one which offers assistance in the event of a breakdown.

If you cover a lot of miles alone, this piece of equipment could prove to be a lifesaver.

Trackstar can be ordered directly over the Internet over a secure connection. There is an initial fitting charge followed by payments which can be made either quarterly, annually or a single payment for the duration you own the car.

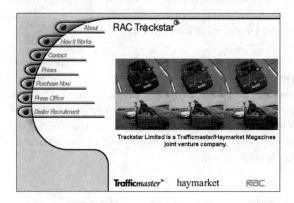

Trackstar Limited is a Trafficmaster/Haymarket Magazines joint venture company.

Traffic Master   **http://ractrackstar.com/**

The most frustrating part of modern driving is getting stuck in a huge stationary queue of traffic. Even more aggravating is joining a queue just after you've passed the exit on a motorway. Traffic Master can help avoid this by giving a constant readout of the speed of the traffic in front on you. Visit this site to get full information about the system and buy the kit online.

Safer driving

Apart from the cost in terms of pollution, motoring accounts for thousands of deaths and serious injuries every year. It seems that for some people, passing the driving test represents the final accolade and they see no point in taking any further lessons or instruction. This attitude is not to be recommended.

Paul Ripley   http://www.paulripley.com

Paul Ripley is probably the most experienced and qualified driver, certainly in the UK and probably further afield. It's well worth looking at his site to get an insight into the areas of your driving that could be improved on. You might then consider taking one of his practical driving courses.

IAM   http://www.iam.org.uk

The Institute of Advanced Motorists offers a test lasting about 90 minutes in your own car. The essential qualities they're looking for are concentration, observation, anticipation and planning. The examiner will be a holder of the Police Advanced Driving Certificate, so you can be sure s/he really knows what s/he's doing. The website feature some IAM accessories and advice packs which can be ordered online.

**The Institute of
Advanced Motorists**

359 Chiswick High Road, LONDON W4 4HS
Telephone - 020 8994 4403, Fax - 020 8994 9249

Registered Charity No 249002

IAM members also attract lower insurance premiums and discounts on a wide range of products.

Servicing and spares

Regrettably, the spending doesn't stop once you've bought a car. It's important to keep it running safely and legally.

Haynes Manuals   http://www.haynes.co.uk/

Some people service their cars themselves because they can't afford dealership prices. Others do it because they don't trust dealers to do it properly. Others just like to tinker for the sake of it. Whichever camp you fall into, a decent workshop manual is essential and Haynes are probably the best known.

Their website lists all of the cars for which there are workshop manuals and you can buy online. IAM members get a 15% discount.

Kwik-Fit   http://www.kwik-fit.com/

"You can't get quicker than a Kwik-Fit fitter" is the quote from the adverts. What is also true is that you can't get much cheaper. If you compare Kwik-Fit prices for exhausts and brakes against the charges made by dealerships, you'll be amazed.

There's a really good section entitled "Trouble starting in the morning?".

The website features a 'Dial-a-Tyre' service. Simply complete the online form stating your requirements, and Kwik-Fit will fax, phone or email a quote telling you when and where you can have them fitted.

National Tyres

http://www.national.co.uk/

The amount of tyre in contact with the road is an area about the equivalent to the sole of a man's shoe. Multiply that by the number of wheels on the car and that's all you've got to get round a corner or stop short of a hazard. It's worth making sure that your tyres are in good condition and National Tyres is one of the leading UK dealers in quality replacement tyres. You can use this site to find the correct size of tyre for your car. Current online information covers tyres, exhausts, shock absorbers, brakes, batteries and oil and filters.

This site has some valuable information on the legal requirements for tyres on both cars and bikes.

236 | Cars and Bikes

Technology

Computers are big business. It's quite astonishing that in such a short time they've developed from a piece of unreliable machinery that fills a room, to a tool that almost anyone can afford. But if you are in the market for a computer, it pays to shop around for the best deals.

Pre-built computers

There are several companies who will supply you with a computer either 'off the shelf' or built to your specification. Complete packages tend to be set up and ready to go (after you've connected all the bits together).

Buy Buddy   **http://www.buybuddy.com/**

The main feature of this US site is computers, in the broadest sense of the word. Everything which is even remotely associated with computers is covered and includes pre-built systems, components, upgrades and software, but also extends to laptops, palmtops and organisers.

Apart from comparing prices, and giving the lowest for your chosen product, Buy Buddy can also provide technical comparisons between rival products.

Computer Prices   **http://www.computerprices.co.uk/**

This UK site offers pricing comparisons for pre-built PCs and components. You can customise how the results will be displayed in several ways, including by choosing to have the prices displayed with or without VAT and to show mail order and/or online retailers. Products can also be shown in alphabetical order by distributor, or ordered according to price.

A particularly useful section is the discussion area which shows the best deals for particular products, but also outlines what you should look for when choosing a product.

Crucial   http://www.crucial.com/

This US site has international links, including one to the UK. It carries details about a wide range of computer equipment with prices. You can find the best memory price in seconds and the site also offers advice about upgrades

Dabs   http://www.dabs.com/

You can buy computers and peripherals from all the top names at the Dabs website. The site opens with the current top bargains and a series of links at the side takes you to areas like Hewlett Packard, Toshiba, Epson and Compaq. Carriage is free for all Internet orders delivered to a UK address.

Discounts Online   http:/www.discounts.co.nz/

This New Zealand store not only sells computers, but a huge range of peripherals and software.

ETEC Solutions   http://www.etec-solutions.co.uk/

Apart from building 'off-the-peg' computer systems, ETEC also build computers to order as well as supplying spares and upgrades.

Fujitsu Siemens   http://www.underagrand.co.uk/

Advertised in the UK as the first 700MHz computer under UK£1000, the Fujitsu is a powerful machine but excellent value for money.

Gateway   http://www.gateway.com/

This US site has links to 15 other sites around the world. You can buy quality, hi-spec desktop and laptop computers at low prices.

Look out for re-manufactured computers at knock-down prices.

Apart from buying online, the site also features tips about buying and using many popular peripherals including scanners and digital cameras. There's a useful feature entitled 'Build your own website'.

Hal Computers   http://www.halonline.com/

Hal make a range of hi-spec and budget computers, including custom-built PCs. They also sell peripherals and upgrades at very competitive prices. All products are described on their website and are available with secure online ordering.

Jungle.com   http://www.jungle.com/

When you get to this site, click on the link to Jungle Computers. Once there you can check out the current best buys or browse through the stock which is indexed under both brand (3Com, Acer, Adobe, Apple, Brother, Canon, Corel, Creative, Diamond, Epson, Hewlett Packard, Intel, Iomega, Kodak,

You can also buy software and download it from this site.

Lexmark, Lotus, Macromedia, Microsoft, Sony, Symantec, Toshiba and UMAX) and type (software, computers, printers, scanners etc.).

Jungle is also a good site to visit for consumables like paper and discs.

Micro Warehouse   http://www.microwarehouse.co.uk/

There are some huge savings to be had at this UK site which stocks just about everything a computer user/enthusiast could want.

> *It's worth visiting this site if you fancy either upgrading your existing computer or building a computer yourself.*

All items can be purchased online, but you'll need to register first. Once you have registered and recorded all your details, future visits will require you to simply log-on with a user name and password.

Modern Computers   http://www.moderncomputers.com/

This company builds a small range of budget and more advanced systems, but offers the end user some options such as choice of processor. So, if you have something special in mind, get a quote from Modern Computers. Products can be viewed online, but ordering is via email.

PC World   http://www.pcworld.co.uk/

The most famous PC store in the UK is online and orders can be made over the Internet.

> *http://pcworld.com/ takes you to PC World (the magazine) where you can get lots of information about the latest trends in the world of computers.*

The online stock is the same as that found in the stores although there are discounts for online ordering.

Quantex   **http://www.qtx.co.uk/**

People tend to buy computers in much the same way as they used to buy hi-fis: they choose the models with the largest numbers associated with them. If there's a choice between 600MHz and 633MHz, they buy the one with the larger number, even though it might be impossible to tell the difference.

You can buy budget, low-spec computers, the very latest computers with the latest gizmos attached and just about everything in between from this UK store.

Simply Computers   **http://www.simply.co.uk/**

One of the big names in computers in the UK, Simply Computers also stocks software and offers a free three-day delivery on most products.

When you get to this site you can choose to select a customisable computer system, a non-customisable computer system or a pre-configured system. There are also links headed software licensing and printer consumables.

Tiny Computers   http://www.tiny.com/

With more and more stores springing up, Tiny is actually quite large. The site splits into three sections for UK, US and Asia/Pacific customers. You can view and order a computer online for either home or office use. Tiny also produce 'First Computers' and 'Entertainment Computers' which are specially equipped with particular software or hardware to meet a specific need.

21 Store   http://www.21store.com/

This UK/US/Canadian store stocks a wide range of computers, organisers, digital cameras, MP3 players, GPS receivers and a whole host of other hi-tech products. The prices are well below those found in the high street and there are often free gifts with your purchases.

Used computers

If you buy a computer this week, you can bet that in a few months, weeks or even days the price will have dropped because a newer model has made your one obsolete. There is a school of thought that suggests that rather than buying a new computer which will halve its value in a very short space of time, it's better to buy a computer that's already obsolete and save yourself the depreciation.

Pre-owned or second-user computers can be bought very cheaply from a variety of outlets. The hardware is mainly that discarded by companies when they upgrade, or ex-lease stock. Don't buy something too old because it just won't be able to run modern software, but if you look around, you can pick up some real bargains. If you're looking for a pre-owned system, go for at least a Pentium 133MHz processor or equivalent.

Games Terminal   **http://www.gamesterminal.com/**
Claimed to be the Net's largest resource for second-hand console and PC games, there are also some amazing deals on new games for Dreamcast, Playstation, N64 and PC.

M M Trading   **http://www.mmtrading.co.uk/**
This company specialises in buying and selling computers. You can check the latest stock list and prices online and complete the online order form to buy.

PC2GO   **http://www.pc2go.co.uk/**
This UK company occasionally have new items for sale, but it is mainly pre-owned desktop and laptop computers with some printers. Stock and prices are regularly updated on the Web pages, but you'll have to order via email.

RDC Shop   http://www.rdcshop.co.uk/

Secure online ordering is a key feature of RDC who specialise in the management of redundant IT assets. This website details a large range of pre-owned laptops, desktops, printers and monitors for sale.

Computer upgrades and peripherals

The cost of computer parts fluctuates dramatically. Prices of some components can change by significant amounts almost overnight. This is particularly true of RAM and so to ensure you get the best (and the latest) price, it makes sense to use the Internet.

Fujitsu   http://www.fujitsu.com/mall.html

Apart from complete computer systems and peripherals like scanners and printers, you can buy good quality hard drives and memory from this website.

You can download software such as printer drivers from the Fujitsu website.

G2   http://www.gsquared.net/

Although you can't actually order online at present, visiting the G^2 website will provide you with all the facts and figures about their stock which includes monitors, hard discs and processors.

Micrologic   http://www.micro-logic.com/

Whether you're building a system or upgrading an existing computer, a visit to Micrologic should prove financially beneficial. All the bits you're likely to need are here and reasonably priced. Secure online ordering has recently been added to this site making it even more worth a visit.

Midwest Information Systems   http://www.midwest-it.com/

You can buy a complete system or the components and do it yourself from this UK store. All the stock can be viewed online, but at present orders can only be taken by phone.

Mustek   http://www.mustekdirect.com/

You can buy most of Mustek's scanners and digital cameras online. Look out for special offers including some refurbished models at ridiculously low prices.

Planet Micro   http://www.planetmicro.co.uk/

Everything you need to build your own PC is available from this site, and at prices that make you wonder why pre-built computers are so expensive.

 You can also buy complete systems from Planet Micro.

There is a good selection of cases, processors, motherboards, hard disc drives and all the rest of the bits you need. Online purchasing is available with a secure connection.

Quantum   **http://www.quantum.com/**

The world famous hard disc drive manufacturers now produce QDT (Quiet Drive Technology) – about the quietest drives available. All Quantum's products, including their disc drive and tape drive range, are available online.

RL Supplies   **http://www.rlsupplies.co.uk/**

Although you can't buy online at present, you can view all of the products and specifications on this regularly updated website. The stock is comprehensive and very competitively priced. It's worth looking here before trying to buy elsewhere.

Worldspan Communications   **http://www.span.com/**

For a wide range of quality hardware at rock-bottom prices, visit Worldspan. Everything for the home-builder is available here including SCSI and IDE hard drives, memory, motherboards, cases and video/sound cards. All prices are quoted on their website and secure online ordering is available.

Organisers

Portable computing is very much the order of the day for business people on the move. A computer that runs on batteries frees the user from the desk and enables him or her to work at times when they would otherwise be passing the time of day, possibly being bored. A train journey is a typical example.

Level 1   http://www.level1group.com/

This dedicated one-stop-shop for Psion computers and organisers offers just about everything you could possibly need including the computer itself. All products can be ordered online and delivery is fast.

Look out for the special offers which include both hardware and software.

Although not the most artistically inspired website, it is efficient.

Palm Pilot   http://www.palm.com/

The Palm series of computers are quite different from most other organisers in so far as they don't have a keyboard. Instead they have just half-a-dozen buttons positioned around a touch-sensitive screen. For text entry there is an on-screen 'virtual' keyboard and hand-writing recognition. The Palm models connect to either PC or Apple Mac so that data can be moved between them.

Widget   http://www.widget.com/

Widget are one of the leading companies for palmtop computers and organisers. If you want to buy a Psion, Palm or Windows CE computer, or you want a peripheral, an accessory or some software for one, this will probably be your first port of call.

The website links to US, UK and Canadian sites.

You can now download Psion, Palm and Windows CE software from Widget.

Mobile phones

The number of mobile phones being used worldwide is staggering, and increasing by the minute. But I'm not convinced that everyone who owns a mobile phone actually needs one. For the vast majority, it's merely a fashion accessory and/or a status symbol.

Carphone Warehouse   http://www.carphonewarehouse.com/

If you want a mobile phone but you're not sure which one, this is the place to go. The Carphone Warehouse has built a fine reputation for providing unbiased advice to would-be mobile phone users.

If you know what you want, you can buy almost any phone connected to any of the providers. You can also buy a bewildering array of accessories including batteries, cases and ring tones.

Ring tones are the tunes or sounds played by your mobile phone when someone calls you. Phones are supplied with an ever-increasing number of tones built-in. If these aren't enough, you can get more.

This site will lead you through the minefield and advise you on which phone is most suited to your needs. You can then order and pay for it online and it will be delivered free of charge in one to two days.

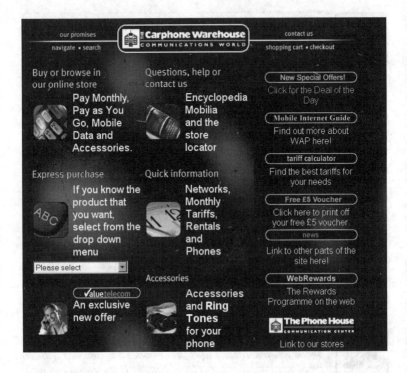

Mobile Phone Store   http://www.themobilephonestore.com/
All the mobiles phones are here for you to peruse. When you've decided, order online.

Mobile Phones   ttp://www.buy.co.uk/moneysm/mobiles.asp
To find out which is the best mobile phone to use for your particular circumstances, visit this Money Supermarket site, enter the information including the number of calls you're likely to make per day or per month and the calculator will sort out the best deal for you.

The Pocket Phone Shop   http://www.pocketphone.co.uk/
You can search for the exact phone and connection agreement best suited to your needs at this UK site. You can get the latest prices on the major service providers and the best deals on hardware.

Cameras

Like computers, to become involved in photography seriously requires some serious money, and in many cases some serious training. But even for the hobbyist, there can be a lot of equipment to buy. Once again, the Internet could provide the tips and the sources for cheaper hardware.

Jessops   http://www.jessops.com/
Jessops is the UK's leading photographic retailer with over 20,000 products including cameras, darkroom equipment and film, backed by a network of over 180 UK stores. They have an enviable reputation which has been built on excellence of service, value for money and unbiased advice to customers. Unlike many stores of this type, Jessops staff actually know what they're talking about as most are themselves dedicated photographers.

In its online guise you have access to the same stock and the same dedication. Look out for links to classic and collectable photographic equipment, pre-owned cameras and courses on a wide range of photography-related topics.

Computer consumables and supplies

The cost doesn't end when you buy a computer. If nothing else, you'll need paper. You may also require hardware add-ons and other consumables like floppy discs.

The rise of the home computer has also seen the rise of companies offering peripherals and consumables.

Online ordering is frequently faster, but it can take longer to fill out the online order form.

Action   http://www.action.com/

A new Action catalogue seems to arrive on my doormat every other month. And it's getting so large it only just gets through the letter box. Postmen all across the UK will, I'm sure, be delighted to learn that you can now view the entire Action catalogue and place orders online.

Lindy   http://www.lindy.com/

If you need a piece of cable to join A to B, this UK site will probably have exactly what you want. Lindy specialises in ready-made cables (i.e. cables of precise length with a connector on each end) that will join virtually any piece of computer equipment to any other piece. Their prices are very competitive, but to qualify for free postage you must spend over a particular amount.

Misco   http://www.misco.co.uk/
This company sells just about everything related to computers including some hardware, but mainly paper, labels and storage media.

Paper Direct   http://www.paperdirect.com/
This company produces a huge range of pre-printed 'designer' papers onto which you add your own text to produce high quality professional documents. All of the paper is extremely good quality and will go through most laser and inkjet printers. Each design has a number of different components including envelopes, brochures, labels and business cards, all carrying a common design feature. You can also order online from *http://www.vistapapers.co.uk/*.

To enable you to position your text in exactly the right place, Microsoft Publisher has several document templates based on some of Paper Direct's designs. Other templates are available from the company on CD ROM.

The Clocktower Paper Company   http://www.clocktowerpaper.co.uk/
This small UK-based shop stocks innovative products for the small office or home office. Also featured are gift ideas, picture frames and photo albums.

TT Digital   http://www.tt-digital.co.uk/
For the best prices in recordable CDs, visit TT Digital.

Viking   http://www.vikingdirect.com/

Viking sell a wide range of computer consumables including plain paper, designer paper and labels, as well as an enormous amount of office equipment. If you want a telephone, a stapler or an office chair, Viking will have it.

Printer ink

The cost of printers is dropping almost daily, but there is a hidden catch. Some cheap printers require special toner (laser printers) or ink cartridges (inkjet printers) that are very expensive. But even for top line printers like Hewlett Packard and Canon, replacement ink or toner can be an expensive item.

Many companies have sprung up who 're-manufacture' laser toner cartridges and in some cases, inkjet cartridges. Some do little more than refill empties with ink or toner that may or may not be contaminated. This can significantly reduce the life of the printer, if they actually work.

ACS Ltd   http://www.printer-cartridge.co.uk/

You can order both original and compatible printer cartridges online from ACS, who accept most credit and debit cards. There are frequent special deals to look out for.

Cartridge Club   http://www.cartridgeclub.co.uk/

You can get some really good deals at the Cartridge Club, although at present you can only view the prices online. If you wish to place an order, you may do so by phone or email.

Inky Fingers   http://www.inky-fingers.co.uk/

Inky Fingers stock a huge range of printer refills which (as they themselves claim) may be able to be beaten on price, but not quality.

Imperial Images   **http://www.imperialimages.com/**

If you don't fancy trusting someone else to refill your ink cartridges, you can buy the ink from Imperial Images and do it yourself. All prices can be viewed online, but at present orders can only be taken over the phone or by fax.

Consumer electronics

We live in an age of mass consumer products, and amongst the most popular are the hi-tech electronic gadgets. Televisions, videos and hi-fi have never been so sophisticated or cheap, and there are dozens of outlets just waiting to sell it all to you.

Best Stuff   **http://www.beststuff.co.uk/**

This site has three key features: Quality, Information and Value. All of the products are high quality, there is an adequate supply of useful information about each and everything is marked well below the usual high street prices. The company also offers fast delivery, a promise that your credit card will not be debited until after the goods are dispatched and a 28 day money back guarantee.

Comet   **http://www.comet.co.uk/**

I can't imagine there's anyone in the UK who hasn't at least heard of Comet, if they haven't actually visited one of the stores. This huge online site has just about every product that requires either a plug or a battery to work. All of the products have been carefully indexed and can be purchased online using one of the usual plastic cards.

Crazy Electric   http://www.crazyelectric.com/

The name refers to the prices of the products rather than the condition of the people who will operate them. This UK site has hundreds of items from all the top names in home entertainment and includes TV, video, DVD, camcorders and hi-fi at incredibly low prices. There is a search engine, but the goods are so well indexed it's hardly needed.

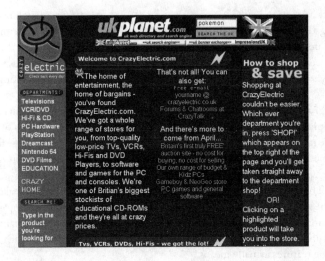

Dixons   http://www.dixons.co.uk/

UK shoppers will need no introduction to what is probably the most famous high street consumer electronics retail outlet.

Of all the online shopping sites, there are few which are easier to use, considering the number of products on sale and the level of technical information about each one. On the first page you're asked to choose the overall category of product you wish to purchase (computer, hi-fi, portable hi-fi, communications etc.). You then select a specific item within that category.

Further information on each product is available (including text and pictures) before deciding whether to purchase online. Payment is by the usual credit and debit cards and delivery is very fast thereafter.

Firebox   http://www.firebox.com/

To gadget and gizmo freaks, Firebox will seem like heaven. On sale on this UK site are all the boys' toys that are apparently widely available overseas, but not yet seen in the UK. Some of the prices seem a little steep, but I suppose that's only to be expected with goodies of this type. UK delivery is free though.

Helpful Home Shopping Company   http://www.helpful.co.uk/

Helpful is certainly an appropriate title for this UK company which offers a wide range of electrical and electronic goodies at prices way below those found in the high street. In addition, the price includes delivery, installation and 3-year warranties.

The clever part about the website is that it give a comparative breakdown of the various features of similar products so you can, for example, compare the features of two DVD players. As a bonus, if you don't understand the terminology, you can click on the headings to get an explanation of what each of the features actually means.

Powerhouse   http://www.powerhouse-online.co.uk/

Formerly the Electricity Showroom, Powerhouse, as it is now known, sells all manner of domestic electronics including TV and video, laundry aids and white goods as well as countless smaller items like radios and vacuum cleaners.

QVCUK http://www.qvcuk.com/

This UK site sells a wide range of goods, but look out for special deals on consumer electronics like videos and camcorders.

Remote Controls http://www.remotecontrols.co.uk/

Remote controls are essential with some TVs as the remote control functions are not always duplicated on the TV itself. This means that once the remote control is lost or broken, some of the functions of the television are lost.

If your remote is missing, visit Remote Controls, enter the make and model of the TV and they'll try to supply you with a new one.

More Remote Controls http://www.remotecontrols.com/

If you're bored with remote controls that look as if they've been carved from a house brick, then visit this site for some of the wildest TV remote controls imaginable. If you've ever felt like firing a gun at the TV, then try the space gun shaped controller that actually has accompanying sound effects.

Tempo   http://www.tempo.co.uk/

This is another high street store with an online branch. Some selected items can be ordered online and delivered anywhere in the UK. Some of the stock can only be ordered online if you happen to live in one of the delivery areas.

Unbeatable   http://www.unbeatable.co.uk/

You should register when you first visit this site and then on subsequent visits you can simply log-on with your user name and password.

All items carry a brief but adequate written description with an accompanying photograph. The prices are low, except the special offers which are very low.

Value Direct   http://www.value-direct.co.uk/

This UK online store sells a range of discount electrical goods. When you place an order you collect Web rewards which can be used against future purchases. The items are indexed and there is a search engine to help you locate the item you're looking for.

Web Electricals   http://www.webelectricals.co.uk/

Research, compare and then buy from this UK online electrical store. All items are categorised into TV, DVD and Video, Hi-Fi, Palmtops (computers), Camcorders and 'Cutting Edge', the latest ultra hi-tech products.

Software

One of the major growth areas of Internet selling is computer software. It makes a great deal of sense for both the seller and purchaser to buy over the Internet. From the seller's point of view, there are fewer overheads. Programs are now so large that they have to be distributed either on a pile of floppy discs or a CD ROM – which is now the cheaper of the two options, providing you have enough sales to warrant the cost of producing them.

Selling software over the Internet eliminates the need to hold any stock. When someone buys a program, they merely make a copy of the file and pull it across the Internet. For the seller, transportation costs are now nil.

As for buyers, they're not paying for huge quantities of fancy packaging which goes straight in the bin. That, of course, significantly reduces the cost. Quite complex programs can be packaged into a single file, which, when the end-user runs it, will self-unpack and decompress. This feature, together with faster and faster Internet access times, means that software can be downloaded very quickly. Furthermore, the buyer doesn't need to physically go anywhere to buy the software. It can all be done from the purchaser's home.

This effectively means the end of the printed manual. What happens now is that, wrapped up in the downloaded software package, is the manual as either a text file or an HTML file (which can be viewed with a browser). Sometimes both. The end result is that the user has to either juggle the new software on screen with the software manual, or print out the manual.

For the user this may be seen as a disadvantage. In global environmental terms it must be considered as a major saving.

Downloading

Computer applications (often referred to as software or a program) typically comprise several files. These files, together with any installation software, are packaged together in a single compressed bundle to be moved from one computer to another via the Internet.

Only download software from a reliable source. If you're not sure, don't do it: it could contain a virus.

You'll find many websites that contain links that offer you the chance to download a piece of software. Some will charge, others are free.

There are some programs that are worth downloading immediately rather than waiting until you need them. Look out for these in this chapter.

When you click on the link, a dialog box will open asking you to confirm that you do really want to download the software. You can usually either run it directly, or save it onto a disc. The latter is usually the safest option.

If you choose to save it, you'll be asked to choose a location to place the file, and this will normally be the Downloaded Documents folder. When you've chosen the location to save, click the 'Save' button and downloading will commence.

When downloading begins, a new dialog will open telling you the current status of the download process. The computer will sometimes show the estimated time left and the current transfer rate, and the location the file is being saved in. When it's finished downloading, a message will pop up telling you so.

Take a note of where you saved it and/or what the file is called. It can be quite tricky to find it if you can't remember either of these things!

All you will have done is to copy the file from one computer to yours. To use it, you'll need to install it. To install a downloaded program you'll need to locate the file and double click on it. The packaged application will 'self-extract' and installation should proceed in the usual way – as if you were installing from a CD or floppy disc.

Sometimes you may find that files you've downloaded are too large to fit on a single floppy disc; not unnaturally, this has the effect of making them difficult to use on another computer. Fortunately, there are websites that recognise this potential problem and respond to it by offering you the chance of downloading multiple files. In this way, each of the files can be stored on an individual floppy disc.

Browsers

In order to access the World Wide Web, you'll need a browser. Of those available, Explorer and Navigator are by far the most popular and advanced. With respect to the others, if you run either of these, you won't go far wrong. They both undergo frequent revisions and it's worth keeping up to date with the latest version. Web developers will certainly take advantage of new browser features.

You must first get a browser on a CD to allow you to access the Internet to enable you to download future versions of the browser.

Many websites have a link to enable you to download the latest version of a particular browser.

Whichever browser you decide to use, stick to your choice. There's no point in running more than one and chopping and changing between the two could cause problems.

Netscape   **http://www.netscape.com/**

Netscape Communicator is a suite of Internet programs that includes a browser, email application (Messenger) and Web page builder. At the time of writing, version 4.8 was current with version 4.9 around the corner.

Netscape downloads as a single file of about 18Mbytes. To put that into perspective, a high density floppy disc holds about 1.4 Mbytes of data. So 18Mbytes is roughly the equivalent of 13 floppy discs' worth of data.

Internet Explorer   **http://www.microsoft.com/**

Like its main rival Netscape, Internet Explorer is updated regularly with new features. At the time of writing, version 5.01 is current. Internet Explorer is a suite of applications which includes the browser, an email application (Outlook Express) and a Web page design application (Front Page Express).

Always run the latest version of the browser of your choice.

When you download Internet Explorer, all that arrives at your computer is a small installation module. When this is run, the software determines which of the available Microsoft websites is the best to use, bearing in mind your location and the chosen language of the software (English, French etc.). It then downloads the software and installs it for you.

Plug-ins

Your browser can support a huge range of multimedia file types, but every so often you'll stumble across a website which uses something your browser can't recognise. Usually you'll be told about this when you first visit the site. If the site has been well constructed, it will detect that your browser can't support a particular feature it uses and so suggests you install a plug-in. A plug-in is a small program that extends the functionality of your browser, usually to enhance the sound or video qualities. Most sites will suggest you download a plug-in, but others may offer you an alternative location which doesn't use the plug-in.

You could ignore this section and just download the plug-ins as and when they are required. The trouble is, all too frequently you find that it's inconvenient to download at the time because you have a specific task to do and you don't want to be side-tracked by getting involved downloading yet another piece of software which could tie up your computer for several minutes.

It's better to take an hour out to download some of the most important plug-ins now.

Many plug-ins come with a viewer so that you can use the features outside of a browser.

iPIX®   **http://www.ipix.com/**
This player is becoming very popular with estate agents and travel companies who want visitors to their website to be able to go on a virtual tour of a house or holiday resort. iPIX enables the user to see a 360° view of the surroundings, controlled by the user. Simply click and hold the mouse button by an edge of the viewing window, and the picture will scroll. Alternatively hold the mouse button whilst moving the mouse in the viewer.

This plug-in downloads and installs automatically although there is a manual version should the automatic version fail.

Macromedia   **http://www.macromedia.com/**

To see special animated effects at their best (or at all), you need Macromedia's
Flash Player which has become the Web standard for animation. To see what's
possible, just visit Macromedia's website - it's filled with clever animated
effects. Many top companies use Flash to create compelling websites and the
gallery shows the work of some outstanding website design by companies such
as Comedy Central and Sony. Flash player is free and should download in less
than a minute. You can also get to the Flash download section by going to *http:/
/www.flash.com/*.

*There are instructions on the Macromedia website to show you
how to produce animations using Flash.*

QuickTime   **http://www.quicktime.com/**

This software is owned by Apple and entering this address takes you onto the
Apple website. If you haven't got QuickTime installed in your computer,
visiting this site will automatically detect the fact and you'll be prompted to
download it.

Quicktime is Apple's technology for handling video, sound, animation and
360° virtual reality scenes and enables you to experience over 200 types of
digital media on both PC and Apple computers. The basic QuickTime is free,
but you can, for a small fee, upgrade to QuickTime Pro which, in addition to
the features of the free version, enables you to play full screen video, create, edit
and save movies and audio.

The 480 Kbyte file (QuickTime) should take less than 5 minutes to
download.

Real Player   http://www.real.com/

The Real Player is one of the most popular plug-ins for enhancing audio and video playback. There is a basic version which is free, but there is also a Plus version which carries a charge of US$29.99.

When it's installed, an icon sits on the right of the task bar and provides access to videos with audio. The Plus version has superb video playback with picture controls, superb audio with graphic equalising and over 150 live radio stations built-in.

To go with the Real Player, there's also a Real Jukebox. Amongst other things, this allows you to record digital music onto a variety of media including writeable compact discs and the high capacity cartridges used by Iomega in their Jaz and Zip drives. (For more information about Iomega, see the chapter about technology or visit the Iomega website at *http://www.iomega.com/*.

Media Player   **http://www.microsoft.com/**

Microsoft's free Media Player will play a range of file types including the digital audio format, MP3. The downloading file is under 3Mbytes so it shouldn't take long, even with a slow modem.

Installation doesn't take long either and when it's installed you can go for a test drive to the MSN Media site at *http://windowsmedia.com/*.

Shockwave   **http://www.macromedia.com/**

Macromedia's Shockwave delivers interactive Web content. In other word, you can act and react to a feature on a webpage. You'll see the whole range of amazing interactive features on the site.

The plug-in is less than 2Mbytes and is free. You can also get to the Shockwave download section by going to *http://www.shockwave.com/*.

There are a variety of Shockwave games freely available on this site including some classics like Frogger and Paintball.

Utilities

These programs are frequently free and provide the user with some useful additional functionality by either working as a stand-alone application or by enhancing another program.

Acrobat   **http://www.adobe.com/**

More and more people are using the so-called PDF file format to transport documents. The advantage is that it produces a compact file which is easier to email or download from the Internet and can be read by a free program – Acrobat Reader by Adobe. The full version of Acrobat includes the facility to create PDF files but for this there is a charge. Acrobat reader can be freely downloaded.

The Adobe site is the obvious place to go to download Acrobat, but you will find that the majority of sites that offer downloadable files in PDF format, provide a link to download Acrobat.

Acrobat is one of the programs that should be downloaded immediately as manuals supplied with downloaded software are often in this format.

Avery label template   http://www.avery.com/

If you can stand going through the lengthy application form, you'll get a really good piece of free software that will significantly enhance the label printing

Use the Avery program to print sheets of labels for your Christmas card list.

facilities within Microsoft Word. The main problem with the label printing feature of Word is that it's not easy to produce a sheet of labels with different names and addresses on each label. With the Avery Label Template it's a simple task. The program downloads as a single file of just under 3Mbytes.

There is also an application form to order free sheets of labels.

Callwave   **http://www.callwave.com/**

This free Internet Answering Machine lets you hear who's calling while you're online. If callers leave a message, you can hear it instantly on your PC speakers. It takes less than a minute to download but is for US customers only.

Genie   **http://www.genie.co.uk/**

Visit this site and find out how to get emails redirected to your mobile phone.

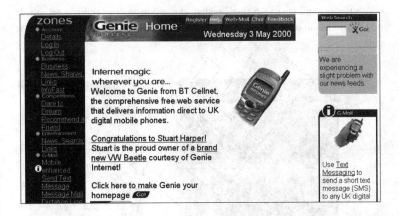

ICQ

Instant Messaging (or 'buddies' as it is sometimes referred to) is becoming increasingly popular. There are several available and most of the big names have a version of it (AOL's Instant Messenger, Microsoft's Messenger, etc.), but top of the pile is ICQ (I seek you). The idea is that you set up a list of contacts (buddies) and when you and they are online, you can 'talk' to each other in private. When it's running, you have a window with two areas – one that you type into, and one to display the text your buddy enters.

You need to download the program from the ICQ website which is available free for a trial period, after which there is a small fee for the licence.

Once ICQ has been downloaded and installed, you'll need to register after which you will be given an ID number. You'll also need to choose a name which you will be known by. ICQ loads automatically when you switch your computer on and it sits on the Taskbar at the bottom right of the screen. It doesn't do much until you go online when it 'announces' itself to the world at large.

When it's active, the icon changes to a flower, which can also be seen in the ICQ menu, displayed by clicking the icon on the Taskbar.

You can 'hide' yourself so the rest of the world doesn't know you're there.

From time to time, if you're online, you'll get a request to have a chat. The request will pop-up on the screen and contain details of the person requesting the chat. If you agree, the dialogue window will open and you can now chat.

ICQ will announce when one of your buddies comes online, so you'll be able to decide whether to have a chat. Similarly, when you go online, you'll be told which of your buddies is also online.

If you get tired of random people trying to strike up a meeting, you can put ICQ into dormant mode which means it's still running, but nobody can see you, although you can still see them.

It's worth knowing how to switch this off. If you're online and working it can be very distracting to have people 'dropping-in' for a virtual chat.

If you're bored, you can try to set up a chat with someone else. This could be a random chat, or a chat with one of your buddies.

Again, this is real-time chat, but the real fascination is watching the other person typing. The letters come up one at a time as they are being typed. You can even see when they've made a spelling mistake and are trying to correct it.

NetSonic   http://www.web3000.com/
Voted as one of the Top 10 of Best Products of the Millennium, NetSonic is a browser companion that works with any browser and requires no setting-up. It allows you to access frequently visited sites faster and will alert you if there is any new content. Visit the site and download it free.

Sandra   http://www.3bsoftware.com/
Sandra is a suite of diagnostic programs developed by SiSoft who have their website at *http://www.sisoftware.co.uk/*. There are two version of Sandra: one free, the other not. The freebie is a cut-down version of the full 'professional' version. For most users, the free version will be more than adequate.

If your computer is a little sluggish, try downloading Sandra to get tips to improve it.

Sandra will tell you about your computer system and will help you make it work better by providing tips to optimise it. Most of the basic bits are covered in the free version including memory check, processor check, disk drive diagnostics, system bus tests and port benchmarks. When you've downloaded and installed Sandra, you'll have a window with over 40 diagnostic tools.

Both versions are available from 3B Software as downloads.

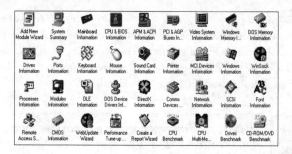

Talking Buddy   http://www.talkingbuddy.com/

Talking Buddy is a cartoon character that will read text and speak it out. It can, for example, read your emails to you, read your letters and documents and Web pages.

It can send animated messages to friends, speak greetings and even announce the time at certain intervals.

This program is now available with support for 30 different languages.

The free 7.75 Mbyte file is fully functional, but you'll only get 10 goes with it. To get it to work for longer (i.e. always) you'll need to purchase the licence, which is currently US$29.99.

Voice EMail   http://www.bonzi.com/

The rise in modem speeds has meant that you can now send much larger files across the Internet. One of the more recent developments has been Voice email. There are several programs capable of recording and then sending the recordings, but the easiest is Voice EMail by Bonzi.

If you've got a microphone connected to your computer this is a fun program to play around with.

The program is available free from Bonzi's website as a limited use evaluation version. If you like it, you can purchase and download the full version.

When the program has been installed and run, a small toolbar will be displayed in the top right corner of the screen. To create a message, click on the 'Create' button. This opens the window in which you can create your voice email. Creating the message is a simple matter of entering the email address of the recipient and speaking into a microphone to record your message.

When it comes to receiving Voice EMail, the recipient collects their email in the usual way, with the normal email program (probably Outlook Express or Netscape Messenger). Among the new messages will be a message informing you that a voice email is attached. The text message is automatically generated to tell the recipient the s/he will need Voice EMail to read it.

When the recipient has installed Voice Email (either the evaluation version or the full version) they will be able hear your message and, if you included a picture, see who sent it.

Webwacker   **http://www.bluesquirrel.com/**

You can spend a great deal of time browsing through the Web, during which time you could be running up an enormous phone bill. One possible solution is Webwacker, a limited-use version of which can be freely downloaded from Blue Squirrel's website.

This could save you a great deal of money in Internet phone charges.

Webwacker captures a whole website and saves it onto your local hard disk so that you can browse through it as frequently as you like, offline.

The free 'limited-use' version is really little more than a demo to prove to you that it works and does what it says it will do. But it only saves a limited amount of the website being 'wacked'. If you like the software and you think

Some people don't like you lifting their entire website.

it will be of use, you will need to pay a small charge for the upgrade to the full version.

WinZip   http://www.winzip.com/

Sending pictures with your emails is a great idea, but the size of some pictures (the amount of memory they use, rather than their physical dimensions) means that emailing pictures can take a long time to both send and receive. In fact, including any file along with an email will increase the time taken to send it. In addition, some Internet Service Providers put a ceiling on the size of emailings because having too many large mailings tends to clog up the system.

What is needed is a way of reducing the size of the files you send. Enter WinZip. WinZip is variously called a compression tool, an archiver or a packer. All descriptions are true. WinZip will take one or more files and package them

WinZip is one of the programs that should be downloaded immediately.

into a compressed archive occupying a fraction of the space they originally occupied. Packaged files can also be unpacked with WinZip.

You can freely download WinZip and try it for a limited time to see if you like it. If you do, there is a small charge.

The Mac version is called StuffIt and is available from http:// www.stuffit.com/.

Beware when receiving attachments. Ensure you have a good virus protection program running before you attempt to open them. Even so, treat unsolicited mailings with attachments, especially from unknown sources, with extreme suspicion.

Software updates

Before the Internet was widely used, software houses used to send upgrades to their programs on floppy disc(s) or latterly on CD ROM. Now, most prefer to use the Internet and allow customers to download upgrades as and when they want.

MS Windows   **http://www.microsoft.com/**

The vast majority of the world uses Windows on their computers. The various versions of Windows are hugely complex and under continuous development. Software upgrades are available from the Microsoft site as well as a huge number of answers to questions and solutions for particular issues.

Also available on the site are updates for most of their other titles including the Office suite which includes Word, Excel and Access.

Linux   **http://www.linux.com/**

If you're frustrated with the force-fed diet of MS software, then why not try Linux? Linux has traditionally been used by the hobbyist at home, although it is creeping into businesses. This site provides everything you could possibly want to know about this operating system and even provides the facility of freely downloading the software.

Apart from downloading the actual operating system, there are several other programs to download from this site including some games.

> *Linux is absolutely free from this website. You can legally give it away and even modify it. But you must not attempt to sell it.*

Printer drivers

When you buy a new printer for your PC, it will come with driver software. In simple terms, the software 'tells' the computer what the product is, what settings are available and how the computer is to communicate with it.

Although the hardware itself doesn't change (until the manufacturer brings out a new model) the software drivers are regularly updated and improved upon. It is usually in the user's best interests to run the latest drivers for their computer hardware and the best place to get the latest driver is from the manufacturer's website.

All of the top manufacturers have websites on which they store the latest versions of their drivers. In most cases, the upgrades are free. Once they have been downloaded, double-click on the file to open and install it.

> *When you buy a new printer, find the manufacturer's website and check it regularly for printer driver updates. Even when you buy a new printer you may find there's a later driver on the Web than the one supplied with your printer.*

Brother   http://www.brother.com/

When you first get to this site, choose the country in which you reside. When the next page opens, choose 'software' under the Printers and Scanners banner to take you to another page where you choose the operating system you are currently using. You can then choose the type of printer you have and click on the download link.

> *There's also a link on the Brother website to tell you how to upgrade your printer driver.*

Epson   http://www.epson.com/

When you get to this site, choose 'Driver and File Downloads' under the 'Support' banner. Choose the printer you have from the list in the dropdown menu and then choose the file for the operating system you are using.

Canon   **http://www.canon.com/**

Click on 'Download Services' and then select the region you are currently working in from the map or dropdown menu. You'll then need to click on the floppy disc picture at the centre of the screen to enter the download site. Choose the type of product you wish to get the driver upgrade for and then the specific model.

Many of these companies produce hardware other than just printers. If applicable, drivers for these are also available online.

Finally, choose the operating system and click on the download link.

Hewlett Packard   **http://www.hp.com/**

This site is a model of clarity and although it includes printer drivers for just about every printer ever made by Hewlett Packard, and on all operating systems, it's easy to find what you're looking for. Whether it's a LaserJet printer or a DeskJet model, the driver will be here.

Sometimes you're given the choice of American English or European English. Make sure you select the correct one.

When you visit the site, choose 'Drivers' from the left of the screen. Then choose the type of product, the product model number and the operating system. Click on the 'Downloads and Drivers' link to download the correct driver.

Lexmark   **http://www.lexmark.com/**

If you are visiting this site for drivers, don't bother to choose your location, but instead click on the 'Drivers' link and then choose 'US Drivers' or 'International Drivers'. You can then choose your printer's name and operating system to download the appropriate driver.

Panasonic   **http://www.panasonic.com/**

Panasonic/Matsushita is a huge company and this website reflects that fact. When you open the site, first choose 'Computer Products' and then select 'Device Drivers'. This will take you to the area where you can select your printer and download the new driver.

Other drivers

Most hardware for PCs needs driver software and manufacturers find that the Internet is a convenient way to distribute upgrades as there are virtually no overheads like media costs and no postage.

3Com   **http://www.3com.com/**

One of the top names in networking products, 3Com's website features drivers for their extensive range of network cards. You'll need to know the exact model as the range is large and includes products from several years back.

ATI   **http://www.ati.com/**

ATI is one of the leading manufacturers of graphics cards for PCs. Driver software for their Rage cards is available from this site, together with some other free goodies like screensavers.

D-Link   **http://www.dlink.com/**

Another famous name in networking products, D-Link's website features drivers for their range of network cards. As with 3Com, this site includes drivers for many products, some dating back several years so you'll need to know the exact model of the card you're using.

Fujitsu   **http://www.fujitsu.com/**

All the downloads for their printers, scanners and other hardware are available here. There's also lots of other free software and an online store.

Microtek   http://www.microtek.com

Amongst the numerous products produced by Microtek are scanners. The latest drivers are available from this site for free download.

Mustek   http://www.mustek.com/

This US company are famous for digital imaging including scanners and cameras. Free drivers are available for all products.

Seagate   http://www.seagate.com/

The Seagate site holds all the driver software required for their tape backup systems as well as a number of utilities including DiscWizard.

Software for palmtops

Both Psion and Palm have a huge following of supporters who not only use the computers, they produce software for them. There are several sites which distribute software which is either free, or very cheap.

PDACentral   http://pdacentral.com/

This US site holds a vast array of free, nearly free and chargeable software for just about all Personal Digital Assistants, including Psion and Palm. They also have a great deal of information available as text documents.

Psion   http://www.psion.com/

Psion and their website are a mine of information about their hardware/ software products and importantly the ability to link their computer to others.

There are several programs on this site that will be invaluable to Psion users, especially Message Suite which enables you to access the Internet and send/receive emails using a mobile phone or land line to make the connection.

Purple Software   http://www.purplesoft.com/

Quality is a byword for this company specialising in software for Psion computers, but also some Palm products and Windows CE computers. The site features links to free downloadable software (as well as software which is chargeable) and to hardware. You'll need to register before downloading.

Software for mobile phones

Surprisingly, many mobile phones can store software to enhance their functionality.

Dial-a-Ring   http://www.dialaring.com/

For some, a mobile phone is more of a hobby than a requirement. If you fit into that category, and you own a Nokia mobile phone, this is the place to come.

Dial-a-Ring offers ring tones, caller group graphics and operator logos that can be downloaded into your mobile phone.

Ring tones are the tunes or sounds played by your mobile phone when someone calls you. Phones are supplied with an ever-increasing number of tones built-in. It these aren't enough, you can get more.

To download a graphic or a ring tone, select the appropriate link and choose the one(s) you want from the indexed list. When you've found what you want, click on the 'Get it' icon to put it into your shopping basket. There is a small charge for this service which is paid for using a credit or debit card. When the transaction has been completed, your graphics or ring tones will be downloaded into your phone.

This site only supports Nokia mobile phones, but not all of them are capable of receiving ring tones or caller group graphics. And those that do are restricted to the number that can be installed at any one time. The table on the site shows each of the phones' capabilities.

If you fancy drawing your own caller group logo, click on the 'Make Logo' link and you will be presented with a grid onto which you can draw your logo. When you've finished, click on the 'Save' button and you will be issued with a special code to enable you to download your logo into your phone.

IOβox   **http://www.iobox.com/**
If you have a mobile phone, it's worth logging on to this site as it will provide you with additional services to enhance your use of the phone. Once you've registered, you can buy services like forwarding email to your phone, receive calendar reminders, and download icons and ring tones. There is also cheaper text messaging and you can send a 'postcard' from mobile to mobile.

If you've got a WAP (Wireless Application Protocol) phone, there are even more services available.

Pagemail   **http://www.dialogue.com/**
SMS (Short Message Service) is a method of sending text messages from one mobile phone to another. The trouble with trying to compose text messages on a mobile phone is that you've only got 10 keys with which you must be able to enter all 26 letters of the alphabet in upper and lower case, all the numbers as well as several punctuation marks. It can be done, but it is a challenge.

When sending an SMS message, you are restricted to 160 characters including spaces. But you can send a message over more that one SMS by ending the first part of the message with an ellipse (...) and beginning the next message with the same.

Pagemail enables you to compose and send SMS messages from a PC using the 100+ keys available on the PC keyboard.

There are two versions of the software, one is free and the other carries a small charge. The free version will allow you to send text messages to subscribers to Vodafone UK, BT CellNet, One-2-One or Orange, within the UK only. The paid-for version allows you to send to subscribers of some international mobile phone services and to most pagers.

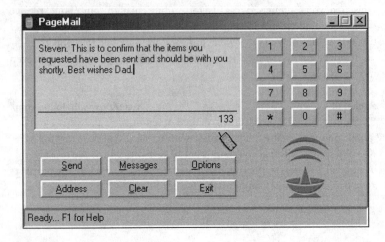

Ringtones Online   **http://www.ringtones.co.uk/**

If you own a Nokia mobile phone, then visit Ringtones Online to buy some additional goodies for it. To buy a ring tone for your mobile phone, select the 'Ringtones' link and select the tune you want. If you have Windows Media Player or an MP3 player installed in your computer, you can preview the ring tone. To buy the ring tone, click on the link and enter your name, address, mobile phone number, credit card number and the ring tone(s) you want.

Make sure your phone is compatible with the software being downloaded. Not all phones are and those that can receive ringtones vary in the number they can hold at any one time.

Your ring tone will be downloaded shortly after the order has been completed.

You can also download graphic icons for your Nokia phone and order Nokia accessories.

Educational software

As soon as you mention education, everyone pricks up their ears and thinks about the perceived benefits for their offspring.

The Learning Store   http://www.learningstore.co.uk/
After receiving some alarmingly incorrect advice from high street retailers, Louisa Gilboy started The Learning Store which sells educational multimedia products. Programs are reviewed so that potential buyers can see what they are going to get and what it will actually do. Only the best PC programs are featured but they can all be purchased online.

Computer games

OK, I admit it, I occasionally play computer games but if computers were just about games, I would stick to a pencil and paper. Or even blackboard and chalk. For some, it is exactly the opposite – computers mean games. Like music, it's not always necessary to have to go to a shop to buy a new game. Many are available to buy online and some PC games can be downloaded.

Freeloader   http://www.freeloader.com/
You can now enjoy the thrills of video-gaming classics such as Grand Theft Auto, Rat Attack and Blastion for free. It's all perfectly legal. You log onto the website and download the full version with no charge. The catch? Well there isn't one except that you'll be blasted with adverts all through the download. No, you can't walk away and leave it because each advert features a 'Click here to Continue' button. The company get a commission for each advert they shoot at you. As there're no further costs involved to the company such as producing flashy boxes and packing discs into them and then shipping them around the world, they can afford to give the games away.

Game Dude   **http://www.gamedude.com/**

Claimed to be the world's largest online video games store, this US site stocks all the top games for all the popular platforms including PC, Playstation and Dreamcast. They will also buy video games, games systems, accessories, DVD and CD ROMs.

If you're more interested in playing than browsing through this site, select the text only website which just features lists of games without the graphics.

Game Play   **http://www.gameplay.com/**

There's free UK delivery on games for PC, Playstation, Nintendo, Gameboy and Dreamcast. Games are divided into categories according to type, price and format. All prices include first class postage, delivery times are normally within 2 days and your credit card is not debited until your order is despatched.

Game Play also sell a range of systems and accessories at competitive prices.

Games Street   **http://www.gamesstreet.com/**

This is part of the same organisation that runs Alphabet Street (books), Audio Street (Music) and DVD Street (films on DVD). This UK store stocks lots of video games for all the top games systems with secure online ordering over a secure connection and fast delivery.

Games Paradise   http://www.gamesparadise.co.uk/

This massive UK site has a huge selection of games in all common formats which can be ordered online. Many of the games are reviewed so you can get an idea of what they're like before you splash out. The prices are well below those in the high street.

The Game Zone   http://www.thegamezone.co.uk/

Not the most inspired website – it's, well, functional rather than riveting. But who cares. You can buy PC and PlayStation games at competitive prices from this site, which has secure online ordering. You search for the game or games you want to buy and place the order in much the same way as if you were buying a book.

thegamezone   **£20**   **Strongnet**
                                      For 2 Years!   Click to join
Updated Thursday11th May 2000   UK BANNERS

Contents   **PC and Playstation Games & Leisure**
                                      Software
Home   Discount Prices - Fast & Free UK Delivery - Credit
                              PC   Card not debited until despatch - Order Online with
                                      confidence - 100% Secure
Search Shop   We are pleased to ship orders to anywhere in the
PC CDROM   world. For shipping costs, select buy button against
Playstation   product and select destination.
Forthcoming   Enter Title to search for [   ] and click
Reviews   Search Shop
Special Offers
Contact   **SALE SALE**   Joysticks
Service   Game Pads
Secure   **SALE**   Steering Wheels

Checkout   Charts w/e 6th
                                                                 May00

Software Warehouse   http://www.software-warehouse.co.uk/

Apart from a wide range of software, this online store sells just about everything for the computer user including hardware and consumables with lots of special online offers.

One of the offers is a subscription to Soft Gold (ISP) which, for a small monthly payment, provides the user with free software every month, expert technical support on an freephone number, 50MB Web space for your own Internet pages and unlimited e-mail addresses.

You can download trial software from this website as well as buying software from the online shop.

Special Reserve   http://www.reserve.co.uk/

Apart from a huge selection of PC software, computer hardware and DVD, this UK store sells all the top games for all the top games platforms.

It's often worth visiting the classified ads section to see if you can pick up a second-hand bargain.

Jungle.com   http://www.jungle.com/

When you arrive in the Jungle, choose 'Jungle Play' and then select the games platform from the list at the top of the next screen. You can then search for a particular game or browse through until you find something that looks sufficiently challenging.

A huge amount of work goes into this site. Use the information to select a game which is right for your age-range.

All of the games have a brief but adequate description and a screen shot or a picture of the cover artwork. Click on the graphic and you get a full description including an outline of the plot, advanced information and the recommended age range for the game. The prices are really keen.

URWired   http://www.urwired.com/

More fantastic games for the major platforms at really low prices. If you get bogged down with a game, visit the cheats section which shows you how to get unlimited lives and invincible weapons as well as showing you how to overcome that seemingly impossible problem to get you onto the next level.

Subscribe to the newsletter and get the chance to enter exclusive competitions.

There is free UK delivery on all items from this site.

Books

Using the Internet to sell books has become very popular. The retailer can operate from a single outlet and yet their doors are open to the whole world. Stock can be rationalised and, apart from packers, there are relatively few staff. The result is lower prices for the consumer. For this reason, Internet booksellers were among the first really successful commercial Internet websites.

Amazon

If imitation is the sincerest form of flattery, then Amazon must be one of the most flattered Internet websites. Amazon's success made its founder a multi-millionaire and has generated a whole host of imitations.

But Amazon is much more than just a bookshop: it is a reference site about books and their authors, with very powerful search facilities.

When you first enter the site you're presented with a screen advertising some of the latest offers. On the left of the screen is a search engine and an index to take you to the part of the site you want. Either click on the drop down menu, choose the area you want to search and click 'Go', or select a topic to browse through from the list of links below.

Apart from books, Amazon sells videos, DVD, toys and games, and several other miscellaneous items.

Searching

When you choose to search for a book, you first need to decide what information you want to submit for the search. This could be the author, the title of the book, the ISBN (International Standard Book Number), even a keyword from the book.

When making a search, you must spell everything correctly. You do have some choices when entering, for example, the author's name.

When you've entered the information in the correct box, click on the 'Search' button and you should get a list of books that fits your search entry.

You'll get fewer entries in the search results if you are more specific – e.g. entering 'Preston, Geoff' will return about six books (in the UK site) whereas entering 'Preston' will give a list of several dozen authors.

Each book listed appears in the same format. You'll get the title, the author, a brief description, the price and the availability. Clicking on the title takes you to another screen which gives more information about the book, including a picture of the cover and ISBN.

If you scroll down the screen a little way you may find some reviews written by either the publisher, the author or by someone who has simply read the book and feels they want to comment on it.

Other links visible will take you to either other books by the same author or other books in the same category or of the same type.

Writing a review

If you fancy yourself as a book critic, you can submit a review which will be displayed on the site. Simply click on the 'Write a review' link and follow the instructions. You'll need to rate the book by giving it a star rating out of five, you'll need to enter a one line comment and follow this up with up to 1,000 words of critical review.

It's worth writing your review in a text editor like WordPad whilst you are offline. When you've got your review done, log on and copy and paste the text into the space provided on the website.

Buying a book

Before you can buy a book from Amazon, you need to register, providing your name, address, email address and credit/debit card details.

When you've found a book you want to buy, click on the 'Add to Shopping Basket' button. When you've got all the books you want, click on the 'Proceed to Checkout' button and complete the online form to complete the purchase. To save you having to complete the form each time you buy a book, you can click on the 'One-click-purchase' button which requires you to enter a username and password. In future, logging on with your username and password eliminates the need to enter your details again.

Your order will be confirmed by email within minutes, your books will be dispatched and you could receive them the next morning.

<u>As a Gift</u>

You can elect to have your purchase delivered to a different address enabling you to send a book as a gift. They will even gift-wrap it for you if you wish.

Residents in the UK should visit http://www.amazon.co.uk/. Otherwise, visit http://www.amazon.com/.

This is the easiest way to send a present to a friend.

Waterstones

This famous UK bookstore carries a huge selection of books which can be searched for and ordered online. The search facility is fast, but for best results you should select the category of book you're looking for first. You can then enter a title or the name of the author.

Apart from the usual selection of popular books, you can download e-books from Waterstones. To be able to read an e-book you'll first need to register by giving the usual details including your email address. You'll also need the software to read e-books and this is Glassbook, which is available as a free download from Waterstones' website. (For more information about downloading and installing software, see the chapter on software.)

Once you've installed Glassbook you can then download e-books straight into your computer. When you find an e-book you wish to download, click on the download link and Glassbook will automatically open and the book will be downloaded into it. For reasons of copyright, you can't print from Glassbook, nor can you mark and copy text into the clipboard. You can download limitless

books into Glassworks and when the program opens you'll be able to choose the book you want to read from the list of downloaded books.

If you install Glassbook into a laptop computer, you can choose to rotate the book which will enable you to hold your laptop as if it were a book with the hinge on the left like the spine of a book.

Visit Nuvomedia at *http://www.nuvomedia.com/* to find out about Rocket eBook: a standalone e-book reader.

Buttons at the side of the Glassbooks window allow you to turn pages and the magnify feature is particularly useful for those with poor eyesight.

Some e-books are free, but some are chargeable. Waterstones carry a selection of e-books including some books which are only available in e-book format. If you want more information about e-books you can subscribe to Waterstones free emailing list.

Visit http://www.waterstones.co.uk/.

Reading books on screen is not always as convenient as reading them on paper.

Other book stores

There are scores of online bookstores throughout the world. Many are similar to Amazon and Waterstones but some offer additional or slightly different features.

Apart from books, many of these sites sell videos, DVD, toys and games, and several other miscellaneous items.

The Absolutely Weird Bookshelf   http://www.strangewords.com/
This absolutely weird US site sells sci-fi, fantasy and horror books.

Alphabet Street   http://www.alphabetstreet.co.uk/
Alphabet Street has similar features to Amazon – you can search for and buy books online. To search for a book you need to enter either the name of the book or the author. The search is very fast and when you have located the book

In the UK there is no VAT on books.

you want from the list, you can click on the title and get some more information including a brief description, or you can add it to your shopping trolley.

Once you've collected all the books you want, you can proceed to the checkout and, before paying, make adjustments to the contents of your virtual trolley by removing unwanted items and specifying the quantities required on all the other items. You then enter your details including name, address and card number, and complete the transaction by clicking on the 'Buy' button.

Within a couple of hours you will receive an email confirming your order and the books will be dispatched, usually within 24 hours depending on the availability.

This popular and friendly UK bookseller offers free delivery within the UK and a loyalty bonus system.

Alibris   http://www.alibris.com/

With access to over 3 million old or used books, this is the site for collectors.

Art2Art   http://www.art2art.com/

This US Arts & Crafts superstore stocks over 2000 books on everything art-related including candle making, jewellery making and glass painting.

Audio Book Club   http://www.audiobookclub.com/

Whatever your reason for not reading, whether it be lack of time or lack of sight, this US site can provide books on cassette tapes for you to listen to. If you join the Audio Book Club, you'll receive a free tape player and 4 audio books.

Barnes and Noble   http://www.barnesandnoble.com/

This is the world's largest online bookseller. If it's not here, it probably doesn't exist. Once you've chosen a category, you'll be taken to another index which further sub-divides. You can either browse or search for a particular book by entering the author's name or book title in the search engine. The results can be huge, but you can sort them by title, author or publication date. There are lots of online adverts highlighting new books or books on special offer.

For e-book fans, there's a huge number of titles indexed in categories which include: Biography, Business, Fiction, History, Horror, Kids, Mystery, Nonfiction, Religion, Romance and Women's History. Most (but not all) are chargeable. There are reviews and an indexed top ten e-books.

This site also features reviews where you can read what other bookworms from around the world think.

Rocket eBook

More convenient than reading e-books on your computer is to use a dedicated e-book reader. The Rocket eBook is a portable device that allows users to download books and magazines from the Internet. The basic version can store up to ten full length books, whilst the 'Pro' version can hold at least four times that amount. Users can annotate the texts, search for words or phrases, look up words in the built-in dictionary, and bookmark pages easily using the touch screen. It also supports audio and has graphics capability. There is a link to buy the Rocket eBook from this site. For more information about the Rocket eBook readers, visit the Nuvomedia website at *http://www.nuvomedia.com/* The Barnes and Noble site can also be accessed at *http://www.book.com/*.

B.T. Batsford   **http://www.batsford.com/**

Apart from being world leaders in Chess publishing, this UK site also specialises in books on Archaeology, Art, Bridge, Business, Crafts, Design, Embroidery, Fashion, Film, Gardening, Lace, Practical Crafts and Woodwork.

Better Life Books   http://www.betterlifebooks.com/

If you're in search of a better life, this US bookseller might be able to help as they specialise in religious and philosophical books.

Bibliofind   http://www.bibliofind.com/

There are more than ten million used and rare books and periodicals offered for sale by thousands of booksellers around the world. Use this site to locate and buy that rarity you want without trudging round dozens of shops.

Blackstone Press   http://www.blackstonepress.co.uk/

Blackstones are specialists in legal books, all of which can be ordered online.

Books are very heavy and carriage charges can negate any saving you might have made. Look out for sites that offer free delivery.

Blackwells   http://bookshop.blackwell.co.uk/

This is the online branch of the UK high street chain of bookshops, offering free delivery in the UK.

BOL   http://www.bol.com/

This huge site sells music and gifts as well as a huge selection of books. To locate the book you want to buy, first click on the subject from the index on the left. This may take you to another index to further divide the category.

Once you've narrowed down your search, you can then enter either the author's name, book title or ISBN in the search engine at the top of the screen. The matching books are displayed with some additional information including delivery time and possibly a review or two from one of the previous purchasers.

Apart from paper books, BOL also sell e-books. Look out also for a wide range of music.

The books you wish to buy can be added to your shopping basket and when you've got enough, click on the 'Checkout' button. As usual, enter your name, address and card details to complete the order and a confirming email will be sent shortly.

You can also write a brief review of any book by following the link, 'Review this Book'. There are carriage charges, but you can order up to 10 books and pay a small flat rate.

If you wish, you can use a password so that in future, you do not need to re-enter all your details.

The Book Garden   http://www.bookgarden.com/
Claimed to be the Earth's Smallest Book Store, the entire online inventory can be searched by author, title, and keyword. Books can be purchased online using Visa or Mastercard. Key features include used, collectible books and first editions.

BookNook   http://www.booknook.com/
This US discount bookstore has over half a million titles including bestsellers and used books. There's a good search facility where you can search by author, title, ISBN or subject.

Books A Million   http://www.booksamillion.com/
This US site offers regular everyday price discounts of 20% to 50% off selected
titles, and by joining the Millionaire's Club, you could save an additional 10%
off every book. Typical discounts are 55% off bestsellers, 46% off features and
37% off in-stock hardcover books.

Books are Magic   http://www.booksaremagic.com/
This US site offers over 2 million book and audio book titles. There's a section
for children and a reviews section with regular contributions from publishers
and critics.

Booklovers   http://www.booklovers.co.uk/
For quality second-hand books, the UK-based Booklovers have a huge
selection available to buy online.

The Book People   http://www.thebookpeople.co.uk/
This site can be viewed at two resolutions enabling those with less than perfect
site to see a large version, whilst the rest of us can choose to see a smaller, more
detailed version. Categories include Sports, Hobbies, Health, Reference and
Cookery books, and also includes a section on books for children and for
toddlers. The site also features weekly handpicked bestsellers which are
discounted.

The Book Pl@ce   http://www.thebookplace.com/

The Book Pl@ce features full searching by author, title or keyword. Once you've found the book you're looking for, you get all the blurb and jacket artwork. There's 10% off over a quarter of a million titles with fast shipping direct from stock.

1Bookstreet.com   http://www.1bookstreet.com/

This US online bookstore has divided its stock into streets at 1 Bargain Book Street, 1 Mystery Street, 1 Romance Street, 1 Cookbook Street, 1 Audio Street, 1 Kid Street and 1 Jesus Way.

Chapters   http://www.chapters.ca/

This Canadian site offers videos, software, electronics, CDs and a huge range of books. When you enter the site, click on the 'Books' tab at the top of the screen and you can either browse the index or search for books by title, author, ISBN or keyword. There are some huge discounts usually around 40% on selected titles but sometimes as much as 75%.

Children's Book Centre   http://www.childrensbookcentre.co.uk/

The CBC features a comprehensive catalogue of books categorised by age. There are six age ranges from 6 months to 15 years. There's also a Top 20 index.

If you've got children, introduce them to this site.

The Children's Bookshop   http://www.childrensbookshop.com/

Children should be encouraged to read and this site contains details of most children's books. Carefully divided into reading ages, books can be searched by author or title. The files are in text format and can be searched off-line. When you've found what you're looking for, you can place an order there and then.

Computer Books Online   http://www.computerbooksonline.com/

This US site offer new and used computer books, with up to 20% discount.

Computer Step   http://www.ineasysteps.com/

Buy titles from the leading UK computing publisher's 'in easy steps' and 'in easy steps.compact' series. Watch out for great special offers!

Country Bookshop   http://www.countrybookshop.co.uk/

This independent UK bookstore has over 1 million books categorised in Arts, Business, Childrens & Educational, Computing & Internet, Discover UK, Family, Home & DIY, Fiction, Literature & Biography and Sport. There is also an out-of-print section and a place to search for old books.

Edge Book Shop   http://www.cumbria1st.com/biz/books/

To find out more about the history of England, Scotland, Wales, Ireland and the Isle of Man, visit this UK site. There is a huge selection to choose from, all available online and a 10% discount if you buy five or more.

If it's a hard-to-find book, visit a seller that specialises in books of the genre you want.

The English Book Centre   http://www.ebcoxford.co.uk/

This UK company provides a specialist service supplying all types of materials for teaching/learning English for non-English speakers.

Funorama   http://www.funorama.com/

This US site is an online activity centre and bookstore for children. It's a great place to find educational projects and some quality books for children.

Innocom   http://www.innocom-ltd.com/

Innocom provide a simple way to purchase books via a secure server. You can search by keyword, author, publisher, category or title.

Internet Bookshop   **http://www.bookshop.co.uk/**
Now owned by WH Smith, the Internet Bookshop includes CDs, videos and over 1.5 million books divided into about a dozen categories. The site includes an index of the top twenty best sellers and there's some good discounts to be had.

James Thin Booksellers   **http://www.jamesthin.co.uk/**
Established in 1848 and soon becoming Edinburgh's largest bookseller, this UK site features fiction, educational books, maps and Scottish books.

John Smith & Son Bookshops   **http://www.johnsmith.co.uk/**
This huge site has over 1 million books and is Scotland's oldest booksellers. In 1999 it was awarded the title of Academic Bookseller of the Year.

Lion Publishing　　　　　　　　　　http://www.lion-publishing.co.uk/
This UK company publishes and sells online books for all ages, but specialises in Christianity, the Church, and the Bible.

Long Barn Books　　　　　　　　　　http://www.longbarnbooks.co.uk/
This small independent UK publishing company sells their titles online and produces a quarterly journal about books.

Macmillan Computer Books　　　　　　　　http://www.mcp.com/
As the name implies, this US store offers a huge selection of computer books.

Maps Worldwide　　　　　　　　http://www.mapsworldwide.co.uk/
The UK's largest Internet map shop. Most of the 10,000 maps etc. have cover images and full product notes. Many are offered with savings.

Millennium Books　　　　　　　　http://www.meridian-experience.com/
This UK online bookseller offers a good range of books in the usual categories.

The Mulberry Bush　　　　　　　　http://www.mulberrybush.com/
Specialising in books about dolls and teddy bears, The Mulberry Bush is now one of the world's largest stockists of collector books.

OK UK Books　　　　　　　　http://www.okukbooks.com/
OK UK Books is one of the best places to choose children's books. Not only do all of the entries show front cover pictures and full jacket information, but many of the books have reviews written by children who have read them. The search engine is simple but effective and there's also a section on future books and links to book series like Paddington Bear, Goosebumps and Asterix.

Ottakar's   http://www.ottakars.co.uk/
This superb UK website features a huge range of books with information about forthcoming titles, experts' recommendations, competitions and lots of discounts.

Oxford University Press Bookshop   http://www.oup.co.uk/
This is the world's largest university press, selling a wide range of academic books online. OUP currently publishes over 150 journals, covering a wide range of academic disciplines. This site also carries a link to the home of the Oxford English Dictionary.

Pan Macmillan   http://www.panmacmillan.com/
Fiction, Music, Science, Technology, Natural History and Crime & Mysteries are the main themes from this quality UK publisher.

PC Bookshops   http://www.pcbooks.co.uk/
The name gives it away – a UK online bookshop selling books about computers and computing.

Penguin Books UK   http://www.penguin.co.uk/
Is there anyone who hasn't heard of Penguin books? The name synonymous with paperbacks has an ordering system where you can buy any of the Penguin titles online. The site also features a history of the company, details about the authors and competitions. You'll need a good monitor and/or good eyesight if you visit this site. Some of the text is very small and sometimes rendered against a dark background.

Pickabook   http://www.pickabook.co.uk/

Pickabook holds almost a quarter of a million titles, many of which are heavily discounted. The site also features a news section containing the latest news about the publishers, authors and titles.

Powell's   http://powells.com/

This US site claims to be the largest new and used bookstore in the world. The books are plentiful and cheap, with free shipping on all orders over US$50 wherever they are shipped throughout the world.

Red House   http://www.redhouse.co.uk/

The online branch of the discount mail order book club.

Richard Nicholson of Chester   http://www.antiquemaps.com/

This long established UK company sells antique maps and prints.

San Diego Technical Books   http://www.booksmatter.com/

This US bookstore carries a huge selection of technical books including computer, construction and medical.

Saxons http://www.saxons.co.uk/

All the books for sale on this UK online bookstore cost £1.

The Scholar's Bookshelf http://www.scholarsbookshelf.com/

Over 12,000 books, many at discounts of up to 70% are available from this US online bookstore. It specialises in History, Military History, Fine Arts and Music.

Sci-Fi http://www.sci-fi.co.uk/

This UK online retailer specialises in science fiction related merchandise, but stocks an excellent assortment of books on the subject. So whether it's Dr Who, Blake's Seven, Star Wars or The X-Files, you'll find all the books here.

Sportspages http://www.sportspages.co.uk/

This website, which uses an open book as the backdrop, sells nothing but sports-related books and videos. The books are categorised in an amazing 92 different sports. The obvious ones are there, but so are the less obvious like Crown Green Bowls, Petanque and Real Tennis.

Just for fun, see how many sports you can think of.

Tesco http://www.tesco.co.uk/books

With 1.2 million books available online, you should find something you want although they tend to be only the top selling books. There is a special section for the best cook books and for the best children's books.

Titanic Incorporated   http://www.titanic-leisure.com/books.htm

This is the book section of the website devoted to the Titanic. There are some fascinating books about the disaster, and the subsequent discovery of the wreck.

Varsity Books   http://www.varsitybooks.com/

This US online site sells college textbooks at up to 40% discount. 350,000 textbooks, fiction and more.

Virgin Books   http://www.virgin-books.com/

The UK's leading publisher of books by top authors on music, sport, biography, TV, film, reference and erotic fiction. There are some good bargains available and you can subscribe to a free e-mailing list.

Watkins   http://www.watkinsbooks.com/

This UK site specialises in books about healing, mysticism, mythology and the occult. They also stock videos, cassettes, CDs and Tarot cards.

WH Smith   http://www.whsmith.co.uk/

The famous high street bookstore actually sells a great deal more than books, but if it's books you want, this is a good site to visit.

When you get to this site, go to the bottom of the home page and choose 'Books' from the index. You can then choose the type of book you want from the drop down menu on the right and then enter the title or author in the search engine to get a list of the books fitting your entry. The list of books is displayed and clicking on one gives further details about the book. At the bottom of the 'further details' screen is a useful feature enabling you to search for other books by the same author, by the same publisher or on the same subject. You'll be emailed the information as part of a regular newsletter from WHSmith.

At any time you can add books to your shopping basket and proceed to the secure checkout.

The advantage of buying online is that your book will be un-thumbed: something that is sadly not always the case when you buy from a shop.

Music

If you like to listen to music by a particular group, singer or composer, the chances are you'll go to your local music shop and buy a plastic disc containing recordings of your chosen music. It will come in a special protective case, probably with pictures and information about the artists. The shop will carefully wrap your purchase and you'll pay for it before trundling it back home to insert it into a special player.

The only variation with this activity in recent years has been the change from black discs (vinyl records) to silver discs (compact discs).

Since the advent of affordable record players, this is how we have collected and played our favourite music. But getting music you like doesn't have to be like this, and if some people have their way, it won't be for much longer.

Use the Net

More and more music lovers are using the Internet to buy their CDs, vinyls, cassettes, videos and DVDs. There are scores of sites supplying music over the net, but top of the list is 101CD.

101CD   http://www.101cd.com/

Boasting over 1 million titles, 101CD is the site for searching and ordering music. The first time you visit the site, you'll need to register. This involves entering not only your name and address, but also your credit card details. You'll also need to choose a username and a password. Naturally, this is done over a secure connection.

At the top of the screen is a row of tabs which takes you to the different sections of the online store. Clicking on *Music* will take you to the department which deals with CDs and the like.

I really don't like visiting music shops to buy CDs. The choice you have is to either ask an assistant or wade through the racks of discs which never seem to be in any particular order, as previous 'waders' have put them back in a different place from where they first got them. I never seem to establish whether a group such as The Who is listed under 'T' or 'W', and music that is listed under headings such as 'Easy Listening' tends to be rather subjective. (My son recently bought a CD from the Easy Listening section, but personally I found that listening to it was anything but easy.) Headings such as 'Garage' and 'BeBop' are a complete mystery to me. Finding an assistant is often easier said than done, and when you do track one down, it's always so embarrassing. I once went into a record shop and asked for a CD by the 60's group Herman's Hermits. The girl who was serving looked about 12, and had no idea who they were or even if I was referring to the group or the title of a song. I, of course, felt every bit my age, even though I told her it was for my wife.

It's less embarrassing asking for 'old' music online.

The privacy and preciseness of the Internet eliminates all of these problems. Just below the shopping trolley on 101CD's home page is the search panel where you can enter the name of an artist, a song, a publisher or a catalogue number. *Search options* allows you to select which of the four search parameters you wish to use and also allows you to choose an inclusive or non-inclusive search. Simply, if you enter 'Queen' as the artist, an inclusive search will return only those artists whose name contains the word 'Queen' and nothing else. In other words, the search will provide you with all of the music by the group 'Queen'. If, on the other hand, you enter 'Queen' as a non-inclusive search, you'll get everything by artists that include 'Queen' in their name. So you'll get things like 'Trooping of the Colour by Her Majesty the Queen'. In general terms, if you know what you're looking for, use an inclusive search. If you're not sure exactly what it is, then use non-inclusive.

Spellings are important. If you don't spell the name correctly it's unlikely you'll get a match.

Entering a non-inclusive search can result in several screens full of information, but it is ordered information. That is, all the products by the pop group Queen are together, all the products about Her Majesty the Queen are together and so on. But further, all the products for each artist are ordered according to their media (CDs, vinyl LP, vinyl singles and so on). This means that even if your search results in masses of information, it's fairly easy to locate your particular interest or requirement from the list.

Each product has a link which will take you to more information about the product. The amount of information held here is variable, but always contains details of the product, artist, catalogue number and where the product was sourced. Most is UK or US, but a great deal is imported from Europe and Japan. If you want to buy it, click on the 'Add to Basket' button and it will be added to the list of items you want to buy.

When you've finished browsing round the store, you go to the checkout where you can alter the number of items you have in your trolley. In most cases, this means deleting the number '1' in the *Quantity* column and replacing it with a '0'. Once you're happy with the contents of your trolley, click on the 'Pay' button and your order will be confirmed. If it is correct, click on the *Proceed* button, your order will be processed and the money will be taken from your account when the goods are shipped, not before.

This is then followed up by an email confirming that your order has been accepted and providing you with an order number should there be any queries. The goods arrive a couple of days later.

The service provided by 101CD is really faultless. It's simple to use and is very secure. But there are other ways of going about collecting music.

Cook your own CDs

The trouble is that the contents of each CD or record have been determined by someone else and although you may like most of the tracks on a given disc, there may be some that you don't like. But that's tough because they're on the CD and you've either got to buy all of them or none at all. The result of this is that you find the track-skip button on your CD player needs to be replaced fairly frequently because it's worn out due to excessive use. If this is the case, you might care to try selecting your own tracks.

This is a good way of collecting music to play in the car.

Customdisc   **http://www.customdisc.com/**

This is a custom CD service which allows you to put songs of your choice onto a CD. When you log onto Customdisc, you can search through their database for the songs they have available. The number of tracks they have is growing rapidly and you're certain to be able to fill several discs. You can preview any of the songs by clicking on the link alongside the name of the song, and you get about 10 seconds listening to an excerpt of the song. Those tracks you like can be added to your shopping trolley. You can collect up to 25 tracks or a little over an hour's worth of music. The system not only keeps track of how much you spend, but how many minutes of songs you have so far collected. Clearly, you cannot go over the allotted time as the amount of music you can fit onto a CD is finite.

You are charged a basic price for the service which includes local tax and postage, and there is also a cost per track charge, which varies according to the royalty for each track.

When you've chosen the contents of your disc and paid for it, the company produce the CD and post it to you. What you get is a Compact Disc containing only the songs you like and in the order you want them. Typically, a custom made CD will be cheaper than a standard price CD, and you'll also get exactly what you want. Just think how much you'll save by not having to replace the track-skip buttons on your CD player.

Razorcuts   **http://www.razorcuts.co.uk/**
This UK site offers a similar custom CD service.

MP3

Even more hi-tech is to download the songs yourself. The current trend is towards music files called MP3, which, by the way, is the most searched-for phrase on the Internet. Yes, even more than 'sex'. MP3s are computer files of digital recordings which can be downloaded from the Internet and played on your computer. Previously, digital recordings stored as computer files used copious quantities of disc space and clearly were not really suitable for downloading from the Internet. The average track on a Compact Disc is about 35MBytes.

MP3 recordings are much smaller, but as far as the average human is concerned, no less perfect. This is because they have been created with all the sounds that humans can't hear removed, which reduces them to about one-tenth of their original size. This works out at just over 1MByte per minute of music. The average song track is about 3 minutes i.e. about 3-3.5 MBytes which doesn't take too long to download, but the quality is still excellent.

Software MP3 players

All you need to play MP3 files on your computer is a software MP3 player, of which there are several and mostly free.

Sonique   http://www.sonique.com/

Top of the list of MP3 players is Sonique which is distributed free by several other websites including Lycos which can be found at *http://music.lycos.com*.

Quite why someone wants to give away such a superb piece of software which must have taken untold hours to develop is unclear, but give it away they do. More details about downloading software can be found in the chapter on buying software.

Looking as though it were carved from a solid piece of granite, Sonique does not run in the usual and familiar Microsoft window, but it does behave in much the same way as a window (you can move it around, place it behind other windows etc.). The controls allow you to play any number of tracks and there is scope for repeating tracks as well as skipping. The audio enhancement panel provides scope for setting the balance and the speed and pitch of the playback.

MP3 files that have previously been downloaded and saved onto your computer can be dragged into Sonique and played through your computer's sound system. Although you can use previously downloaded MP3 files with Sonique, this program will log onto the Internet and search for particular files if you wish. This is generally a better way of downloading and importing files as Sonique can do it all in one operation.

Once you have amassed your collection of MP3 files you can 'tell' Sonique where they are and they will be played whenever you run it. The songs can be changed around just as you would do with CDs or MiniDiscs.

The interesting feature of Sonique is the fact that a small industry has sprung up producing files to change the way it looks and behaves. You can change the appearance of the player by downloading special plug-ins called 'skins'. These small files can be freely downloaded and incorporated into Sonique, which effectively changes its window. So, if you don't like the 'carved from a lump of granite look', you can change it for something that looks like an intergalactic spaceship or a 21st Century instrument of torture. The graphics feature of Sonique, which works in much the same way as an oscilloscope but keeps in time with the music, can also be changed by downloading special 'plug-ins'. Like the skins, there are dozens and dozens available, which can also be freely downloaded from sites like *http://www.mp3players.co.uk/*.

Xing   http://www.xingtech.com/

If Sonique is too gimmicky, then try Xing's MP3 player which is also free as part of their CD ripper software, AudioCatalyst. Xing's MP3 player is much more straightforward, although it doesn't have all of the flashy features of Sonique. Xing can be downloaded free from several sites including Lycos and Xing's own website.

A CD ripper is a program that will take tracks from a music CD and convert them into MP3 files. Once the CD ripper is running in your computer, you place a music CD into your CD ROM drive and the software will catalogue it. You select the track or tracks you want to rip, and then go off and have a cup of tea. Although most rippers will convert CD tracks faster than real-time, to convert a whole CD still takes several minutes. Once the ripper has done its job, the resulting files can then be renamed and stored for future use.

If you like the AudioCatalyst CD ripper, there's a small charge for the fully working version.

To get the full value of digital sound on your computer you'll need a good sound card and very good speakers. Most multimedia computers are sold with only a passable sound card, and speakers that often aren't up to even that standard. But these will be good enough to get you going. Ideally you need a 32bit sound card and good quality mains powered and amplified stereo speakers, preferably with a sub-woofer to really bring the sound alive. Anything less will produce sound which is less pure, but still very acceptable. You also need a fast modem, otherwise downloading will take a long time.

Many of the tracks are free, but these are only songs that have either never been heard of and/or by artists that have never been heard of. For everything else, you have to pay, although the cost can work out much less than you think.

Voice Activated Player   http://ghs.ssd.k12.wa.us/~pdavis/

For users of the Linux operating system (see the chapter on software), you can get this superb MP3 player that uses IBM's voice recognition software. You can turn your computer into a jukebox by issuing verbal commands. It has a powerful search engine so that you can search through your library of MP3 files and play the tune of your choice just by speaking to it. Best of all, it's free.

BURBs   http://www.burbs.co.uk/

If the British Underground Rock scene is your scene, then this is the site to visit. Of particular note is the fact that MP3 clips can be downloaded enabling you to have your ears blasted whilst you're working on your computer.

Crunch   http://www.crunch.co.uk/

For those collecting MP3 files, this a good site for UK music. Lots of choice and good prices. Most software MP3 players are available for free download, and some MP3 hardware players can also be purchased online.

Lycos   http://www.lycos.co.uk/

Although Lycos is a search engine, it's also the place to visit if you're collecting MP3 files.

MP3 Central   http://music.lycos.com/mp3/

There are dozens of sites from which you can download MP3 music files, but one of the most popular is MP3 Central. At MP3 Central you can search for MP3 recordings by either song name or artist name. The library is huge and is getting larger by the hour. Once you've selected a track, you can either download it, or pay and download it.

Either the name of song or the name of the artist can be searched for, but as with all searching, you need to exercise a little thought or you could find yourself presented with a list running to several screens.

Avoid sites which contain illegal copies of songs which they do not have the authority to distribute.

Other legitimate MP3 sites exist, but so do several less legitimate ones. Some sites contain huge quantities of pirated music which is either being sold off cheap or given away. These should be avoided at all costs, as should individuals who attach MP3 files to news postings or to emails.

MP3.com   http://www.MP3.com/

MP3.com is another popular site which offers a good selection of songs in MP3 format which can be downloaded. Also worth investigating is *http://mp3.box.sk/* which has a list of all the best MP3 search engines.

Vitaminic http://www.vitaminic.com/

Wide selection of MP3 software available for download conveniently divided up into operating systems categories. Also provides a Top 10 MP3 download chart.

Hardware MP3 players

First there was the portable cassette player. Then came the portable CD player. Next came the portable Mini Disc player. Now comes the portable MP3 player.

Empegear http://www.empegear.com/

Does your car stereo run Linux? If not then visit this site to find out why it should. Actually it's all to do with playing MP3 files in your car.

Look at some of the sites which specialise in consumer electronics for more MP3 players.

MP3 Players http://www.mp3players.co.uk/

If you collect MP3 files and want to play them on something other than your computer, this site will be of interest to you as they sell everything associated with MP3 including portable players and adapters for the car. Also available are most of the top software MP3 players including Sonique as a free download. If you haven't got into MP3 yet, but think you might like to, this is the place to visit.

CDs and vinyl

There are literally hundreds of online stores that specialise in selling music, mainly on CD but sometimes on vinyl. For some, it's not their main stock-in-trade, but selling music accounts for a significant amount of their business. As with all websites, the quality varies enormously.

Abbey Records   http://www.abbeyrecords.com/

Lots of CDs and vinyl records, both new and used and links to other related sites. This site is also accessible via *http://www.abbeyrecords.co.uk/*

Action Records   http://www.action-records.co.uk/

Yet another music shop with an online ordering service, but this one also sells vinyl and has its own music label. The catalogue is huge and so, conveniently, you can download it and browse at your leisure offline. Non-EEC customers don't have to pay VAT on these orders.

Amazon   http://www.amazon.com/

This site is included here because of its music department, but a fuller description is given in the section about buying books. Along with 101CD, Amazon is the yardstick by which other sites are judged.

Audiostreet   http://www.audiostreet.com/

Unlike many others, this store has an excellent search facility which should enable you to track down exactly what you're looking for. The advertised CDs have track listings included in the description which makes buying more certain. The prices are significantly cheaper than high street prices and if you review a CD, you could win a free one.

Beat Museum   **http://www.thebeatmuseum.com/**
This site specialises in Jazz and all of the incomprehensible variations.

Black Music   **http://www.blackmail.com/**
Relatively small, but Black Music is a good reference site and online store with descriptions, pictures and track listings of a wide selection of CDs. As the name suggests, this site specialises in black music and so is the obvious place to go for Reggae, BeBob, Hip-Hop etc.

Blockbuster   **http://www.blockbuster.co.uk/**
One of the best known names in UK high-street entertainment, Blockbuster is a video library in its shop guise. Online it's a place to choose and buy mainly films on video tape and DVD. The site opens with a pleasant introduction from a welcoming female.

BOL   **http://www.bol.com/**
This huge operation contains a wealth of information and stock for sale online. Like Amazon, you can review products and send them in for everyone to read.

Borrow Or Rob   **http://shop.borroworrob.com/**
Not the easiest address to enter, and when you've typed it, it still looks wrong. Over half a million CDs at reasonable prices. They offer free worldwide delivery and information about the featured artists include track listings, about the artist and cover artwork.

Boxman   **http://www.boxman.co.uk/**

This site's most notable feature is the fact that each CD description includes
a picture of the cover. Some others also provide this, but not always as
consistently. There's also free delivery on some discs.

CD Now   **http://www.cdnow.com/**

A massive selection of CDs are available from CD Now.

Chart CD   **http://www.chartcd.com/**

Effectively the antithesis of CD-Wow in that this site specialises in the current
Top 10 US albums, and the Top 75 UK albums. You'll find the prices much
lower than many high street stores, and the prices include local tax and carriage.

CD Paradise   http://www.cdparadise.com/

It is incredible how times have changed. WH Smith, I recall, was little more than a newspaper stand on railway stations before expanding into the giant chain of high street shops. CD Paradise is their online shop for music. There's a great selection and the prices are very competitive.

CD-Wow   http://www.cd-wow.com/

Apart from the top selling current CDs, this site features a good selection of records from days gone by. If you think you're paying over the odds, tell them, or look on the price comparison chart which compares their prices with others.

CD Zone   http://www.cdzone.co.uk/

This is one of the largest online stores in the UK for CDs, DVDs, videos and cassettes. Oh yes, and Minidiscs. Simple, but effective searching.

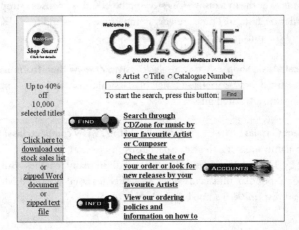

Cheap or What!   http://www.cow.co.uk/

Claiming to be the first online CD store in the UK, this site uses a simple search and ordering system. These are very competitive prices and free UK delivery is one of the plus points.

Classical Music Shop   http://www.thegiftofmusic.co.uk/

This relatively new store has a range of classical music and even some bright ideas for music-related gifts.

Compact Classics   http://www.compactclassics.co.uk/

As the name suggests, this site specialises in classical music, so a search for music by The Sex Pistols is unlikely to result in many matches. But you can find some popular musicians here. Recently featured was Paul McCartney who had just finished some classical work.

Classical Choice   **http://www.cdchoice.com/**

New and used classical CDs are this site's main stock in trade. You can also offer your collection for sale. One interesting feature is that you can email them your wish-list.

Classical Insites   **http://www.classicalinsites.com/**

Classical Insites features classical music on most media, with the chance to listen to some extracts. There are also some good gift ideas.

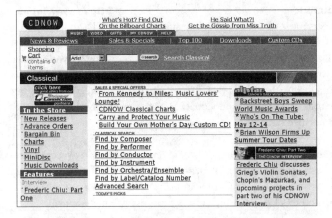

CMS Music   **http://www.cmsmusic.co.uk/**

It's worth visiting CMS, especially if you like the idea of buying some second hand CDs. Better descriptions would be welcome though. You can sell your CDs, International orders are welcome and there are some hot links to other related sites.

Crotchet   **http://www.crotchet.co.uk/**

This site specialises is what is best described as classical. Heavy classical. But also Jazz, Orchestral and an interesting area called Historical.

Dalriada   **http://www.argyllweb.com/dalriada**

The passion these folks have for their music clearly comes out of this site. For lovers of traditional Irish and Scottish music, a visit to Dalriada is essential. Wide choice, good prices and good delivery service.

Dotmusic   **http://www.dotmusic.com/**

This is more of a chat and gossip site, but it sells CDs too.

E-Dance   **http://www.e-dance.co.uk/**

If you want a piece of dance music, look no further. The choice is a little limited, but there is both CD and vinyl. There are also some interesting pictures of unknown individuals having (apparently) lots of fun at various unspecified dance venues.

Entertainment Express   **http://www.entexpress.com/**

Albums are listed under a variety of headings including Top 50 Albums, Top 50 Artists and Top 25 Compilations. There's also a good selection of DVD films on this UK site which offers free postage on all items.

Entertainment Express features advance release information so you can buy that new CD as soon as it's available.

Fusion Records   **http://www.fusionrecords.co.uk/**

Another online store selling not only music in the form of CDs, and DVDs but also a whole lot of collectable odds and ends to go with it. This site offer free postage and packing.

GB Posters   **http://www.gbposters.co.uk/**

Although not strictly speaking music, this site does sell a huge range of pictures and posters of favourite musical artists.

GEMM   **http://www.gemm.com/**

If you're trying to track down an elusive title, this site should be high on your list of visits as it searches other sites that specialise in new and second-hand discs. It claims a massive 7 million titles. I would have thought that if you can't find it here, give up.

Global Groove Records   **http://www.globalgroove.co.uk/**

As the name suggests, this store specialises in vinyl records and holds a fairly large stock of new and used records. Reminiscent of 1960's record shops, there is a listening booth where you can hear what you're buying before you've paid for it.

Hard To Find Records   **http://www.htfr.co.uk/**

Self-explanatory: rare CDs and vinyl records, but also some bits and pieces for the budding disc jockey. They receive orders from all over the world.

Heyday Mail Order   **http://www.heyday-mo.com/**

I've never been really sure what psychedelic music actually is. If you know, and you want some, this is the site to visit.

HMV   **http://www.hmv.co.uk/**

It's a long way from the dog and the phonograph which was the trademark of His Master's Voice. The dog is still there, but it's become more stylised. Now referred to simply as HMV, the online store offers CDs and videos for sale.

Internet Music Shop   **http://www.musicsales.co.uk/**

Apart from the usual diet of CDs etc., this site contains lots of sheet music as well as some books for tutoring for a range of popular instruments.

Jungle   **http://www.jungle.com/**

Quite why they've chosen a Jungle as the theme running through this site, you can decide for yourself. But this site has some superb deals for music and movies (amongst other things) which includes free UK delivery and an order tracking service. The products are well described, including pictures.

Magpie Direct   **http://www.magpiedirect.com/**

Original recordings by original artists from the 1940's onwards.

MDC Classic   **http://www.mdcmusic.co.uk/**

A huge selection of classical CDs, well organised and easily searched.

Mello Yello   **http://www.melloyello.co.uk/**

A good place to buy CDs and DVDs at below high street prices.

Ministry of Sound   http://www.ministryofsound.co.uk

Sounding like something from Monty Python, the Ministry of Sound has a huge catalogue of past issues. You can access Web radio through this site, there's a download section as well as the almost obligatory special offers and competitions.

Moving Music   http://www.movingmusic.co.uk/

The stock list is best described as 'budget', but it does have a large selection of music on all media as well as special offers which include getting a free CD.

Music 365   http://www.music365.com/

Music 365 is a sort of online magazine with chat and news about groups and clubs and offers for concert tickets, CDs and videos. It includes some good reviews on a wide range of titles.

Music Box   http://www.musicbox.uk.co/

Note the address, it's '*uk.co*' and not '*co.uk*'. The Music Box is part of the high street store that sells discounted CDs.

Music Capital   http://www.musiccapital.com/

Apart from the usual range of products for sale, there is also plenty of news, reviews and comment on this, Capital Radio's online store.

Musicmania   http://www.musicmania.co.uk/

The mania certainly comes from the music and not the Web design. This online store has a good selection of CDs and cassettes at reasonable prices, carefully catalogued for easy searching.

Music Metropolis   http://www.musicmetropolis.com/

I would have thought that a company with the resources of Cable and Wireless, might have come up with something a little more inspiring than this. But it does the job of selling CDs reasonably well.

Music Stop   http://www.music-stop.co.uk/

Not the most inspired title, but nevertheless an adequate description – another online music shop selling a range of CDs covering most genres. There are also some useful links to other related sites.

New World Music   http://www.newworldmusic.com/

Visit this site to discover the very best Relaxation, World, Celtic, Native American and Uplifting music. The Artists include Medwyn Goodall, Terry Oldfield, Phil Thornton, Stephen Rhodes and many more of the very best musicians in the world. For lovers of New Age music, this site has everything you could possibly want. You can even listen to some the tracks before buying.

NME   http://www.nme.com/

The New Musical Express website offers a good selection of CDs and videos, but also sells tickets for concerts, or 'gigs' to use the popular parlance.

Online Records   http://www.onlinerecords.co.uk/

This site specialises in black music as diverse as Reggae and Gospel. You can join the mailing list as well as buy the music and other merchandise.

Past Perfect   http://www.pastperfect.com/

Do you remember the early gramophone records which included lots of crackling? What this site offers is digitally re-mastered versions of the same but without the crackles. Recordings from the 20's, 30's and 40's which were previously thought to be useless have had their crackles removed and are now sold on CD.

Plantagenet Music   http://www.plantagenetmusic.co.uk/

There's something rather stirring about military music, but it's not everyone's taste. If it's not your cup of tea, don't bother visiting this site, because that's about all they sell. But it does include some of the finest military and brass band music from some of the top bands like The Band of The Royal Irish Regiment and The RAF College Big Band, who have a CD entitled Swing Wing. Very droll.

Record Store   http://www.recordstore.co.uk/

The Record Store specialises in dance music, of which they have a great deal with stacks of useful information.

Riffage   http://www.riffage.com/

The strategic vision behind Riffage is to revolutionise the way music is distributed by using the Internet to allow bands to sell their music directly to their fans. Riffage is staffed by people who genuinely care about music and includes musicians, former radio DJs and record company veterans, as well as fans. There is a large selection of downloadable authorised digital music, both free and for purchase.

Seaford Music   http://www.seaford-music.co.uk/

Seaford Music specialises in imported classical CDs, sheet music and some instruments.

Sentimental Records   http://www.sentimentalrecords.com/

The name says it all – oldies but goldies. Order a full catalogue online but orders for the music are currently via email.

Shop DVD   http://www.shopdvd.co.uk/

Not the best title for this shop which actually sells all the latest CDs, Minidiscs and videos. Oh yes, and DVDs.

The Lobby   http://www.thelobby.co.uk/

A sort of bargain basement of all sorts of miscellaneous products, including some cheap music.

The Muse   http://www.themuse.co.uk/

Compared to some of the other online stores, The Muse is quite small, but you can download samples of the music before you buy.

Timewarp Records   http://www.tunes.co.uk/timewarp

The name to me implies oldies, but actually Timewarp Records specialise in more modern music like BeBop.

Uptown Records   http://www.uptownrecords.com/

Another online music store that is efficient and reliable, but otherwise fairly unremarkable, apart from the fact that it deals mainly with black music.

VCI   http://www.vci.co.uk/

Yet another up and coming store selling a range of books, videos and CDs. There are some special offers to look out for as well as the odd competition.

Vinyl Tap Records   http://www.vinyltap.co.uk/

Otherwise known as World Wide Rarities, this online store is especially for collectors. Lots of vinyl.

Virgin Megastore   http://www.virginmega.com/

Britain's most popular entrepreneur has found his way here too. It's just like the high street shop, but less walking around.

WH Smith Online   http://www.whsmithonline.co.uk/

There are some good deals to be had from this high street shop, but you do have to watch the postage which can make some CDs cost more.

Y2K Music   http://www.y2k-music.co.uk/

Y2K Music have set themselves up as an alternative way of obtaining and then reselling music. It specialises in a range of weird and wonderful sounds that some people rave about. But not I.

Yalplay   http://www.yalplay.com/

Billed as Europe's premier online music store, Yalplay boasts over a quarter of a million titles, mainly CDs.

Ynot Music   http://www.ynotmusic.co.uk/

The smart readers will immediately notice that 'Ynot' is 'Tony' backwards and they (or he) stocks music for aerobics classes. The trouble with visiting the local Gym is that it's so boring peddling away and not even being able to enjoy the fresh air and scenery. Ynot provide music especially for rowers and press-up artists, as well as those people who like to burn off their surplus calories on a treadmill.

Musical instruments

Anyone can put a CD into a slot and press a button, but playing a musical instrument takes lots of practice. These sites sell all manner of music-making equipment.

ABC Music   http://www.abcmusic.co.uk/

This site opens with a lively sound track and eye-catching animation. You can buy and sell a musical instrument at this online store based in southern England. Also available are instruments to rent and a selection of tutorials covering most popular instruments.

Axemail   http://www.axe.music.co.uk/

For budding pop groups, get yourselves equipped at Axemail with guitars, amps and drums. Remarkably, Axemail actually offers a reduction if you pay by credit card.

Chappell of Bond Street   http://www.shopyell.co.uk/chappell

The opening page carries the banner, "Suppliers of fine musical instruments and printed music for almost 200 years. Beethoven, Richard Strauss and Charles Dickens have all been regular clients of the unparalleled Chappell service". Chappell's is also one of the largest sheet music sellers. Orders are dispatched worldwide.

Churchill's Music   http://www.churchills-music.co.uk/

If you're a keyboard player, everything you want and need is here. Not just the keyboards by Casio and Technics, but all the accessories to go with them.

Drum Central Superstore   http://www.drumcentral.com/

It must be everyone's nightmare – a young lad living next door who's given a drum kit for his birthday. Best not tell them about this site, which seems to sell nothing but drums, which are guaranteed Y2K compliant.

EL Music   http://www.elmusic.co.uk/

EL Music sells everything from Grand Pianos to banjos.

Gibson   http://www.gibson.com/

If you're a fan of guitars, you will have heard of Gibson. The famous guitar maker from Kalamazoo, Michigan, USA has been at the forefront of guitar development, with help from Les Paul who helped them develop the electric guitar. This site provides a wealth of information about the famous guitars, and an online auction where you can buy or sell.

Guitar Superstore   http://www.guitarsuperstore.com/

You can buy new or used guitars and all the paraphernalia that goes with them from this superstore. The stock list is huge, but it's easy to find what you want (if you know what you want) and you can even download a sample of the sound of the guitar you're interested in.

KB Music   http://www.kbmusic.co.uk/

This online store sells a wide range of music including sheet music, karaoke, CDs and instruments including guitars and keyboards.

Look Music http://www.lookmusic.com/

For those who fancy strumming out ABBA songs on a cheap guitar, take a look at Look Music who specialise in sheet music and book music.

Macaris Musical Instruments http://www.macaris.co.uk/

Apparently this is the oldest established musical instrument store in London. Its other claim to fame is that it's the birthplace of the fuzzbox. All sorts of musical instruments for sale, as well as amplifiers etc. Almost as interesting as browsing round the shop itself, but the site contains lots of fancy sound samples and animations and so can take a while to load.

Maestronet http://www.maestronet.com/

Maestronet specialise in downloadable sheet music. The files come in Adobe Acrobat format and so you'll need to have that in your computer to be able to print it out once its been downloaded. If you haven't got Acrobat, you can download it free from this site. They also have a stolen instrument registry.

Musician Shop   http://www.musicianshop.co.uk/
This online shop specialises in accessories for most musical instruments, but guitars seem to come out on top. There is an advice section on buying strings and an online guitar tuner. A neat feature is the facility to hear some of the guitars and special effects.

Oxfam   http://www.oxfam.org.uk/
You can pick up some good deals on musical instruments at the site. The stock is not large but worth visiting. When you get to the site, click on the Fair Trade link and then the Musical Instrument link.

Recollections   http://www.recollections.co.uk/
Pop Memorabilia is very popular, and Recollections is the Internet site to visit for just about any item from the 1960's on. All the top bands are featured and items for sale include programmes and commercial artifacts.

Regent Guitars   http://www.regentguitars.co.uk/
For guitar fans, this is a great site to visit with lots of quality guitars by all the top names like Fender and Gibson. The instruments are well described with both technical specifications as well as subjective views, each carrying a good quality picture.

Saxophone Rental Company   http://www.saxophones.co.uk/
Rather than buying an instrument to learn to play, rent one. If it doesn't work out you haven't lost anything. If you do take it up, then buy. The Saxophone Rental Company will help, but not just with saxophones – they supply flutes and clarinets too.

Sheet Music Direct http://www.sheetmusicdirect.com/

You can buy and download sheet music from this site. You must first download the free Musicpage Viewer before you can either preview or buy music, which is also downloaded.

Sounds Great Music http://www.soundsgreatmusic.com /

Another great online store for guitarists. Apart from lots of guitars (both new and used), they carry a comprehensive stock of accessories too.

Stafford Classical Guitar Centre http://www.staffordguitar.com/

Not the place to come if you want a guitar with a battery in the back. Classical guitars are the speciality here. And only quality classical guitars at that. You can buy and sell but there are also courses and details of forthcoming concerts.

Tutti http://www.tutti.co.uk/

Tutti is the musical term used to indicate that everybody is to play, and this site aims to do exactly that – enable every musician with a CD, sheet music, book or other musically related item to distribute it to a global market.

Tutti is a Web shop-window for classical music. Composers, musicians, record labels and publishers offer their goods for sale by credit card transaction on a digitally secure site provided by Impulse.

You can buy just about anything related to music from this site run by two professional musicians/composers: Sarah Rodgers and Geraldine Allen.

When you enter the site, choose the category you want from CDs, sheet music, books and gifts. Alternatively enter a search word into the search engine to find what you're looking for. When you've chosen something you want to buy, click on the 'Add to Basket' button and when you get to the checkout you can pay for your goods using either Visa or Mastercard.

Leisure

Organising leisure activities can sometimes be so stressful that you need a break to get over it. Let the Internet take away the strain.

Evenings out

Listening to music on a CD or watching a play on TV is fine, but to really get a thrill you need to be there. Ordering tickets for pop concerts, football matches, cinemas and theatres isn't always straightforward and on more than one occasion I've felt that the hassle wasn't worth it. Finding out about what's on, choosing an event and booking tickets using the Internet is easy.

Lastminute.com   **http://www.lastminute.com/**

A brilliant idea, and a site that has made its founders multi-millionaires. There are a few ways to fix an evening out with this site.

To book a last minute trip to the theatre, click on the 'Entertainment' link which will open a page offering categories including concerts, musicals, sporting events and theatre productions. Click on a category and you'll get a list of events. If you fancy one, click on it to find out more, and then to book.

Alternatively you could choose the location and/or date you want to book and the computer will search out some possible shows or events. Again, you've got the choice to find out more about a particular show before you book it.

lastminute.com

To buy from Lastminute.com you'll need to register and log on at each visit.

Yet another way is to click on 'Going Out' which is under either the 'What can I do Tomorrow' or 'What can I do at the Weekend' headings on the home page. You'll get a list of lots of last minute bargains which you can select to get more information, or buy. Another route is to click on the 'VIP Tickets' button at the top of the screen to get another list of events for which tickets are required.

Scoot   http://www.scoot.co.uk/

Scoot is a search tool which can be used to locate UK cinemas and theatres. Once you've located a venue near to you, you can find out what's on and book tickets online.

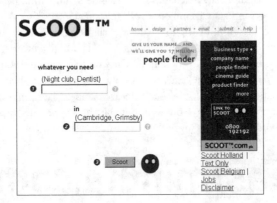

Tickets Online   **http://www.tickets-online.co.uk/**

To find an event you want to go to, enter the details in the search window, or browse through the index of events under the headings region, new events, best sellers, rock, dance, classical, theatre, pop, club, comedy, special events, motor racing – cars, motor racing – cycle, sport, jazz and festivals.

Full details of each event are provided, frequently with special notes about transport and parking. All tickets can be ordered online and will usually be sent to you before the event.

Ticket Master   **http://www.ticketmaster.com/**

If you want tickets for the theatre, a top sporting event, a stage show or a family show in the US, Ticket Master will probably have a lot to choose from.

When you first get to this site, choose the State you are in (or the State in which you wish to see the event or show) and you'll get a list of top events for which tickets are available. Selecting one of those featured will give you more information with the chance to book if you wish.

Look out for Deal of the Week which is a special discount on a top show or event.

Instead of clicking one of the listed shows or events, you can use the search engine to find what you want, or you can select one of the letters of the alphabet to get a list of events beginning with that letter. UK residents (or those wishing to see a show in the UK) should visit *http://www.ticketmaster.co.uk/*. Here, you can either choose the type of event or show you want to see or you can search for something specific either by venue or city and date.

Theatre

Dress Circle   **http://www.dresscircle.co.uk/**

Many people, when they've seen a good show, want to buy a little souvenir like a CD or a keyring. There's almost always a shop within the theatre which sells bits and pieces, and there's almost always a massive crowd gathered round ensuring you don't get a look in.

Billed as the greatest showbiz shop in the world, Dress Circle sells memorabilia from all the great shows worldwide. There's secure online ordering and the prices reflect those you would expect to pay in a theatre. There aren't many pictures of the merchandise so you need to know what you want to buy.

What's on Stage   **http://www.whatsonstage.com/**

This site opens with a news page telling you all the latest gossip about newly appointed casts, new shows and stories of general interest.

If you wish you can join the free weekly theatre news service. Once you've subscribed you'll get a regular email giving you all the latest gossip and hot stories from theatre land.

Clicking on the grey button labelled 'Open Ticketshop' takes you to a screen where you can enter the day and/or the type of show you want (play, musical etc.). Alternatively you can enter the name of a show, either as well or instead of the previous information. To start the search, click the 'Go' button and the search result will appear very quickly. You can get more information about any of the shows listed, and if you like the look of it, book online.

Gigs

In addition to the websites that also offer booking for all types of event and production, there are some sites which specialise in music concerts, or 'gigs', to use the popular parlance.

Aloud   http://www.aloud.com/

Details of all the top UK gigs are on this award-winning website with online booking. When the site opens you can search for the name of a band or artist by entering just the first three letters of the name. You can also find out what's happening on particular dates including today, the next 14 days and the next 6 months.

You can see what's happening in virtually every major town and city in the UK.

When you've booked your tickets, they'll either be sent to you or, if the event is only a couple of days away, you'll pick them up at the box office.

Concert Breaks   http://www.concertbreaks.com/

Why not make a trip to the theatre into a long weekend? Concert Breaks can organise travel and accommodation with a visit to the theatre or concert in European cities like London, Paris, Amsterdam or Dublin.

Many of the concert packages are organised in conjunction with fanclubs and take thousands of people to concerts all around Europe every year. Their ticket and hotel packages include the very best concert tickets and quality hotel accommodation.

The Fab Beatles   http://www.fabbeatles.com/

I saw the Fab Beatles by chance when I visited the Beatles Story in Liverpool. If you like Beatles music, it's worth seeing and listening to The Fab Beatles.

If you're thinking of booking this group, you can hear them first by downloading samples of their songs from this site.

Their website gives dates of their tours and lots of information about the band. If you want to book the band for an event you're organising, complete the online form. You can see their diary including when they're definitely booked and the days when they're definitely not available.

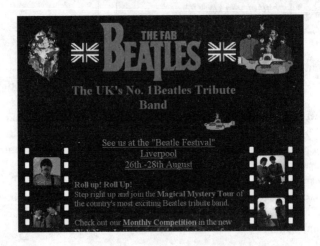

Music 365   http://www.music365.co.uk/

Apart from all the latest news and views, this site can supply tickets for all the top outdoor concerts including Glastonbury, Homelands, Gatecrasher, V2000, Roskilde, T In The Park, The Fleadh, Reading, Leeds and many more. You can also buy CDs and DVDs online.

Ticket Zone   http://www.ticketzone.co.uk/

If you want to go to a pop concert at either an arena or at an open air venue, visit Ticket Zone who always have a good choice of tickets for all the top gigs.

Wayahead   http://www.fortunecity.com/wayahead

This UK website can supply tickets for just about every event for which tickets are required. Whether it's a sporting event, a musical event, theatre, dance, exhibitions, whatever, Wayahead will probably have it.

Wayahead can supply tickets for concerts in the UK and overseas.

You can search for events by date, artist or region – there are new events, special events and special offers.

World Pop   http://www.worldpop.com/

When you open this site, click on the 'Tickets' icon at the top of the screen. You can then search for an artist and/or a venue and/or dates to get a list of concerts matching the criteria you entered.

If you see something you like which has an 'Order Now' icon by it, you can click the icon and you'll get to a screen showing the availability and price range of tickets. If you want to book, click on the Order button and your seats will be reserved.

Cinema

British cinema was hit hard in the 1970's and 80's by the rise in popularity of home video. But now they're hitting back with modern complexes which often include a variety of entertainment, places to eat and several cinema screens.

I daren't think of the amount of time I've spent hanging on the phone trying to book cinema tickets. Now the Internet is here, booking online is so quick and easy.

Odeon   http://www.odeon.co.uk/

You'll need Flash 4 to run this site properly but if it's not installed you'll be given the chance to download it as soon as you visit this site.

You should begin by choosing the Odeon cinema nearest to you and then clicking on the 'Now Showing' button to get a list of the current films. Alongside each film title is a 'Details' button which gives details about the actual film and lists the times when it is being shown. Choose the date and time you want and click on the 'Book Now' button.

You can only order tickets online. Popcorn and drinks have to be bought at the cinema.

To get more information about a film, you can click on the 'Odeon Recommends' button to get the Odeon's view of the film you have chosen. You can also get information about forthcoming film releases.

ODEON

Warner Village   http://www.warnervillage.co.uk/

The website opens with the current top 5 films which you can select to begin the booking process. Having chosen the film, you'll then be asked to select the cinema and you will then get a list of times the film is being shown during the next seven days. Choose the showing you want and complete the online form.

This ticket booking system will automatically select the best available seats for the selected film performance.

Tickets are collected from the automatic ticket machines in the foyer of the cinema and you'll need the credit card you used to pay for them as authorisation, so remember to take it with you. Student tickets require a valid NUS or ISIC card, and can only be collected from the Box Office.

Sporting events

In addition to the ticket websites that also offer theatre booking, there are some sites which specialise in sporting fixtures.

Arsenal   http://www.arsenal.co.uk/

Not all clubs in the football league have their own website, but of those that do, Arsenal's must be regarded as one of the very best. Built onto a background of a piece of electronic gadgetry, presumably something to do with their sponsor, the design and layout of the site is a model of perfection.

The site is regularly updated with in-depth stories about recent matches as well as previews of forthcoming matches. Although you can't actually buy tickets online yet, you can check their availability and view the stadium plan to see where you'd like to sit.

The online shop enables supporters to buy kit, videos and miscellaneous merchandise using their Visa or Mastercard credit cards.

Manchester United   http://www.manutd.co.uk/

In total contrast to the Arsenal site, Manchester United's website is much more romanticised, but equally well executed. Like Arsenal's website, you can't buy tickets online, but you can buy all the goodies like replica kit and other useful everyday objects emblazoned with Manchester United's emblem.

There are full match reports and previews, and your chance to vote for the player of the match.

Silverstone Racing Circuit   http://www.silverstone-circuit.co.uk/

You can book tickets online for all major events at Britain's premier motor racing circuit. Or, if you prefer being part of the action, you can book a drive in a classic Jaguar XKE, a Lotus Elise and a Formula First single seater race car.

Outdoor activities

For some people, leisure means sitting in an armchair watching the telly. For others it means getting involved in some sort of white-knuckle pursuit.

Acorne Sports   **http://www.acorne.co.uk/**

If you'd like to try something different, why not visit the Acorne website. At Acorne you can book a flying lesson, gliding lesson, helicopters, motor racing, rally driving, military vehicles, off-road, vintage aircraft, simulators, parachuting and ballooning. Browse through the site and look at what's on offer. When you absolutely know what you want, select the button labelled 'Ordering' and complete the online order form.

Read the terms and conditions carefully before applying. If necessary, consider taking out extra insurance.

ARDS   http://www.aintree-racing-drivers-school.co.uk/

Here is your opportunity to drive a really fast car, including a Formula 1 car, around the Aintree race circuit. You can also join the Aintree Racing Drivers' School and learn the art of racing single seaters, karts and saloon cars. There is an online enquiry form to get more information about the various schemes and availability, including corporate days out.

A corporate activity is a great way to boost staff morale and hence boost output.

Once you've decided precisely how you want to pump up your adrenaline, use the online booking form.

Bespokes   http://www.bespokes.co.uk/

Bespokes has a fleet of over 60 classic sports cars which they will hire out for anything from a day to 3 months. Use the online enquiry form to check on the availability.

eXhilaration   http://www.exhilaration.co.uk/

"Adventure activities", the introduction reads, "are a fantastic way of experiencing life to the full." Indeed they are and if you fancy some high speed fun in a power boat or your idea of a jolly break is scaling the side of a near-vertical mountain, eXhileration have a range of programmes which can be purchased online.

Ian Taylor   http://www.iantaylor.co.uk/

Drive high performance cars around Thruxton. For more details, contact Ian Taylor using the email link on the website.

Silverstone Rally School   http://www.silverstonerally.co.uk/

If you fancy yourself broad-sliding a works rally car down a disused cart track through a forest in the middle of nowhere, first visit the Silverstone Rally School and get a few lessons. The full range of options are described on this site and when you've decided what you want, book online.

Tangerine   http://www.tangerineuk.com/

If you fancy getting behind the wheel of one of those fast exotic sports cars that you've always dreamed about, visit Tangerine. They will give you instruction and then let you loose on a variety of high performance cars including a Porsche 911, Dodge Viper, Lotus Elise and a Ferrari. The circuits on which you drive are notable for their absence of policemen (especially those carrying radar guns) and a total lack of speed cameras and other traffic calming devices.

tangerine®

CLICK FOR
LAST MINUTE DEALS

Warbird Flying   http://www.warbirdflying.com/

For something really different, take to the air in a genuine WW2 US aircraft.

Phantom Simulation   http://www.yorkshireflightcentre.co.uk/

Experience the thrill of flying a Phantom jet fighter without leaving the ground. Book online for this exciting ride or balloon flights.

Staying in

Sometimes, just sometimes, what you really need after a hard week at work is to curl up on the sofa with your loved one on one side and a glass of Scotch on the other. And a good film to get lost in.

Home entertainment

First was the wireless, then came TV. The 1970's saw the advent of the video recorder which enabled people to watch movies at home. The latest is DVD (Digital Versatile Disc) which can store a whole movie on a disc the size of a CD. The advantage of DVD over video cassette is that it's lighter, much more robust and you can get to any part of the film instantly without having to rewind or fast forward.

Blackstar   http://www.blackstar.co.uk/

This huge site contains search facilities for every video ever made. Blackstar has over 100 of the biggest box-office movie titles, as well as some of the most acclaimed films of all time. The films are available to buy online or rent.

Blockbuster   http://www.blockbuster.co.uk/

One of the best known names in UK high-street entertainment, Blockbuster is a video library in its shop guise. Online it's a place to choose and buy mainly films on video tape and DVD. You can also view the top 20 rentals.

The Blockbuster site contains a huge amount of additional information about the films, the stars and the directors.

Discounts online   http://www.discounts.co.nz/

This New Zealand site has a wide range of audio/visual products for sale online.

DVD Box Office   **http://www.dvdboxoffice.com/**

This US site has an enormous range of DVDs and will ship them around the world free. All of the films are categorised using headings like Action, Musicals and Sci-Fi, or you can enter the name of a film in the search engine to locate it.

Note that DVDs from a different market may not run on your DVD player.

DVD Express   **http://www.dvdexpress.com/**

This US site has a huge selection of DVD movies which you can locate using the search engine or browse through the indexed titles. The site also hosts an online auction.

DVD Street   **http://www.dvdstreet.com/**

You can buy all the top DVD films from this UK online store. All items are delivered free in the UK and there's a guarantee that any personal information you provide is kept secure.

Filmstore   **http://www.filmstore.co.uk/**

This is the Odeon Cinema's marketing site where you can buy films on video and DVD. Titles include some television programmes as well as cinema releases. You can pre-order forthcoming releases ensuring that when they're released you'll be among the first to have them. You can search for the movie you want by film name, actor or director.

Film World   **http://www.filmworld.co.uk/**

This UK site has a huge selection of videos and DVDs at very competitive prices. Apart from the actual film there's also film memorabilia for sale so that you can see the film and read the book and wear the 'T' Shirt.

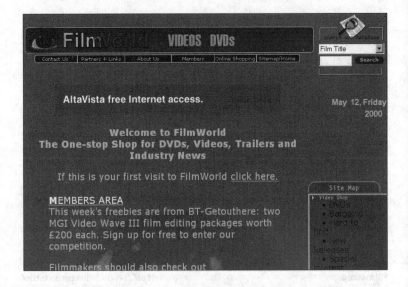

Jungle.com   **http://www.jungle.com/**

When this site opens, click on the 'Jungle Vision' link at the top of the screen to access a huge range of Videos and DVDs at knock-down prices. The searchengine makes it really easy to find the specific movie you're looking for but there is an index if you want to browse.

Toys, games and hobbies

It seems that every Christmas a new craze hits the shops. Since my son was born we've had Ghostbusters, Mutant Turtles, Tamagochi, and Buzz Lightyear. The advertising in itself is bad enough, but the fact that you can never actually buy the item makes it all the more desirable and so the young ones want it all the more. The result has been stories about parents travelling miles to track one down, queues outside toy shops and over inflated prices.

Barbie   http://www.barbie.com/

The famous doll that most girls seem to own has her own website laid out, appropriately, in candy colours. The Barbie Doll site is effectively an online catalogue where you can view Barbie's wardrobe and buy clothes online. There are also safety tips, registration and a section entitled *Enjoying barbie.com* which gives some useful advice about using the site.

Dawson & Son   http://www.dawson-and-son.com/

You won't find any guns or laser zappers here. In fact, you probably won't find much with a chip inside. This traditional UK toyshop sells quality traditional toys online.

Beanie Babies United   http://www.cherryade.com/

I wouldn't mind if Beanie Babies were actually attractive, but they are hugely popular. This is Europe's premier site for Beanie Babies which gets a claimed 450,000 hits per week, offering online shopping, collector's chat and much more.

Doll's House Emporium   http://www.dollshouseemporium.com/

My daughter had finally reached the stage where she wanted a doll's house. When she got one it became a sort of family hobby with everybody chipping in with ideas and help. This site is packed with furniture, wallpaper and figures to make your doll's house extra special. Everything can be bought online and the prices are realistic.

There are some great ideas for doll's houses on this site.

You can also access this site by entering *http://www.dollshouse.co.uk/*.

Early Learning Centre   http://www.elc.co.uk/

This high street store is popular with mums and dads who want to buy something with at least some educational content. The Early Learning Centre has some excellent toys and games which kids wouldn't necessarily think of themselves but which will amuse them for hours and teach them something into the bargain. Check out the science kits with safe experiments for the home and garden.

eToys   http://www.etoys.com/

One of the US' premier toy sites. Items are organised by age/brand, or you can search for what you're looking for. UK residents should go to: *http://www.etoys.co.uk/*.

Funstore.co.uk   http://www.funstore.co.uk/

This is Hamleys online – probably the most famous toyshop in the UK. This fun site features many of the toys available in the store which are indexed according to age range and gender

If you're really stumped for a present, go to the Personal Shopper section and enter the age and the sex of the child you are trying to buy for together with the price range, and it will suggest some possibilities. There is also a gift-wrapping service for which there is a small fee.

You can purchase online but delivery is in the UK only.

Hornby   http://www.hornby.co.uk/

Apparently, when I was born and my father told his brother that he had a nephew, his response was, "Oh good, we can buy him a train set!" Five years on, I got my train set, but didn't get much of a look in for some time. When my son was born, it was a similar story but regrettably the pull of computers, Star Wars and other modern pastimes meant that railways didn't get a look in. I suppose it's largely because, having never seen a steam engine in service on a regular basis, having a model of one did not really appeal to him.

Hornby is still going strong and have a constantly changing catalogue of steam, diesel and electric trains with a large selection of rolling stock and track. Their website is rather like an extension to their catalogue, with copious pictures of engines, carriages and goods wagons. There's a news page and a very interesting section outlining the history of the company.

Rather cleverly, the page links are built into an overhead signal gantry.

MacTeddy Bears
http://macteddy.hypermart.net/

This is not so much a toy shop as a place for collectors to visit. They will accept UK and International orders for this range of teddies in Highland Dress.

Magic by Post
http://www.magic-by-post.co.uk/

Amaze your friends and confound your enemies with a range of magic tricks. But only if you live in the EEC. The tricks and instruction books are categorised so you can find the right stunt for your ability. Order a catalogue online, but orders are currently by email only.

Meccano
http://www.meccano.com/

When Frank Hornby invented Meccano, he launched an engineering system that would retain its popularity for decades. The clever system of beams, brackets, bolts, nuts and washers continues to maintain its popularity with middle-aged children, but the rise in popularity of plastics has meant that some of the more recent construction products have taken a substantial proportion of Meccano's market.

In spite of this, Meccano continues to sell in large quantities and has a loyal following amongst would-be engineers of all ages. Cleverly, Meccano frequently showed pictures of fantastic creations in their advertising campaigns to demonstrate what could be done. Some models would probably require a small mortgage to buy all the parts required to build them.

This site shows you where to buy Meccano online (and offline) so that you too can build one of the amazing models in the comfort of your own home.

Scalextric   http://www.scalextric.co.uk/

Slot car racing started in the mid 1950s and reached its height of popularity in the 1960's. At that time there were countless manufacturers of slot car sets for the home. Today, very few remain and Scalextric is probably the largest, certainly in the UK.

The website details the models, the sets and even offers limited edition cars that cannot be purchased anywhere other than on the Scalextric website.

SmarterKids.com   http://www.smarterkids.com/

This US site features games, toys and books all categorised into 5 age bands. You can search for a product or browse through the indexed items before buying online.

Toycentre   http://www.toycentre.com/

You can buy toys online and this UK store will deliver them anywhere in the world. The Toycentre has an excellent range of toys and games for all ages and interests. Products are indexed under Early Age, Girls' Toys, Boys' Toys, Boxed Games, Jigsaws & Puzzles, Collectibles, Outdoor, Construction Toys & Kits, Diecast Toys and Soft Toys. There's also a section featuring special offers and a link to batteries and wrapping paper.

Lots of toys require batteries. You should also buy a spare set.

Toy Chest   http://www.toychest.co.uk/

This independent family run toy shop offers quality toys for babies and children up to 10. Order online and they will dispatch your toys within 24 hours.

When you've finished your shopping, they have thoughtfully provided some links to some educational sites.

Toy City   http://www.toycity.com/

Available in 15 languages, Toy City is a superb site for children of all ages, from 4 to 104.

You can search for information about the toys and their suitability for particular children. You can search by age, make and type so that parents can be sure they're buying something which is appropriate and that will last more than a couple of weeks. The toys offered on this site are priced very competitively.

Toys R Us   http://www.toysrus.com/

This site is as huge as the stores. Toys R Us sells every conceivable toy and game for children and adults. Products can be selected by age range, brand, category or theme, but it's fun to just wander round and browse at all the things you wish had been available when you were young.

UK residents should enter *http://www.toysrus.co.uk/*.

The Toyshop   http://www.thetoyshop.com/

There are some excellent bargains to be had at this online toyshop. At the time of writing, Pokemon cards were very popular and these were being offered at well below high street prices.

The site also features a look at the history of toys and you can sign up to receive regular free updates on a variety of toy-related topics.

Toytown   http://www.toytown.co.uk/

Toy Town offers you a range of toys and activities which will entertain you and your family for hours. The prices are keen, but look out for the special offers.

VIP   http://www.viponline.co.uk

A large range of toys and baby goods for your Very Important little People from the world's finest manufacturers, with an emphasis on educational value from childcare specialists. Toys are indexed by brand, category and age range. There are also child-related items like prams, nursery items and car seats.

The Great Outdoors

If you're taking up a sports pursuit seriously, you need the proper kit.

Explorers Online   http://www.explorers-online.com/

Everything you need for the outdoor life can be bought online here. Tents, trekking poles, stoves and drinks bottles – ah… the Great Outdoors.

Orvis   http://www.orvis.co.uk/

If you really want to venture into the wilds of the countryside, then get properly equipped. Orvis have everything you need to stay dry and warm, or cool, depending on what you're doing and where you're going to be doing it.

Quadro Toys   http://www.quadro-toys.com

This is rather like a giant construction kit which enables you to build vehicles you can sit in and buildings you can climb on. For more information about this range of outdoor toys visit the site and complete the online form. If you want to buy, you can now do so online.

Shore Watersports   http://www.shore.co.uk/

If your sporting pursuit has anything to do with water (either getting in it, or riding on it) then Shore Watersports will have something for you. Items for sale include equipment for snowboarding, surfing and bodyboarding, and all the paraphernalia that go with it. Most important, they also stock fashion clothing so that you can really look the part.

Wheelie Serious   http://www.wheelie-serious.com/

If you're really serious about biking, you can't afford to ignore this UK site. Everything associated with pedal powered transport is here. Bikes, bike parts, accessories and clothing can be purchased online. There's also news and reviews about bikes, manufacturers and events.

Wiggle   http://www.wiggle.co.uk/

This site features a good range of bikes, bike parts and clothing, including Oakley glasses. They also sell tools for repairing bikes (and condoms).

Travel

The annual fortnight's migration to foreign parts is a way of life for millions the world over. This is also the time when travel agents rub their hands together as money begins to flow like water from a tap.

Booking holidays can involve countless hours trudging round travel agents to organise flights, ferries, accommodation, insurance and, if you're travelling abroad, currency.

If you have access to the Internet, you can do all that and more without even standing up, let alone leaving your house.

One-stop shops

These websites allow you to book everything (or almost everything) from the same place.

a2b Travel   http://www.a2btravel.com/

This service allows customers to find and book complete holidays on the Internet. But it's not just complete packages: you can also locate and book accommodation as well as finding the times of trains, planes and ferries and then booking them. You can even get the local weather report.

Bargain Holidays   http://www.bargainholidays.com/

Open seven days a week, Bargain Holidays lets you choose your ideal getaway at sensible prices. Everything is here from a weekend break to a full holiday including travel. There are also several last minute deals.

Bon Voyage   http://www.bon-voyage.co.uk/

This site offers some of the best ways to get to America from the UK. Simply complete the Quote America form and you will get a response with a detailed, illustrated itinerary together with a guaranteed fixed price, usually within 48 hours.

America

NEW YORK BREAKS 2 nights from	**£299** per person	• **96 page colour brochure**
HOMES Florida, California, New England & more from	**£49** per night	• **TAILOR-MADE AMERICA:** fully detailed, illustrated itineraries in 48 hours.
CARS "All Inclusive" from	**£149** per week	
4-STAR HOTELS	**£49** per room per	• **LOWEST fares on 11 TransAtlantic airlines**

Concierge   http://www.concierge.com/

Some people love shopping around for their holiday, buying a bit here and bit there. If you have neither the time nor inclination to operate this way and want to get the whole holiday from one place, take a trip to the Concierge website.

This US site has online booking, special travel deals and US bed and breakfast places. You can choose your location, make your travel plans and even chat to other would-be holiday makers in the Forum section. There's a help and advice section, a quick airfare finder and a currency converter online.

Expedia   http://www.expedia.co.uk/

You can book virtually anything through this superb UK site. Apart from the full holiday deals, you can book hotels, hire cars and flights.

You can get a price on a holiday by entering the date you want to leave, the duration of your stay and the destination. There are also several of the now familiar last minute deals.

Fly Drive   http://www.flydriveusa.co.uk/

Visit this site to find out about air fares, car hire and combined journeys in the US known as Flydrive. All the details are on the site including destinations and prices. Online booking is not available at present, but you can email your request at *enquiries@flydriveusa.co.uk/*.

Holiday Auctions   http://www.holidayauctions.net/

As the name implies, you can bid for a holiday in an online auction. Holidays are categorised by location, so you decide where you want to go and you'll find several holidays to suit. As well as auctioning off complete holidays, you can also visit this site for car hire, travel insurance and complete fixed price holiday deals. For more about auctions, see the relevant chapter.

Holiday Deals http://www.holidaydeals.com/

Not just full holidays, but short stay deals at low prices. For a bargain break, visit Holiday Deals.

Kuoni http://www.kuoni.co.uk/

For a dream holiday, visit the Kuoni website where you'll find details about over fifty exotic locations. Choose the time and place and book online.

Lastminute.com http://www.lastminute.com/

Some people like to leave their bookings to the very last minute in the hope of picking up something cheap. If this is your style, a visit to 'lastminute.com' could prove beneficial. This is a brilliant idea and a site that has made its founders multi-millionaires.

You can browse through the hundreds of last minute offers before placing your order online. If your order is accepted, you will be sent an email or you will receive a telephone call confirming acceptance of your order. You will also be informed whether the deal was through 'lastminute.com' or with a third party acting on behalf of 'lastminute.com'.

Last Stop   http://www.laststop.co.uk/

This website features a wide range of holiday clearance bargains to browse through. At present you can't book online, although you can email or phone to confirm.

The Passport   http://www.thepassport.co.uk/

"Get away without getting stressed!" is the opening statement. Part of Freeserve, The Passport is the Internet travel site for women where you can collect objective up-to-date information and advice on everything from days out to package holidays. Online booking is available, as well as a family hotel guide, and holiday horrors.

1Ski   http://www.1ski.com/

If you like to get away for the winter break, 1Ski is a complete one-stop-shop for all your skiing and snowboarding needs. There are even links to webcams on the pistes so you can see what you're letting yourself in for.

Sun Seeker Holidays   http://www.sunseekerholidays.com/

If you like lounging around on a sun-drenched beach, visit Sun Seeker holidays to arrange your trip. Don't forget the sun-cream.

Thomas Cook   http://www.thomascook.co.uk/

Thomas Cook is probably one of the most famous names in travel, certainly in the UK. Their website contains everything you need for a holiday which can then be booked online. You can browse for the best bargains, arrange flights and ferries, buy currency and even arrange travel insurance.

Travel Bag   http://www.travelbag.co.uk/

This website has just about everything you need including car hire, flights and travel insurance. Once you've chosen your holiday you can complete the online quotation form which is emailed to Travel Bag who will provide you with a quote usually within 24 hours.

Travelbreak   http://www.travelbreak.com/

This New York based website auctions everything associated with travel including flights and complete packages. Everything for your travel needs.

Travelbreak is the world's first open-to-all online leisure marketplace. It is a meeting place where travel and leisure providers can sell directly to consumers from around the world.

World of Travel   **http://www.worldoftravel.net/**
The World of Travel is a search engine for travel related Web content. Simply place a search word or words into the search box on the right and click the 'GO' button. Alternatively you can jump to the category that interests you. The site is comprehensive to say the least and includes accommodation (hotels, guest houses) advice, airlines and airports (European, UK and Worldwide), car hire (European, UK and Worldwide), Coaches (European and UK), information about countries, cruises (Caribbean, Mediterranean, Worldwide), ferries (European, UK and Worldwide), railways (Channel Tunnel, European, UK, Worldwide), specialist holidays (activity, safari, winter sports) and travel goods (clothing, equipment, health, luggage).

Cruises

If all this seems too tourist oriented, and the prospect of fighting for a plot on an over-crowded and over-heated beach is too much, then how about a cruise? For some, the peaceful sound of the waves interrupted by the occasional stop at some exotic destination is the holiday to die for. Cruises are big business and for those that think it's little more than an extended ride on a slightly upmarket ferry, think again. Some of these cruise liners are as luxurious as top hotels. The difference is that when you look out of your cabin window, you get a different view each day.

Cunard   http://www.cunard.com/

In 1840 Samuel Cunard established the British and North American Steam Packet Company to carry Royal Mail from the UK to Canada and the USA. Over a century and a half later Cunard boasts some of the finest ships at sea including the Queen Elizabeth 2, probably the world's most famous ship.

You can't book a cruise on the QE2 online from this site, but you can browse through the itineraries of all of Cunard's ships, compare cabin features, view fares and look at the various excursions available. When you've made up your mind, you can order a booking request form.

Olsen   **http://www.fredolsen.co.uk/**

If you're not sure what it's like onboard ship, a visit to Fred Olsen's website will give you a better idea. You can have a virtual tour over the Black Watch or the Black Prince and see the amazing facilities on offer. You can then choose your destination and get an online guide.

You can't actually book from this site at present, but you can download an order form which is in PDF format. (You'll need Adobe Acrobat to view it – see the section on software downloads).

Fred. Olsen Cruise Lines

e-Cruise   **http://www.e-cruise.co.uk/**

Whether you've been on a cruise before or this is your first, 'e-Cruise.co.uk' will help you find and prepare for your holiday. With destinations from Alaska to Zante and cruises to suit every budget and theme, there's bound to be something for everyone here. You can even win a cruise by entering one of the numerous competitions run on the site.

You can search for a cruise specifying dates and locations, and you'll be presented with a selection of brief details. Clicking on the 'Info' button provides more details including a picture of the ship and the price. Although you don't book online, you can fill in the online form to make enquiries.

P&O Cruises   **http://www.pocruises.com/**

At the P&O website, you can search for all types of cruise from short breaks to lengthy world cruises. You'll get the full itinerary of all the forthcoming cruises around the world. You can also find out about the ships and life onboard.

Sea View Cruises   http://www.seaview.co.uk/

You can find your ideal cruise from most of the top companies like Cunard, Olsen and P&O. Enter the information about your cruise including departure/destination details and you'll get a list of possibilities.

There's also help and advice about cruises and a link to an 'on-board shopping mall', called a 'shipping mall'.

Swan Hellenic   http://www.swanhellenic.com/

You can get up to 25% off the cost of cruises when you book early with this P&O company.

Cross Channel ferries

The English Channel is the most congested stretch of water in the world. This seems to be largely due to the fact that a significant percentage of the European population want to come to the UK, whilst the British travel in the opposite direction.

Stena Line   http://www.stenaline.com/

Stena operate ferries all around Europe and the UK and when this site opens, you must first choose your country of residence.

You must register as a member the first time you want to make a reservation from this website. Once you've registered, you will be sent a member ID by email.

There are links to take you to the timetable of ferry journeys and the prices. There are lots of different combinations of journey time, with or without car, number of passengers etc. You'll need to spend a little time scrutinising the tables to get the best deal. When you've found what you want, you can book online.

During the booking pages you will always have direct contact with the database and so will have access to the latest information about departures and availability. Bookings will be confirmed by email.

Hoverspeed   http://www.hoverspeed.co.uk/

Flying at an altitude of about 9 inches, a hovercraft is one of the fastest ways to cross the Channel. The other way to move across water quickly is by a Seacat or a Superseacat. These high-speed twin-hulled catamarans are very fast and stable which means that if you're taking children, there's less chance of them becoming sea-sick.

There are four routes to choose from and over 25 departures each day. The tables contain all the information about times and dates as well as the mode of transport (Hovercraft or Seacat). You can find the costs of the crossings but you can't book online at present. There is a freephone number to call instead.

P&O Ferries   **http://www.poportsmouth.com/**
This site is available in English, French and Spanish: the three countries P&O Ferries sail between. You choose your destination, look at the timetable and price guide and finally book online.

Sea France   **http://www.seafrance.com/**
Sailing between Dover (UK) and Calais (France), Sea France has several sailings each day. The website allows travellers to calculate their fares based on sailing times and numbers for both Dover-Calais-Dover and Calais-Dover-Calais. Also featured are details about the facilities onboard ship.

Sea Containers Ltd   http://www.superseacat.com/

With ferries serving Britain and Ireland, Britain, France and Belgium and
between Scandinavia and Germany and Estonia, this company is actually one
of Europe's largest ferry operators. Sea Container's Passenger Transport
division also runs a commuter service between New York, Brooklyn and New
Jersey in the US. You can't book from this site, but it has links to their operators
from where, in most cases, you can book online.

Flights

If you want to get to where you're going quickly, then it's got to be by air. But
there are so many different offers, it's difficult to know which is best.

Booking a flight used to be a painfully long-winded process which always
seemed to require a great deal more paperwork than seemed necessary.
Certainly, given the choice, I'd rather book a train journey than a plane journey
(apart from the destination).

EasyJet   http://www.easyjet.com/

EasyJet proudly boasts that their airline has a ticketless booking system which
you can book yourself over the Internet without having to go and sit in a stuffy
travel agents' shop.

EasyJet's booking system couldn't be easier, especially with the interactive
calendar that helps you choose your flight times. Opening the calendar displays
the current day and the month. Choose a date and click on one of the 'Set'
buttons and the date is automatically entered into the correct place on the form.

Once the booking form has been opened, you are led, step by step, through
a series of screens into which you insert flight times, destination and departure
locations. Finally you are asked to enter your credit card details for payment.
EasyJet will confirm your booking by email.

Other flights

Easy Jet is one of the most well known companies for online flight booking, but there are others.

a2b Airports   http://www.a2bairports.com/

This UK site contains all the information you'll need when planning your trip including airport guides, directions to get you to the airport, telephone numbers for local taxi, bus, and train services, and the latest flight arrival information. It's simple, just click on the airport name on the map, and everything is provided for you.

If you've been coerced into meeting someone from an airport, a visit to a2b could save a lot of waiting.

Austravel   http://www.austravel.com/

Find the best prices to Australia and New Zealand from the UK and US. The site also features hotels.

Buzzaway   http://www.buzzaway.com/

With flights to 12 European cities, plus a further three during the summer months, this budget airline is becoming very popular. Unlike some low cost airlines, the fares include airport tax and all applicable charges. In other words, the price you see is the price you'll pay, unless you want to add extras, for which there will be an additional charge.

Buzzaway offer reductions for online booking and you can also get a reduction if you hire a car at your destination.

Cheapflights   http://www.cheapflights.com/

Holidays can be an expensive business, especially if you've got a couple of children to take. One way of cutting the cost of international travel is to go to a company that specialises in discount tickets. Cheapflights is one such company. Their website lists thousands of seats on hundreds of flights.

Dial-a-Flight   http://www.dial-a-flight.com/

You can search through over three million cheap flights from the UK. When you visit the site, choose the 'Flight Search' link and enter departure/destination details. Within seconds you'll get the best price. At present you'll have to copy the information and then phone through your booking.

There is also information about weather, travel insurance etc.

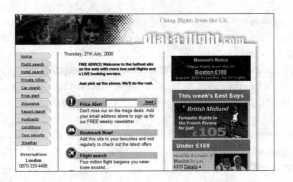

ebookers   **http://www.ebookers.com/**

When you get into this site, click on the link to 'Deals of the Day' to get some amazing discounts.

To book a flight, choose both your place of departure and your destination which can be from most EU countries. Enter the departure date and the return date, number of people travelling and wait for the response.

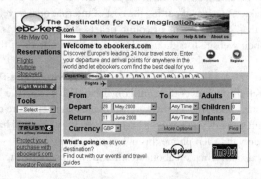

Fly Concorde   **http://www.flyconcorde.com/**

Still going strong after almost 30 years, Concorde is still the pride of British and French avionics.

This site outlines details of Concorde flights including special round-trips. Take the Orient Express to Southampton, UK, sail to New York on the QE2 and then fly home on Concorde. If you fancy something a little more modest, you could try a subsonic flight from London to Manchester. Once you've chosen your flight from this website, you can apply for a booking form.

If you want to fly Concorde, you'd better book soon as the fleet are due to be pensioned off in a few years.

Flights Direct   http://www.flights-direct.co.uk/

Flights Direct is a specialist Service from Thomas Cook Retail Ltd. At present you can't actually book from this website, but you can find out the prices and times and book over the phone.

Travel Bug   http://www.flynow.com/

This website features a fast flight calculator. Enter your starting point, proposed destination and departure and return dates and the database will search for suitable flights. The list returns containing brief details and clicking on the "Info" button will provide you with a full itinerary.

If everything is as you want it, you can book the seat(s) online, provided you have read the online terms and conditions. When you book, you'll need to complete an online form in which you must enter your personal details exactly as they appear on your passport.

Go   http://www.go-fly.com/

This site is available in seven languages and opens with an extended animated introduction. You can browse through the special offers or search for flights to specific destinations.

You'll be sure to get the lowest quote possible for the dates you wish to travel, and the fares include tax. The prices are displayed in the currency of the country where you start your journey.

It's worth noting that when you enter the Go site there is a 'skip intro' button so you can avoid the clever, but time-consuming animation, and get on with the important business of booking a flight.

Monarch Airlines   http://www.monarch-airlines.co.uk/

For cheap flights from Luton and Manchester in the UK to a great number of destinations throughout Europe, Monarch Airlines is hard to beat. You can download all of the current flight times and prices so you can scrutinise them offline.

Because there is less administration work for the airlines, there is almost always a substantial cost saving for booking online.

Once you've found your flight, you can book online over a secure connection. The airline does not issue tickets - the only thing you'll need at the airport is your passport.

Print out the times and prices for the flight you're considering before booking over the telephone.

Ryan Air   http://www.ryanair.com/

Ryan Air is a budget airline flying out of Stanstead and Luton to many European cities. No frills, no gimmicks, they just get you there cheaply and efficiently. Visit their website and book online.

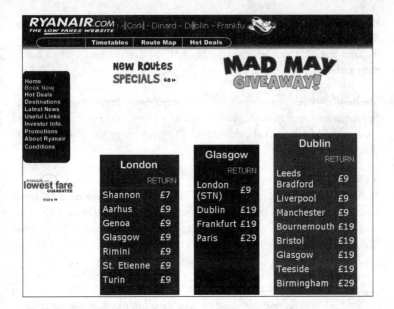

Star Alliance   http://www.star-alliance.com/

More upmarket is Star Alliance who can book you onto most of the world's major airlines, and consequently to most destinations. You'll need to begin by registering and you should login on all future visits. You can search for the flight you want and book and pay online.

Coaches

Travelling overland by coach is much slower than aeroplane, or even car. But you do get to see the countryside.

Wallace Arnold   **http://www.wallacearnold.com/**

Wallace Arnold has been coaching people all over Europe and beyond for years. To find out what they have to offer, including rates and times, take a trip to their website.

Sterling Coaches   **http://www.festiveholidays.co.uk/**

For more information about Sterling coach tours, visit the Festive website and click on the Sterling Coaches icon. Full itineraries are provided with booking details.

Train travel

Eurostar   **http://www.eurostar.com/**

Eurostar is the high speed passenger train linking London, Paris and Brussels. You can use the website to plan your journey and book your ticket. You should begin by choosing the language you want the website to be in and then look up your intended destination which includes Euro Disney.

If you register you can save time later by keeping up-to-date with the latest offers.

You can then choose the time you want to depart by browsing the online timetable and finally book your ticket online.

The Orient Express   http://www.orient-expresstrains.com/

The Venice Simplon-Orient-Express must surely be the most famous train in the world, thanks in no small part to Agatha Christie who organised a murder on it. It's also the most luxurious.

If you book online you'll receive the beautifully illustrated hardback book 'The World's Most Celebrated Train' by Dr. Shirley Sherwood, as a free gift.

Click on the Travel Planner to see details of all the Venice Simplon-Orient-Express dates and journeys. Once you've decided on your itinerary, you can book online.

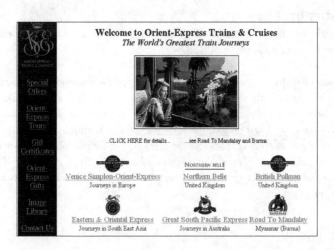

Although the Venice Simplon-Orient-Express is the most celebrated train journey, the company do arrange others including journeys in South East Asia and Australia.

> There is a links page with links to a variety of hotels and other services all over the world.

The Train Line   **http://www.thetrainline.com/**

Let the train take the strain, is the familiar expression. To find out what train services are available, the costs and even online booking for all the UK's railways, visit the website and book a ticket.

Short breaks

The stresses and strains of modern life take their toll and what better than a short break to get away from it all?

Concert Breaks   **http://www.concertbreaks.com/**

Why not make a trip to the theatre into a long weekend? Concert Breaks can organise travel and accommodation with a visit to the theatre or concert in European cities like London, Paris, Amsterdam or Dublin.

Many of the concert packages are organised in conjunction with fanclubs and take thousands of people to concerts all around Europe every year. Their ticket and hotel packages include the very best concert tickets and quality hotel accommodation.

Crabwall Manor   http://www.crabwall.com/

This traditional English country manor house hotel is set in eleven acres of beautiful Cheshire countryside overlooking the historic City of Chester. The facilities are superb and include Health & Fitness Spa, Drawing Room and Billiards Room and private conference and meeting facilities for up to 120 delegates.

The website provides full details of all the facilities with online booking via a secure server.

If you plan arriving by helicopter, the website provides grid co-ordinates.

The Bay Hotel   http://www.thebayhotel.co.uk/

You can relax in the unspoilt countryside of the beautiful Lizard Peninsula on the Cornish coast in the UK. The facilities are extensive and luxurious and full details about the hotel and the area are given on the website. You can't book online but you can make enquiries via email at *enquiries@thebayhotel.co.uk*

De Vere Hotels   **http://www.devereonline.co.uk/**

You can learn all about the hotels in this prestigious chain and make reservations by email.

Gulf Coast   **http://www.florida-villas.co.uk/**

This company represents private owners of the best in Florida property from luxury one bedroom apartments on the beach to villas and houses with private pools just minutes from Disney World. You can book your flights, car hire, tickets and travel insurance by emailing the company on the website.

Holiday Options   **http://www.holidayops.com/**

Apart from flights, Holiday Options offer sports packages where you combine a short break with a visit to a top sporting event. Motor Racing fans will doubtless go straight to the Monaco, Indianapolis or Le Mans breaks, but there are packages for football fans, rugby fans and even golf lovers. There are a variety of options including one where Holiday Options takes care of everything.

Ireland Holidays   http://www.irelandholidays.co.uk/

If you fancy a trip to the Emerald Isle visit this site first. It has a wealth of tourist information and has links to other sites so that you can book accommodation, car hire and flights/ferries online.

La Tarentaise   http://www.latarentaise.com/

Situated at Méribel-Mottaret in France's Three Valleys, hotel La Tarentaise gives you access to this world famous ski area and superb mountain scenery. Méribel is also an excellent venue for mountain biking, hiking and rafting. There are facilities for other sports, including swimming, tennis and golf.

Luccombe Hall   http://www.luccombehall.co.uk/

The Isle of Wight is a popular place for visitors and Luccombe Hall is one of the best hotels on the island.

Originally built in 1870 as the Summer Palace for the Bishop of Portsmouth, this family-run hotel has some of the best facilities of any hotel on the Island. The list is endless: jacuzzi, sauna, solarium, squash court, games room, weights and fitness area, grass tennis court, children's areas, garden walks, beach access and waterskiing.

All tariffs are listed on the website and you can make further enquiries by email at *enquiries@luccombe-hall.demon.co.uk*.

Canvas, villas and gîtes

Self catering holidays provide you with more independence. You can eat what you want, when you want and where you want. Of course it does also mean you've got to do the washing up.

Eurocamp   **http://www.eurocamp.co.uk/**

Personally I've never liked sleeping under canvas, especially when I wake up freezing cold in the middle of the night and remember I've got a perfectly good bed 500 miles away. But with Eurocamp you can, if you wish, detach yourself from nature and not stay under canvas. They have a great many camp sites throughout Europe which provide mobile homes and chalets.

The term 'mobile' is something of a misnomer because there isn't anything mobile about it other than the fact that it can be moved around the site with a great deal of effort and a rather large crane. These are extremely comfortable homes that just happen to be on wheels and should not be confused with a caravan that can be towed behind the family car.

The chalets too, are very spacious and feature all the mod-cons one probably has at home.

Algarve   http://www.algarve-villarental.com/

You can rent country cottages, farmhouses, beach-side apartments and luxury villas in the Algarve from this site.

Bowhills   http://www.bowhills.co.uk/

An alternative to a campsite is a villa or a gîte: a house for one or more families in a picturesque part of France either by the sea or inland. Bowhills specialises in renting villas and gîtes and their website lists many. After opening the site, the first major page contains a map of France with a description about each area. Click on the area of France you're interested in and you get a list of villas with a description and price for each.

Haven Holidays   http://www.haveneurope.com/

Haven offer holidays in France, Italy, Spain and the UK, and touring holidays. As well as offering a wide range of mobile homes, Haven also provide tents, chalets and apartments.

Holcots   http://www.holcots.co.uk/

This website, which is available in five languages, allows you to search and select quality cottages in the UK. Just click on the one you want. There are some 500 cottages to choose from, in locations all over Britain – each personally inspected to make sure that the facilities and equipment are of the highest quality, and that each property offers you genuine value for money.

Hoseasons   http://www.hoseasons.co.uk/

Hoseasons offers self-catering holidays including holiday parks and lodges, country cottages in Britain and Ireland, boating holidays in Britain, France and Belgium and apartments in Holland, Germany and Belgium.

Once you're onto this site, you can choose your holiday, check availability and book online.

Hotels

If you feel you're past the age where laying on damp grass is seen as an adventure and you want something a little more upmarket, then you're looking for a hotel. Booking hotels in advance can be difficult and time consuming if you don't know what is available where you're heading.

Hotel World   http://www.hotelworld.com/
Hotel World lists all the major hotels throughout the world. A hotel can be searched for by either name or location and can then be booked online. Many of the hotels have quite a lengthy editorial about them and the website features special discounts and offers on specific hotels at particular times.

All Hotels   http://www.all-hotels.com/
All Hotels offer similar services to Hotel World.

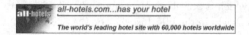

Bed and Breakfast   http://www.beduk.co.uk/
                                                  http://www.visitus.co.uk/

There is something peculiarly British about Bed & Breakfast. Other countries have the equivalent, but when one thinks of B&B it immediately conjures up pictures of seaside towns and little old ladies locking the front door at 10:30 and serving bacon and eggs for breakfast. It's not like that now of course, but to find out what is available, visit this site.

Travelodge   **http://www.travelodge.co.uk/**

The Travelodge chain of hotels are always clean and reasonably priced. They're also all identical inside so when you wake in the morning you may have to remind yourself which city you're actually in. For stop-overs, these are ideal.

When you visit the website, click on the area of the UK you wish to stay at and you'll get a list of hotels. Choose the one you want and you can book it online. If you're not sure how to get there, you can get directions from the website.

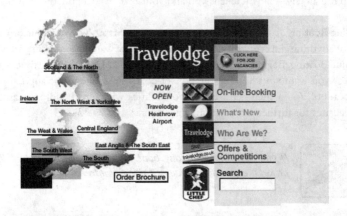

Warner Holidays   **http://www.warnerholidays.co.uk/**

Warner has thirteen historic, character hotels throughout the UK, all situated in beautiful grounds. Each one is different but all have one thing in common: children are not allowed.

Something a little different

For many, package deals are the answer. You buy the whole lot in one go and from one place.

Bicycle Holidays   http://www.kolotour.com/

If you really want to see the countryside, go by bike. There are several companies offering bicycle tours in all parts of the world. Some even arrange for your luggage to be ferried from place to place so you don't have to crank it up hill all day – all you take is you and your bike. And a puncture repair kit.

Blue Boating   http://www.bigblue.org.uk/

For anything and everything to do with any type of water-based transport, visit Blue Boating. Begin by selecting the 'Go Boating' link and then the time of the year you want your holiday, the type of boat you want and the approximate location. You'll then get a list of possibilities with email addresses and/or websites for further information and booking.

If you're hiring a holiday boat, don't forget to also hire life jackets, especially if you're taking children.

Apart from hiring a boat for a holiday, there is advice about buying a boat, with links to sites with boats for sale, competitions, news and even boat shows.

British Holidays   http://www.british-holidays.co.uk/

This site lists all types of British holiday including caravan parks. Select what you want to get a list of operators' websites and/or email addresses.

Costa Blanca Property   http://www.costablancaproperty.co.uk/

The thought of buying a holiday home is very attractive. Visit this site to get all the information you need to buy freehold property in Spain. There's an online form to request further information.

Cresta Holidays   http://www.crestaholidays.co.uk/

Cresta specialise in short breaks and will tailor-make a quality break including transport and hand-picked accommodation in such places as Paris, Amsterdam, New York, and Dublin.

France Afloat   http://www.franceafloat.com/

Enjoy the French countryside cruising along French Waterways. You can't book through this site but you can email your enquiries.

Global Holidays   http://www.globalholidays.co.uk/

If you don't like shopping around buying a bit here and a bit there, visit Global Holidays who can provide everything including flights, accommodation and car hire.

Home Exchange   http://www.wwhec.com/

This is really different. With the spiralling cost of staying in hotels, the idea of an exchange deal is very attractive, providing you don't mind complete strangers living in your house when you're away living in theirs.

You have to subscribe for which there is a small charge and you'll get a catalogue of homes throughout the world. Decide where you want to go and Home Exchange sorts out the rest.

Individual Travellers   http://www.indiv-travellers.com/
Browse through this site to find holidays in England, France, Spain, Portugal and Italy.

JMC   http://www.jmc.com/
JMC have some superb holiday destinations which you can search through online.

Marsdens Cottage Holidays   http://www.marsdens.co.uk/
Located in England's West Country, all of Marsdens Cottage Holidays properties are inspected and graded by The English Tourist Council. Some of the properties border National Trust land and enjoy spectacular views over beaches and the coast.

You can search for a property by location and by the number of people you wish to accommodate, and there is an online form to request additional information.

Shorefield   http://www.shorefield.co.uk/
This site has hundreds of holiday homes on the South Coast of England to rent or buy. There is an online booking form for holiday homes and self-catering holidays.

Skiing   http://www.skiingmail.com/

To find your ideal skiing holiday, choose which country you want to go to, then select skiing or snowboarding (or both). The result of the search will be a list of possible venues with the operator's email address and/or website.

This site contains additional information which will probably be of interest to the skier: like if there's any snow at the resort you've chosen.

UTravel   http://www.utravel.co.uk/

Visit this site to search out holidays at remarkably low prices.

There is now a World Events guide to help you plan your perfect holiday. Get details on everything from film festivals to full moon parties, and then get all the details telling you when, where and how to get there.

Visit Britain   http://www.visitbritain.com/

When you arrive at this site, first enter the country from which you will be departing. You can then find countless ways to spend anything from a few days to several weeks in the UK. There are activity ideas, places to visit, lists of accommodation and the interactive map helps you locate where you are going.

Wine Trails   http://www.winetrails.co.uk/

This is not to be confused with a sort of upmarket pub-crawl. You can explore the wine regions of the world and sample the delights of the locality.

This is a relatively new site and at present does not feature online booking, but there is an email link for further information.

Yorkshire   http://www.yorkshire.ytb.org.uk/
The Yorkshire Tourist Board operates this site which provides a wealth of information about the land of the White Rose. There's a section headed 'What's On' and a search engine to help you locate accommodation.

Breaks for the kids

There comes a time when parents and their children want to do different things on holiday, or at least have different views about what constitutes a holiday. Mums and Dads don't always want to spend all their time in the fast lane, and the kids don't want to spend it with the oldies in the slow lane, or even the lay-by. The answer might be to ship the kids off to a camp, and take a break in a nice quiet village in the middle of nowhere.

Centerparcs   http://www.centerparcs.co.uk/
The trouble with British weather is that it's so unpredictable and you wouldn't be the first to have a holiday ruined due to torrential rain. A break at a Centerparc need not be spoilt by the weather because there's so much to do under cover.

Browse through this site, check on the availability by entering your desired location and dates into the search engine, and if there's a vacancy you can make a provisional booking online.

Superchoice   http://www.superchoice.co.uk/
This brilliant website captures the spirit of the Superchoice experience. The two UK sites (Osmington Bay and Isle of Wight) are packed full of activities

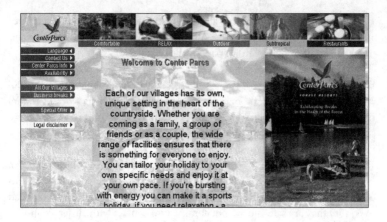

Welcome to Center Parcs

Each of our villages has its own,
unique setting in the heart of the
countryside. Whether you are
coming as a family, a group of
friends or as a couple, the wide
range of facilities ensures that there
is something for everyone to enjoy.
You can tailor your holiday to your
own specific needs and enjoy it at
your own pace. If you're bursting
with energy you can make it a sports
holiday, if you need relaxation - a

for 7-16 year olds. The list is impressive with karts, rock climbing, archery,
computers and sailing among the numerous activities.

Days out

What better than to break up the week with a special day out? It need not be
exhausting making a return journey in one day, and there are some special trips
worth taking. Sometimes, a day out can be just the break needed to let you
forget about work.

Ascot Tickets   http://www.ascot.co.uk/

Horse racing is a hugely popular sport in the UK with meetings every week at
countless sites throughout the British Isles. One of the most prestigious events
is Royal Ascot where outrageous headgear seems obligatory, especially amongst
the women.

This site lists all the meetings at Ascot, giving details about important races and providing online ticket buying. All you need to do is select the meeting and use your credit or debit card to pay for the ticket(s).

Bekonscot Model Village   **http://www.bekonscot.org.uk/**

I used to love going to see model villages, especially if they had a working model railway. Visit Bekonscot's website and get full details about how to get there and what you'll see when you do.

The Blacktie Company   **http://www.blacktie.co.uk/**

Finding a suitable venue for young teenagers to have fun is no easy task. On one hand you want them to enjoy themselves, but on the other hand you need to be sure they are safe and are not coming into contact with either alcohol or cigarettes or worse.

The Blacktie Ball Company Ltd has been organising events for under 18's for over 10 years. They are well attended and relatively cheap. You don't have to live in a big city either as they are organised at small local venues around the UK. The events are well organised and are well staffed by responsible adults.

The Millennium Dome   **http://www.dome2000.co.uk/**

The controversial Dome has had so much publicity, I doubt whether introductions are necessary. But for the handful of people who haven't heard of it, it's a large tent on the banks of the River Thames in London, England, in which all manner of exhibits are on show, many of which you can actually take part in.

You can make an online booking at the website which also features highlights from the Dome.

Ramblers   http://www.ramblers.org.uk/

If you like getting out for a walk, visit this site which provides lots of information about places to walk. You can buy guides for walking routes from all over the UK by using the online email form.

The Royal Horticultural Society   http://www.rhs.org.uk/

The Royal Horticultural Society's website features a wealth of information about everything to do with gardens and gardening. It also includes details of conferences, exhibitions and visits, with information about opening times and ticket details.

Woburn Safari Park   http://www.woburnsafari.co.uk/

I remember the first time I drove through a safari park. A group of monkeys jumped onto the car and immediately began dismantling it. Favourites are windscreen wipers and aerials, a large collection of which the animals accumulate before the keepers retrieve them.

If you want to book, select the link to the online booking form.

Currency

It's easy to buy foreign currency, but if you don't want to chance taking a lot of hard cash on your journey, you could try travellers cheques.

Thomas Cook   http://www.thomascook.com/

If you go to foreign parts you'll need foreign money and one of the best names for currency is Thomas Cook. Their site features a handy currency converter and lots of helpful tips.

Travel insurance

I'm surprised anyone should ever want to consider going anywhere further than the end of their street if half the stories about holiday disasters are true. Apart from hotels that haven't been finished, there are stories about people's luggage arriving at a different destination to the owners. Or not arriving at all. But the reality is that you're more likely to have your holiday ruined by poor weather or illness. Travel insurance won't put it right, but you could get something back which should make next year's break a little easier to afford.

CGU   **http://www.cgudirect.co.uk/**
You can buy travel insurance online from CGU. Their website caters for both annual travel and single trip insurance. Simply complete the online form and, provided there are no complications, you'll get an instant quote.

Club Direct   **http://www.clubdirect.co.uk/**
For all your travel insurance needs, visit Club Direct who offer a range of standard policies, and tailor these to the individual needs of customers.

Animal sitters

The trouble with having pets is that it's not always easy to go anywhere. Some animals you can take with you, but in some cases that is simply not possible. Whilst dogs and cats may be welcome on ferries, horses may not be.

Animal Aunts   **http://www.animalaunts.co.uk**
Animal Aunts will provide a responsible and experienced sitter who will live in and exercise your pet whilst you're on holiday, in hospital or away on business. They will ensure the animal is properly fed leaving you to do whatever you want with total peace of mind.

Gifts

Sending gift to people can take an inordinate amount of time. By the time you've searched around looking for something appropriate, bought it, got it home and wrapped it and then trundled it round to the lucky recipient, you could have spent the best part of a day. Apart from helping you to choose a gift, the Internet can also do everything else.

Flowers

Sending flowers is always regarded as a special way of remembering someone, or saying how you feel about someone. Roses, lilies and tulips are popular.

BloominDales   **http://www.bloomindales.com/**

Bouquets and baskets of flowers can be ordered online at BloominDales. This US company provides a fast delivery service and takes the usual range of credit and debit cards. There is a free consultation service for weddings and funerals.

Flying Flowers   **http://www.flyingflowers.co.uk/**

This Jersey-based company can deliver flowers within a couple of working days, but if it's for Mother's Day or Valentine's Day, you'll need to leave a little longer. Online payment is quick and easy.

Allow extra time on popular flower-sending days.

Flowers Direct   **http://www.flowersdirectuk.co.uk/**

This company offers a superb flower delivery service. When you enter the site, you can choose from a variety of different arrangements, including a single red rose. Enter the name and the address of the person you want it to be delivered to, a greeting for the card, your own name and address and the method of payment. Most cards can be used on this secure payment service.

The flowers are delivered, very carefully wrapped, and if for some reason they can't be delivered, there's an emergency free-phone number for the postman to call.

The card is printed with your message in a script font, which always seems better than a personal message being written in another person's handwriting.

Interflora   http://www.interflora.com/

The name 'Interflora' has become part of the English language, but is an international distributor of flowers. When you enter the website you must choose the language you wish to use (English, French, German, Italian) and then choose the country you wish to view flowers from. You can also choose the currency you wish to view the prices in.

The choice of flowers will often depend on the location and the time of the year.

The next screen will show you the different flower arrangements available which will be based on the location and the time of the year. Choose what you want by clicking on it and then enter the recipient's name and address and a message. Finally, enter your payment details and the job's done.

Flowers are a great way to show someone you care.

If you've ever forgotten a birthday or anniversary, Interflora's message service will help.

Forgetting your wedding anniversary can have dire consequences.

You'll need to register your name and your email address and you can enter dates of special events – birthdays, Mother's Day, anniversaries etc. Each entry requires the date, whether it is an annual event or a one-off, what the date is and who it's for. Finally, enter the number of days before the date that you wish to be reminded of.

You'll receive an email to remind you of the event in time to order a bunch of flowers.

You need to specify a reminder date at least a couple of days before the actual date.

Chocolates

I immediately put on 2 pounds just smelling it. Chocolate was first used by the Aztecs, although it was very bitter. The process by which chocolate is made is a long and fascinating one. Not to mention scientific. There are several websites where you can buy chocolates either for yourself, or as a gift.

Cadbury   **http://www.cadbury.co.uk/**

Cadbury is probably the best known UK chocolate and their website gives a vast amount of information about the history of chocolate, where it is grown,

the modern manufacturing process and its distribution. There is an education section, which is well worth visiting, and a recruitment section.

Chocolate is also a cooking ingredient and Cadbury have included a recipe section which contains some truly mouth-watering recipes.

Choc Express   **http://www.chocexpress.com/**
Browsing this site, I'm told, is almost as good as browsing round the shop. You can search out chocolates by type or by occasion. There are boxed chocolate selections, chocolates for business, chocolates by the case, indulgence baskets and seasonal selections like the Easter range. You can also view by occasion so if you want something for Dad's birthday or just a spontaneous gesture, you can easily find something suitable. Alternatively, you can use the search engine to find the perfect chocolate.

You can join the Chocolate Tasting Club from this website.

Once you've chosen, you can buy online and have them delivered to someone else. Or you can accept delivery yourself.

Geneiva Chocolates   **http://www.geneivachocolates.co.uk/.**
The sister business of Choc Express, this company offers full personalisation of chocolate boxes including inserting your own business cards or compliment slips into the products, or overprinting your own logo into their message cards.

Chocnet   http://orders.mkn.co.uk/choc/.en

Chocaholics will love this. This UK company sells real chocolates which can be ordered online. Choose the product you want from the examples which include full mouth-watering descriptions and arrange for it to be delivered.

Chocolate Store   http://www.chocolatestore.com/

Hand made Belgium and Swiss chocolates for all occasions can be ordered from this UK website. Having made your selection from the huge indexed range, you can arrange to have it delivered to another address and pay by the usual credit and debit cards.

de Spa Chocolatier   http://nzpossumproducts.co.nz/despa/

You can purchase premium quality chocolates from this New Zealand based company. The range is wide and varied, not to mention unusual.

I can recommend Kiwifruit chocolate.

There's also a range of sugar-free chocolates which are so good, you can't taste the difference between them and the real thing.

These make an ideal corporate gift for your clients on any occasion.

Godiva's World of Chocolate   http://www.godiva.com/

Continuing the waist-expanding theme, the World of Chocolate website by Godiva details their range of high-quality chocolates with mouth-watering illustrations. This US company offers online ordering and secure payment using most credit and debit cards.

This site features a gift reminder service. Enter your name and email address and you can then enter anniversaries and special dates. At a pre-determined day preceding the special date, you'll get an email reminding you to get a gift organised.

Thornton's   http://www.thorntons.co.uk/

Enter this UK site and your mouse pointer immediately inherits a trailing Mmmmm. These high quality chocolates can be selected and purchased online and delivered to a friend for a gift. To speed things up, there's a speed shop service where you just get a written list of chocolates rather than the illustrations.

Look out for regular competitions. You'll never guess what the prizes are!

Virtual Chocolates   http://www.virtualchocolate.com/

You can send someone you love a chocolaty greeting from this website which delivers to most parts of the world. In addition to chocolate, you can send greetings and download screensavers and wallpaper for your desktop.

You can also use the Web to send someone a virtual chocolate. If you're not sure what that is, visit Virtual Chocolates.

Jewellery

Diamonds, so the song goes, are a girl's best friend. They suggest love and marriage and giving them is very romantic. And expensive. Some of these sites should help you reduce the latter without diminishing the former.

Cool Diamonds   http://www.cooldiamonds.co.uk/

This is a most appropriate title for this online store. Cool Diamonds features some superb designs, carefully illustrated and explained. Whether it is a ring, earrings, a necklace or loose diamonds, Cool Diamonds should have something for you.

You can order from anywhere in the world and delivery is anything between next day and 7 days depending on where you live.

Gold and Diamond.com   http://www.goldanddiamond.com

Claiming to be America's leading online jewellery store, this site stocks a wide range of diamond solitaires, wedding bands and engagement rings in gold and platinum. There's a good selection of necklaces, bracelets and charms. Ordering is over a secure connection with a 30 day return policy. So if it doesn't work out...

Jeremy Hoye
http://www.jeremy-hoye.co.uk/

Whether it be silver or gold, if you want something really special for the really special person in your life, visit bespoke jeweller Jeremy Hoye. Browse through the online catalogue, choose your gift and place your order over a secure connection.

Hirsh
http://www.hirsh.co.uk/

This Hatton Garden jeweller makes exquisite rings and earrings in gold and platinum with precious stones. There's some really interesting information about diamonds on this site – the four 'C's – cut, colour, clarity and carat.

Icon Jewellery
http://www.icon-jewelry.com/

This UK website offers an exclusive contemporary handcrafted designer jewellery collection including rings, bracelets, necklaces, earrings, bangles, pendants and cufflinks. Search for a piece you like, then buy online.

Jewel Time **http://www.jeweltime.com/**

This well-presented US website sells a selection or rings, pendants and charms online to most parts of the world. Items include engagement, wedding and anniversary rings, pendants, necklaces and earrings. Each item is displayed as a thumbnail picture; clicking on it gives a larger view.

You can choose to view this site in English, French or Italian, or if you prefer, you can order a free catalogue online.

The Rennie Mackintosh Store **http://www.rennie-mackintosh.co.uk/**

This UK store sells quality gifts by Charles Rennie Mackintosh, Scotland's most famous designer. This site offers some of the very best jewellery and watches inspired by Mackintosh.

There's a useful page of links to other related sites.

Rings & Things   **http://www.ringsnthings.com/**

Rings and Things is a US site that ships jewellery to most parts of the world. They also specialise in Tahitian pearls, loose diamonds and Black Hills gold. There is a secure ordering service. You can also access this site at *http://www.liquidweb.com/*

Thompson Jewellers   **http://www.thompsonjewelers.com/**

This might be the place to come for gifts for sailors. Based in the US, this company has a large selection of traditional and nautical jewellery and gifts, including watches and clocks. You can get Lighthouse salt and peppers pots, ships in bottles and even tasteful items like anchor paperweights.

Wishing Glass Company   **http://www.wishingglass.com/**

Glass and charm jewellery, earrings, chokers and pendants are the stock-in-trade of this company that ships to most parts of the world. The site doesn't show all of the products at present, but this is expected to change soon.

Scent

You always have to be careful about giving someone perfume in case they think you're dropping a hint.

Fragrance Shop   **http://www.fragrance-shop.co.uk/**

There's lots of smelly stuff here for both men and women. The Fragrance Shop also sells toiletries and gifts. All of the leading brands are here at below high street prices. Watch out for special offers that save you even more.

Perfume is subject to import duty in many countries.

Island Trading   http://www.island-trading.com/

Free shipping to UK and US makes shopping at this site worth considering. There are perfumes for both men and women as well as cosmetics. The products are indexed according to brand and most of the top names are available. There is secure online ordering and fast delivery.

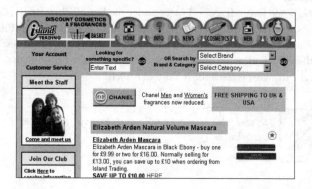

Other gifts

Regardless of the occasion, there's bound to be something unusual to buy for a special present on the Internet.

Alternative Gifts   http://www.alt-gifts.com/

This online UK gift store has a huge selection of wacky, off-beat gifts. The site is divided into gifts for men, gifts for women, gifts for children, gifts for the home and corporate gifts. Some of the highlights include melon soap, an Apollo 11 radio and a giraffe mug. For the man who has everything – a rubber radio that bounces!

The selection of gifts for the bedroom is interesting.

Chiasmus   http://www.chiasmus.co.uk/

This UK site has indexed gift ideas under the heading bathroom additions, candles, greeting cards, incense, kitchen gizmos, living space, on the move, soaps and smellies, stationery and tableware. There's also a list of best savings and the top ten ideas for gifts, new products and multi-buys which would be ideal as birthday presents for twins and triplets.

If you still don't know what to buy, you could try a gift certificate.

Composition by Design   http://www.cbdesign.co.uk/

This UK store offers a wide range of gift items including glassware, jewellery, clocks, candlesticks, vases, paperweights, picture frames, ornaments and calendars that have been specially commissioned by CBD.

The online catalogue is divided into four sections - Elements, Astrological, Angels and Evolution. You can get to each section by clicking on one of the icons on the home page. The products are displayed in a setting with numbered spots for you to click on to get more information about the item.

Confetti — http://www.confetti.co.uk/

Whether you're planning a wedding or you've been invited to one, a visit to this site is almost a minimum requirement.

Apart from lots of advice for the bride, groom, best man, bridesmaids and ushers, there's a gift shop where you can buy just about everything you'll need.

Crafts Of Ireland — http://www.craftsofireland.com/

For some traditional gifts from the Emerald Isle, including jewellery and other hand-made items, visit Crafts of Ireland. The items are indexed under the headings jewellery, Irish wood craft from Con Doyle, luxury handmade Irish soap, Irish bodhran, wooden tableware and handmade jigsaws.

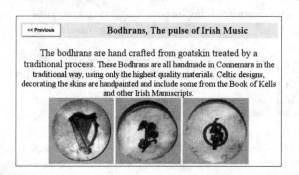

<< Previous   **Bodhrans, The pulse of Irish Music**

The bodhrans are hand crafted from goatskin treated by a traditional process. These Bodhrans are all handmade in Connemara in the traditional way, using only the highest quality materials. Celtic designs, decorating the skins are handpainted and include some from the Book of Kells and other Irish Manuscripts.

Crafts to Buy — http://www.craftstobuy.co.uk/

If you want to buy something for someone who is impossible to buy for, then visit this site. There is a huge range of gifts under the headings arts, books, ceramics, clothes, floral, glass, hobbies, jewellery, knitting, leather, needlecraft, sculpture, soft furnishings and wood.

Designer Stationery   **http://www.ctrlp.com/**

This is a really clever idea, brilliantly executed. If you want business cards or personalised note paper, rather than going to a print shop, you can design it online and the results will be sent to you.

You'll need to register and log on, but once inside the online print shop you'll prepare your job, check the price, place the order and send any artwork as a computer generated file. You can even track its progress without leaving your desk.

You will get an instant price for leaflets, booklets, reports, posters, business cards and labels.

Earth's End   **http://www.earthsend.com/**

If you want a disposable ballpoint pen, don't bother to visit this US site. What you'll find here are the finest pens by the top names. Cross, Parker and

From time to time this site also stocks limited edition pens.

Waterman, to name but three. The prices are very competitive and the service is excellent.

They also stock a range of briefcases, desk accessories and fragrances.

Fifth Sense   **http://www.fifthsense.com/**

When you enter this site, click on the 'Gift Ideas' link to take you to a range of about 20 gourmet-related products which will be ideal for gifts.

The Gift Delivery Company   **http://www.giftdeliveryco.com/**

The Gift Delivery Company is a UK site specialising in quality gifts for him, her or them, for all occasions. Payment is secure using any of the usual plastic cards and they will deliver virtually anywhere in the world.

Gift Delivery   **http://www.giftdeliveryco.com/**

This site features a varied and ever changing range of exclusive presents which can be gift wrapped for next day delivery.

Gift Delivery features a reminder service which will email you when an important date is approaching so that you can organise a present.

Gifts are categorised for him, for her, corporate gifts, weddings and travel gifts. Prices start at under UK£5 and go up to three figures.

Gift Store   http://www.giftstore.co.uk/

This superb UK site features gifts of just about every type and for every occasion. There are ready-wrapped chocolates, flowers, foil balloons, cakes, certificates, herbal hampers, perfumes, ties and much more.

Goto Gifts   http://www.gotogifts.co.uk/

This site has links to lots of other sites with lots of ideas for gifts for all occasions.

Hammacher Schlemmer   http://www.hammacher.com/

This US online store has an assortment of unusual gifts. The products are divided into categories or you can search for a product using the search engine. The 'Unexpected' section contains, well, unexpected items including a robot lawn mower and an all-terrain two-person hovercraft. Just the thing for the man who has everything.

Hawkin   http://www.hawkin.com/

This site sells a large selection of simple gifts for all tastes, pockets and occasions. You can choose from Tricks & Magic, Stocking Fillers & Party Gifts, Puzzles, Wooden Toys, Games, Decorations for Christmas, Outdoor Pursuits, Books, Gifts for Grown-Ups, Science Toys & Kits, Tinplate Toys for Collectors and Yo-yos.

You can order a catalogue which will help when you complete the online order form.

Hugs and Cuddles   **http://www.hugsandcuddles.co.uk/**

Select a teddy bear from this UK based store and they'll send it to anyone, anywhere in the UK for free. You can even include some chocolates with the bear.

Innovations   **http://www.innovations.co.uk/**

This UK website is the online branch of the mail order company who specialise in all manner of things you'd like, but not a great deal you actually need. The gift section includes a search facility where you can look for gift ideas by either price or type. The resulting list is just text, but clicking on one of the item descriptions takes you to a page with full description and picture. Purchase online and pay using the usual credit and debit cards.

Look out for special offers at the Innovations website.

I Want One of These   http://www.iwantoneofthese.com/

This site features a huge assortment of gadgets and gizmos. There's nothing here you will actually need, although there's bound to be plenty that you'll want. This UK site has a 24 hour delivery service and reasonable carriage charges.

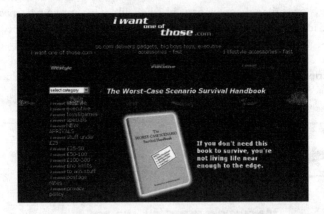

You can search for goodies according to price or type. Just to show the diversity of the products offered here there are a beautiful brushed steel and leather clock for UK£18 and a Panther 64 Catamaran for a cool UK£1,000,000.

My birthday is in July, (and it's not the clock I'm after).

Presents Direct   **http://www.presentsdirect.com/**

This UK site stocks quality products which will make ideal gifts for anyone and everyone. There are picture frames, candles, stationery and photo albums to name but four.

It's Wine.com   **http://www.itswine.com/**

When you enter this site, click on the 'Gift' button to go to a section where you can choose a bottle of wine in one of three price categories. Choose the bottle (or bottles) you want and you can buy online.

Sending wine is a great idea for a business award or incentive but make sure the recipient is neither an alcoholic nor teetotal.

Jomono   **http://www.jomono.co.uk/**

If you're still not sure what to buy, why not try a gift voucher? If you buy one from Jomono, you can spend it with anyone of a dozen or more companies and the list is growing fast. You can buy most vouchers in multiples of UK£10, although a couple are UK£20 denominations.

Just Shetland   **http://www.just-shetland.co.uk/**

Shetland is famous for knitwear, ponies, Vikings, puffins, and fiddle music. Visit this site for a small but select collection of gifts like Fair Isle knitwear, lace shawls, jewellery, smoked salmon and Celtic gifts. If you enter your email address you can receive news about the latest products on sale at Just Shetland.

K2Man   **http://www.k2man.co.uk/**

The site reckons you can save between 10-15% on all purchases. There is a good selection of gifts for men and for women, and for either. Products can be gift-wrapped and delivered directly to the person you want to give it to.

K.C. Gifts   **http://www.kcgifts.com/**

Whether it's for birthdays, Valentine's Day, Mother's Day, Father's Day, weddings, anniversaries or just a spontaneous gift, this US site, which sends gifts to just about every corner of the globe, will probably have something for you. Products include collectibles, jewellery and American figurines with up to 50% off shop prices.

Loch Ness Shop   **http://www.lochness.scotland.net/**

This Scottish Shop has a spectacular range of gifts including a model of Urquhart Castle, a 'Nessie' ornament set, crystal and tartan products.

You can also send an electronic postcard to a friend and see if you can spot the monster by looking at the webcamera.

Made In Sicily   http://www.madeinsicily.it/

You can choose to view this site in either Italian or English. It offers a relatively small but carefully selected range of Sicilian products including sweets, jewellery and olive oil. They will deliver to almost anywhere.

Manx Mall   http://www.manxmall.com/

From the island where cats have no tails, a selection of Manx products including jewellery, crafts and prints.

me2u.com   http://www.me2u.com/

For a truly romantic gift, visit this online gift store and browse through a selection of unusual gifts from around the world.

The random quote generator at the top of this website produces some classics e.g.: 'To desire your wife's happiness amounts to mighty little, unless you are willing it shall be accomplished in her way.'

Amongst the new gifts on offer, there is a collection of lesser known love poetry, a candle depicting the sun and moon kissing and a book entitled 1001 ways to be romantic.

My Mug   http://www.my-mug.com/

This is a clever idea. Upload a picture to this website and they'll put it onto a mug or any of a number of different products. You'll first need to capture a picture and this can be either a photo from a digital camera or an ordinary photo that has been scanned. The picture will be uploaded to the My-Mug site where it can be placed onto a T-shirt, cap or shorts.

Mystical Dragon   http://www.mysticaldragon.com/

The Mystical Dragon site features a range of spiritual gifts and books including Tarot, jewellery, candles, water fountains for the table, aromatherapy kits, figurines, dragons, mermaids, fairies and much more. There is a secure online ordering facility and goods can be shipped almost anywhere.

NZ Gifts   http://nzgifts-souvenirs.co.nz/

This New Zealand-based website specialises in gifts and stocks a wide range including flowers, hampers and baskets, art, greeting cards, toiletries and beauty products, health products, chocolates and sweets, jewellery, perfumes, teddy bears, sheepskin, possum fur, fashion clothing, wine and souvenirs of all descriptions.

Online ordering and payment is via a secure server. This site features a free gift reminder service that will email you in time to buy a present for that special someone whose birthday you can never remember.

The Pen Shop   http://www.penshop.co.uk/

There's nothing quite like a fountain pen. Unlike the disposable ballpens that we've all become used to, a fountain pen shows style, character and individuality. The Pen Shop stocks all the best makes at keen prices.

Propagangsta   http://www.propagangsta.com/

I'm not sure I altogether like this modern trend of misspelling words and substituting numbers for groups of letters. But that is what we have here – Giftz4him, Giftz4her, Giftz4Home, Timepiecez and Fun4all. There's also furniture but evidently they couldn't think of anything to do with that so they simply called it 'furniture'. Really wayout gift ideas from this UK site.

Redmonk   http://www.redmonk.com/

This UK website has the oddest and most incongruous assortment of products I've ever seen. The items are handmade greetings cards, body lotions that are guaranteed not to have been tested on animals, bras, socks, hand-crafted garden products, bicycles and towels. I'm not really sure which chapter to include this site in so I put it here because you could make a gift of just about any of its contents.

Ross-Simons   http://www.ross-simons.com/

You can choose from a large selection of fine jewellery, fine china, giftware and collectibles at well below high street prices from this US store.

Shakespeare Gifts   http://www.shakespeare.uk.com/

Not just for bookworms, this site offers a small selection of quality gifts with a Shakespearean flavour. Included in this is a single red rose, Romeo & Juliet chocolate, a sonnet on parchment and a bottle of Highland Malt Whisky.

Shop Scotland   **http://www.shopscotland.net/**

You can discover your Scottish connections with the online tartan/clan finder and once you've found yourself, you can buy your tartan. If the search engine couldn't match your name, (as was the case when I tried it) you can view a selection of 'generic' tartans. You can either buy the material or a range of garments made from it.

There's also a good selection of gifts, crests, shields and jewellery with a Scottish theme.

Stewart Highland Supplies   **http://www.stewarthighland.com/**

From the hills of Scotland comes this site stocking a range of traditional Scottish goods including kilts, bagpipes, sporrans, highland dress, drums and Celtic jewellery.

Stocking Fillas   **http://www.stockingfillas.co.uk/**

This online store is only open from September to January and is for Christmas gifts.

Virtual cards

This is just a lovely idea. Technically it's little more than an email with a picture, but it could mean so much more to someone. There are several similar sites to choose from, but they all work in much the same way. It takes no time to complete and costs nothing.

All Yours   **http://www.all-yours.net/postcard**

Begin by choosing a suitable picture for the occasion from those provided. This will be the postcard. Then, enter the email address of the recipient, your email address and the all important message. Some sites allow you to add music or use animated cards. Finally, click the 'deliver' button and your virtual postcard is sent.

The recipient receives an email instruction to log onto the site (usually by clicking on the link) and view the card with the message.

Other virtual card sites include:

Blue Mountain   **http://www.bluemountain.com/**
This site has a large selection of really good cards with only a few naff ones amongst them.

ICQ   **http://www.icq.com/**
A good selection from the site that hosts one of the most popular real-time chat services.

Virtual Chocolates   **http://www.virtualchocolate.com/**
If you don't want to give a real chocolate, send a virtual one. Nowhere near as fattening, although not as tasty either.

Real cards

In addition to sending virtual cards, some sites go one further – you can also choose a real paper card, customise it and get it sent. You choose your card and your message in exactly the same way as you would for a virtual card, the only difference is you have to pay for the paper ones.

American Greetings   **http://www.americangreetings.com/**
Lots of free virtual greetings in several categories to help you choose just the right one. You can also choose from a large assortment of paper cards and a great deal more. Like chocolate.

Cybercard   http://www.cybercard.co.uk/

You can create a card that says what you want it to say and this UK site will print it and post it. There's a good selection, and the cards are well designed, and not too pricey.

Hallmark Cards   http://www.hallmark.com/

This site offers both virtual cards and paper cards courtesy of the high street card shop. In addition you can order flowers, cookies and candy, as well as some very expensive, but exquisite crystal.

You can view this site in one of three languages.

CRC Greeting Direct   http://www.greetingsdirect.co.uk/

Of them all, this one gets my vote. There's a good selection of cards to choose from which can be customised with your message. When you've done it and paid for it, it'll be posted. The difference is that some of your payment goes to the Cancer Research Campaign in the UK.

GREETINGS
DIRECT

Auctions

Going, going, gone...

Yes, it's true, you can even take part in an online auction and bid for lots.

Auctions can be great fun, so I'm told, but if you're frightened of finding that you've bought something because you sneezed at the wrong time, or you scratched your ear just before the gavel fell, why not try an Internet auction? There are basically two types of online auction – direct and person-to-person. A direct online auction means that you buy direct from the auction company. You'll usually find that these sites offer end-of-line goods, and occasionally reconditioned or renovated goods.

A person-to-person auction is where an individual advertises one of his/ her possessions for sale, and others bid for it. Sites that operate these types of auction don't actually hold any stock themselves, they merely facilitate the process for others and usually take a percentage of the sale price. As person-to-person sites do not require the company to hold any stock, it means they have few overheads and consequently they make their founders a great deal of money.

Spend time looking at different auction sites and seeing how they operate before embarking on a spending spree.

Some sites operate a sort of 'cyber auctioneer'. The way it works is very clever. Once you've chosen something you want to bid for, you can place a maximum bid with the auction house. Nobody else knows what you will be prepared to bid up to as the information is fed into a computer. When all the maximum bids are in, the computer effectively opens the bidding, takes bids, discounts people who have reached their limit and finally finishes up with a buyer.

Before bidding for an item, find out what it's really worth.

The buyer will have purchased the item by outbidding the other bidders, but will not have gone beyond their pre-determined limit – one of the inherent dangers when bidding in a 'real' auction.

There is also a reverse auction where prices start high and drop until someone presses a button to buy the item.

Visiting an auction house

The number of online auctions is increasing rapidly. Some sell anything and everything whilst others specialise in a small range of items. One of the most successful online auction sites for anything and everything is eBay, which is a person-to-person auction.

eßay   **http://www.ebay.com/**
UK bargain hunters should visit *http://www.ebay.co.uk/*. In Japan it's *http://pages.ebay.com/jpbridge.html*, in Germany it's *http://www.ebay.de/*. If you're

an Australian resident visit *http://www.ebay.com.au/* and for Canada it's *http://www.ebay.com/canada/*.

eBay auction a wide variety of goods under the headings antiques & art, books, films, music, coins & stamps, collectibles, computers, dolls, jewellery, gemstones, photo & electronics, pottery & glass, sports and toys.

<u>Registering</u>

Before you can buy or sell anything at eBay, you must register by entering your name, address and your email address. When you have completed the registration form, click on the 'Send' button and within 24 hours eBay will email a conformation which will include your Registration Code.

Keep your registration code safe, you'll need it whenever you want to bid.

With the registration code will be a user agreement form which must be completed and returned.

<u>Searching</u>

Many people will probably begin by just browsing through the site and stumble across something that takes their fancy. This is probably a good starting point, but once you get into the swing of bidding in online auctions, you'll find yourself actively searching out something to buy.

You can do this in one of two ways. The first is to go through the index of items for sale. If you want to buy, for example, a watch, then click on the 'Jewellery' link and you'll get to a screen that lists various types of jewellery including precious gems and watches. Clicking on the 'Watches' link takes you to a screen that list watches by make. (A recent innovation is a search that covers several sites).

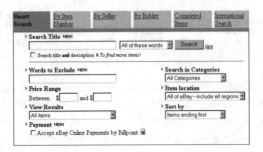

You can choose to display items by currency or by location.

Alongside each item, you'll see a number in brackets – that's the number of items currently under the virtual hammer. Continuing on the search for a wrist watch, click on the make of watch you want and you'll get a listing of watches of that make that are being offered for sale, giving the names, the starting amounts and the time each auction is due to finish.

When the deadline approaches, the time remaining will be highlighted.

Buying

When you find an item that interests you, you can click on the title to get more details about it, which usually includes one or more pictures. You can find out about the vendor's reputation by clicking on the 'Feedback' link which takes you to his or her selling record.

It's worth scrutinising the vendor's record very carefully.

If you want to bid, scroll down the page until you see the section on bidding. You'll be asked for your User ID, password, and the amount of your bid. Then click on the 'Review Bid' button. You should carefully check what you're bidding for, and how much. When you're satisfied, click the 'Place Bid' button to fix your bid. You'll immediately be told whether or not you are the current highest bidder.

The auction for a particular item usually lasts several days, and you'll receive a daily email telling you if you are the current highest bidder or if you've been outbid by someone else. Just like a real auction, you can place another bid.

It costs nothing to bid with eBay, but some sites do charge for each bid you make.

If you are the highest bidder when the auction closes, you've bought the item. You are under contract to pay the vendor the amount of your bid, and possibly any postage costs.

Before you bid, make sure you know what the carriage will be. This should be declared in the item description.

You must contact the vendor within three working days and make arrangements to pay. The vendor is then under contract to send you the item.

Selling an item

To auction an item through eBay you must first gather all the information you have about it. This includes a description of the item, any pictures you have, the category you want the item listed under and a reserve or starting price.

Visit the website and click on the 'Sell Your Item' button. A form will be displayed into which you must enter the description of the item. Again, check the information very carefully before clicking on the 'Submit My Listing' button. You should then see the confirmation page.

Copy down all the information provided, which will include your item number.

When your auction closes, you will be told the name of the highest bidder and you should contact them within three working days. You'll need to confirm the final cost, including any postage charges, and tell them where to send payment.

When the bidder meets your payment terms, you must fulfil your part of the deal by sending them the item you have sold.

Entering an auction forms a binding contract between you and the highest bidder.

When you list your item for sale on eBay, you will be charged a Listing Fee which is based upon the opening value or minimum bid of the item you list for sale. For Dutch Auctions (where you are offering several similar items) the Listing Fee is based upon the opening value or minimum bid of the item you list for sale, multiplied by the quantity of items you are offering. For items where you have declared a reserve (a price below which your item will not be sold) the fee will be based on the value of the reserve.

You can enhance your advert in several ways but these will usually incur an extra fee.

Online auction houses

Some of the other general auction houses of particular note are…

allegro auction   **http://www.allegro.com.sg/**

Both new and used products are listed on this friendly online auction site based in Singapore. There are also regular charity auctions.

AltaVista   http://auction.shopping.com/

Like many other online auction sites, AltaVista auctions are free. At present. This is the place to come to buy and sell collectibles, electronics, software, housewares and travel packages, amongst other things.

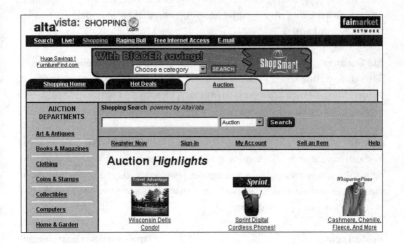

Auction Port   http://www.auctionport.com/

You will be required to open an account to use Auction Port, but this site offers more than just auctions: you can learn how to become an auctioneer. The listings are free, and this site features antiques, collectibles and computer equipment.

Auction-Land   http://www.auction-land.com/

This Canadian site has free registration, bidding and listing.

Auctiontrader   http://www.auctiontrader.com.au/

Auctiontrader Online hails from Victoria, Australia. They offer the chance to trade online under the categories of antiques, antiquities, boats, books, coins, notes & stamps, collectibles, computers, electronics, home & office, house & garden, jewellery & gemstones, motor vehicles, movies, music & sound, musical instruments, photography, sporting equipment & memorabilia, textiles, tools, toys and wine.

Bid Bonanza   http://www.bidbonanza.com/

This US online auction with free registration and listings is based in Pennsylvania. There are a great many categories for sale items and the service is free to the public at present.

Bidn4it   http://www.bidn4it.com/

You can bid for and sell antiques, books, movies and music, coins and stamps, collectibles, computers, dolls and figures, jewellery and gemstones, photo and electronics, pottery and glass, sports memorabilia and toys online. This auction is free to the public at this time.

Boston.com   http://auctions.boston.com/

Use Boston Auctions to buy and sell collectibles, electronics, software and travel packages. There is a fee for listing and for the transaction.

Bullnet online auctions   http://www.bullnet.co.uk/auctions/

Bullnet is one of a growing number of UK Online auctions for personal and business users. The online auction site offers the facility to run an auction from your own website using a bidding robot. There is excellent online help giving a clear explanation of most of the terms associated with auctions.

eBase5   http://www.ebase5.com/

This UK online auction site opens with links to 'hot items' and 'new items'.
A particularly useful link is entitled 'Ending soon' and leads to a list of items
with only an hour or two remaining before the auction closes.

ebid   http://www.ebid.co.uk/

ebid is billed as the UK's finest person-to-person online auction site. You can
sell or bid for anything from clothes to tickets.

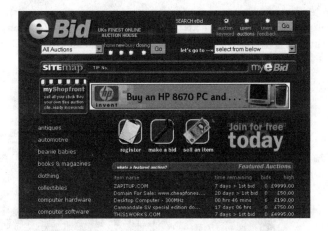

Excite Auctions   http://auctions.excite.com/

Collectibles, electronics, software and travel packages are amongst the categories
on Excite's online auctions. There are seller transaction fees which range from
5% down to 1¼% per item listed, based on the sale price of the items.

Go Ricardo   **http://www.goricardo.com/**

This UK Auction service provides sellers the opportunity to auction anything
from a fountain pen to a motor car.

When you open the site you'll find a list of the hottest auctions presented
at random, whilst on the left there is a list of categories which will take you to
specific auctions. Alongside each index category is a number representing the
number of auctions currently in progress.

You can set up your own auction from this site but you must first register
and accept the agreement confirming you will abide by the rules.

Infinite Horizon   **http://www.infinitehorizon.com/auctions.html**

Registration is free, as is bidding and selling on this online auction. There are
numerous categories into which you can list your items for sale.

Loot   **http://www.loot.com/**

This UK auction house is a spin-off from the UK advertising journal. They
will accept most items for sale, and there is no charge for bidding or selling.

Lycos Auctions   http://auctions.lycos.com/

Lycos run online auctions where you can buy and sell all types of goods under a variety of categories. 'Today's Hot Auctions', 'Local Listings' and 'Just Opened' are some of the helpful links to save you having to wade through the site.

MSN Auctions   http://auctions.msn.com/

MSN Auctions offers a wide variety of different online auction categories including art & antiques, books & magazines, car, classifieds, clothes, coins & stamps, collectibles, computing, electronics & photo, home & garden, jewellery, homes, music & movies, pottery, sports & recreation, sports memorabilia, toys & games and travel. There is no charge for posting your own listings.

Polar Auctions   http://www.polarauctions.com/

Polar Auctions is a person-to-person online auction service based in Canada. All auctions are in Canadian dollars and are free.

QXL   http://www.qxl.com/

This European online auction house has offices in the UK, France, Germany, Italy and the Netherlands and more are opening all the time. It accepts virtually all items for auction under the headings arts & collectibles, cars & transport,

Every day, QXL auction British Midland's airline tickets.

computing, electronics & cameras, entertainment, good causes, home & garden, the travel shop and sport & fitness.

There is no charge for bidding, browsing or searching for items listed for sale on QXL, but there is a charge for selling items, if you successfully make a sale. There is no charge if the item did not meet the reserve and therefore did not sell. The point to note with selling through QXL is that the more you sell, the lower the percentage of commission you'll pay.

ReverseAuction.com   http://www.reverseauction.com/

A reverse auction works in the opposite way to a conventional auction. The price begins high and then starts to drop. When the item gets to the price you're prepared to pay, you bid and if nobody has beaten you to it, you've bought it. This Washington DC site shows the prices declining in real-time.

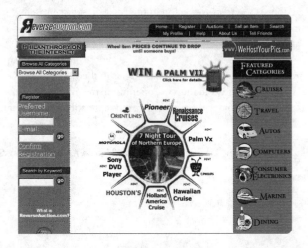

Tag-Star European Auctions Community   **http://www.tag-star.com/**

This European site offers the chance for European online bidders and sellers to take part in an auction. Unusually (at present), transactions are made in Euros. There is a charge for sales which is based on the sale price achieved. Costs begin at 3½% for sales of between €0.01 to €25. The commission drops (depending on the selling price) to about 1¾%.

Trade Me   **http://www.trademe.co.nz/**

This New Zealand site opens with a list of all auctions near to closing, giving you the last chance to make a bid. Apart from the online auctions, there are also classified adverts.

Auction Help

Auctioning is a fascinating subject and if you are considering taking part in an online auction, you can get help and advice online.

Auction Watch   **http://www.auctionwatch.com/**

Auction Watch allows you to manage and track all of your auctions. There is also a free secure payment service and you can find out what your items are really worth. You can visit the auction site directory and browse the database of auction sites.

Auction Guide   **http://www.auctionguide.com/**

You can buy and sell your own goods at this US site in the personal online auctions under a variety of categories including agricultural, antiques, art, collectibles, computer, consumables, estate, household, jewellery, leisure, memorabilia, music, property, tools, transport and travel.

In addition, you can search through the directory to find an auctioneer, get help with the Auction Tips section and learn auctioneering at a specialist school.

Specialist auctions

Some online auctions deal in specific items, rather than handling everything that comes their way. These sites often hold direct auctions and some of the best include:

Auction-Warehouse   **http://www.auction-warehouse.com/**

This direct online auction house holds auctions for computers, computer accessories, peripherals, and games, but also includes electronics and household items. Auction Warehouse also hosts person-to-person auctions.

Beanie Babies   **http://www.ty.com/**

I think it must be something built into our genes – without doubt we are an acquisitive species, and don't the marketing men know it! One of the latest collections is the Ty series featuring dogs, cats, dolls, bears and various other odds and ends. The collection has caught the imagination of kids in a big way and the backup provided by the website is equally popular. Just look at the hit counter!

The site is, in fact, a comprehensive database of the collection which is regularly updated with the latest news as to the status of the individuals. Apparently, after a particular individual has been in production for a given period of time, they retire him (i.e. he's 'discontinued'). This, I'm reliably informed, makes the toys more valuable.

Biddington's   http://www.biddingtons.com/

This upmarket, online art and antiques auction is based in New York. It features established painters, sculptors and printmakers.

Some of the main categories are Paintings & Watercolours, Drawings & Illustrations, Sculpture & Mixed Media and Prints & Posters.

B Squared Coins   http://www.stratamar.com/bsquared/

This family-run coin business deals mostly in collectible American coins. The site features both direct auctions and person-to-person.

Gibson   http://www.gibson.com/

Anyone who plays a guitar will need no introduction to Gibson. The company from Kalamazoo, USA makes some of the most desirable guitars in the world. Their site hosts an online auction where they will accept quality guitars of any make. Although this is a person-to-person auction, Gibson inspect and verify the model, year, condition, and originality of every instrument before it is auctioned. They also handle the financial transactions for sold instruments. For service of this standard, there is a commission of 10% or US$40 minimum.

Heffel.com   http://www.heffel.com/

The Canadian based Heffel.com holds a series of monthly auctions, providing 24 hour bidding access to some of the world's finest art. The gallery provides collectors with the opportunity to view and purchase works from Canadian, European and American artists. Collectors have the opportunity to view and purchase fine works from a constantly changing collection of Canadian, European and American artists. The current collection can be viewed online.

Holiday Auctions   http://www.holidayauctions.net/

As the name implies you can bid for a holiday in an online auction through this UK-based Co-op. The categories include Bargain Flights, Caribbean, Cosmos, Cyprus, Exotic-Bargains, Florida, Gatwick-deals, Gotta-Go and Young-at-

Heart. Click on a category and you'll see a brief description of what's available. Clicking on the name of the holiday will provide further information.

Icollector   **http://www.icollector.co.uk/**
Bid for a huge range of art and antiques from auction houses/dealers worldwide.

Jewelnet Auctions   **http://www.jewelnetauctions.com/**
You can buy/sell jewellery and gemstones at this US-based site. A miscellaneous category covers everything from computers to Beanie Babies.

Nationwide Equine Auction   **http://www.equineauction.com/**
Yes, you read it correctly, horses. This equine online auction from Florida, USA provides bidders with the chance to buy horses via the Internet. You can list your horse(s) for sale for free, but there is a commission charge when the sale takes place. The company accepts most methods of payment.

StampBourse   **http://www.stampbourse.com/**
For philatelists everywhere, StampBourse provide online stamp auctions where you can buy and sell stamps, covers and postcards. The 'shop' part of this site sells philatelic literature and supplies.

The American West   http://theamericanwest.com/

For fans of authentic western Americana of the 1800's to collectibles of the 1950's Hollywood Westerns, The American West is the place to go. You can make online bids for western native American antiques, collectibles and art.

Travel Auction   http://www.travelbreak.com/ostrbr.html

This US site features auctions for adventure travel, airline tickets, car transportation, apartments, cruises, boats, honeymoons, hotels, accommodation, outdoors, activities, merchandise, sports, vacations and tours.

WhatAmIBid Online Auctions   http://www.whatamibid.com/

This real-time person-to-person online auction site specialises in collectibles. They claim over 3,000 items auctioned per week, with no buyer's premium and no insertion fees for sellers. This is a good site for Beanie Babies, Pokemon cards, stamps and coins.

Wine Bid   http://www.winebid.com/

This online auction site has links to the US, UK and Australia and offers fine wines for sale. Wines are carefully categorised making it relatively easy to find what you're looking for.

ZDNet   http://auctions.zdnet.com/

ZDNet Auctions, specialises in auctioning computers, consumer electronics and domain names online.

Personal Services

Not all websites sell something tangible. Many offer services which in most cases will be paid for.

Dating on the Internet

This is not a new idea. Dating Agencies go back years and computer dating is almost as old as computers themselves. And now the Internet can help you find the man or woman to sweep you off your feet.

Blind Date   http://www.blinddate.co.uk/

At the time of writing, this UK site is offering a free trial. You'll need to sign up to become a member, although there is a section where you can try it out. Once you've registered you can enter your details which will then be used to match against other profiles. You can then browse through the details of other people and even search for a particular type of person.

The system works well but as with all systems of this type, it relies on people telling the truth about themselves.

You can email any member anonymously and, if you wish, download software to enable you to have an online conversation.

Caroline Crowther   http://www.carolinecrowther.com/

A small but well established introduction service for professional and business people aged from 28 to 65+ in the South, West and South West of the UK.

Dateline   http://www.dateline.uk.com/

Dateline is the world's largest and longest-established introduction agency. Ever since their foundation in 1966 they have been responsible for thousands of friendships, romances and happy marriages.

When you enter this website, begin by searching the database of clients. Next, take the personality test to find out if you have what it takes for a long-term relationship.

Dateline

How it Works
Database Search
Test Match
Join Online
F.A.Q.
Couples Stories
Members' Area
Dateline Magazine
Contact Details
Press Release

Dateline is the world's largest, most successful and longest-established introduction agency.

Ever since our foundation in 1966 we have been the success factor behind many thousands of friendships, romances and happy marriages.

You could spend a lifetime searching for *your* perfect partner but we may have already found them. Why not search our database now, and see for yourself. Then take this personality test to find out if you have what it takes for a long-term relationship.

Intermate UK
http://www.intermateuk.mcmail.com/

This UK website opens with the story of how the founders (Sarah and Peter) got together. Their relationship was so successful it developed into a partnership.

> *InterMate UK claim that in the USA 72% of women met their present partner through the Internet.*

By entering your details into this site you too could find the ideal person for a lunch date, for a companion or for a long term relationship.

InterMate UK differs from many other introductory agencies as it has been designed for busy people who have a personal email address.

Match
http://www.match.com/

You'll need to register with this site for which there is normally a fee, but at the time of writing there was a free introductory offer. You'll need to fill in your details on the online form and supply a username and password.

Sirius Synergy
http://www.clubsirius.com/

To quote the advert, joining Sirius Synergy, the introduction agency, 'will enable you to be introduced to intelligent and articulate people, through a unique mixture of sophisticated technology, personal service and social events'.

Medicine

From time to time we need some potion or other to help us get better or just to keep us well.

PlanetRx.com   **http://www.planetrx.com/**

PlanetRx is an online pharmacy for prescription drugs, vitamins & herbs, items for your medicine cabinet, beauty supplies and more. This US store stocks quality vitamins, herbs, and supplements, at lower prices than leading brands.

Astrology

It's all in the stars, I'm told. I'm a Cancerian but rarely, if ever, read my stars. It's not that I don't believe it, it's just that I find it difficult to get my head around the fact that all other Cancerians (about one twelfth of the world's population) have exactly the same fortune as I do.

Astrology.com   **http://www.astrology.com/**

Apart from regular news from the heavens, you can choose from up to 30 full-length astrological reports.

Astrology Online   **http://www.chartwise.com**

If you want to find what the future has in store, visit this site to get a reading. You'll need to enter details about yourself, you'll have to cross their virtual palm with gold (well, dollars actually) and you'll get a comprehensive account of your future.

Reality   **http://www.reality.com/**

Visit this site to get a full reading based on your time, date and place of birth. Pay using a credit card over a secure connection and in return you get a beautifully presented document, unique to you, containing your Chart Wheel, Aspect Chart, Element Chart and Quality Chart. Also included is a 20 page interpretation of your character.

Cosmetic surgery

It seems such a shame that so many of us are dissatisfied with the body we've been given. Vanity is a curious thing, but if having your body remodelled makes you feel better, and you can afford it, then why not?

Transform Medical Group   **http://www.transform-medical.co.uk/**

Transform is one of the most popular cosmetic surgeries in the UK. All surgery is carried out in Health Authority Registered Clinics. Transformations include breast enlargement, fat removal, nose reshaping and facial rejuvenation.

Having viewed the possibilities, you can click on the 'call back' button and a representative will call you back to discuss your requirements.

Laser Hair Removal   **http://www.laser-clinic.co.uk/**

As the name implies, hair removal by laser and also by Intense Pulsed Light Treatment which was developed especially for Asian skin types.

You can use this site to make an enquiry about the procedure, get the current prices and email a request to book for treatment.

Pountney Clinic **http://www.cityscan.co.uk/pountney**
The list of treatments offered is comprehensive, to say the least. Providing you have the money, you can have a complete overhaul including breast enlargement, breast reduction, breast uplift, classical facelift, mini facelift, chin tuck, neck lift, eye improvement, nose refinement, ear correction, fat removal and tummy tuck. You'll look like a new person. Get online to order a brochure.

Domain names

If you have an Internet service, then it's likely that your service provider will provide you with webspace so that you can run your own website. The trouble is that its address will probably be a page linked to your service provider's address: something like *http://www.serviceprovider.com/users/gpreston/*. (Don't try to enter this, it's totally bogus, just an example). It's far better to get something shorter and more meaningful *http://www.gp.com/*. This is called a domain name and there is a charge, although not as much as you might think.

Domains Domains **http://www.domainnamesregistry.org.uk/**
Before a domain name can be registered, you must first find out if it already exists. This site will enable you to check and then to register it if it is available. Alternatively you can buy one of the 2000+ domains already registered by this site. You can also access this site at *http://www.domains-domains.com/*.

UK2 Net **http://uk2.net/**
This site includes the facility to check if a *.co.uk* or a *.com* name is available. If it is, you can register it here and pay for it monthly.

Many of the domain registration sites also offer a web design service.

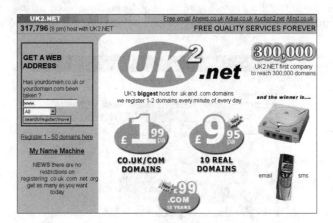

WebDNS   http://www.webdns.com/

This UK site offers international domain name registrations and online brand protection services using a secure online management tool. Domain registrations start at UK£30 for 2 years of service including email and web forwarding services.

Domain Experts   http://www.domainexperts.com/

'Get noticed, get an identity, get a domain name' is the heading on the first page of this UK website who have registered over 1 million domains.

Job hunting

Although you don't have to pay for these services, it is a sort of shopping.

Reed Online   http://www.reed.co.uk/

Apart from searching for jobs or browsing through the index, there's a lot of useful advice for would-be job applicants including producing your CV.

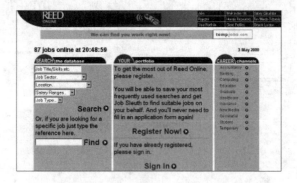

Retail Careers   http://www.retailcareers.co.uk/

Click on the Jobsearch database to view an ever-changing list of career vacancies from many of the UK's top retailers and recruitment agencies. There are jobs for all ages and at all levels including senior executive, middle management positions, junior management and entry level opportunities.

If you select the 'Retailers' link you can find employers' dedicated pages advertising careers in retailing.

The 'Jobsearch agencies' button provides details about recruitment agencies and provides links to their websites.

Scotland Online   http://www.recruitment.scotland.net/
If you're thinking of relocating to Scotland, visit this site where there are countless jobs advertised by some of the top employers in Scotland including NEC, Riley and Scottish Life.

Total Jobs   http://www.totaljobs.com/
There are over 24,000 jobs listed on this UK website which are categorised under almost 50 headings. The powerful search engine helps you to easily seek out the right job for you.

Pets

If you own a pet, you'll know how much it can cost to feed and care for it properly. The Internet has lots of sites that will help cut the costs and/or reduce the inconvenience a little. There are websites that will sell live animals, but these should be treated with caution.

Pet Emporium   http://www.petemporium.co.uk/
This online store for cat and dog gifts, includes beds, carriers, scratching posts and presents for your pet. The online catalogue (and dogalogue) lists a huge range of products, all of which can be purchased online for delivery anywhere in the EEC within 5 working days.

Pet Planet   http://www.petplanet.co.uk/
You can buy everything including food for most common pets. There's also a list of services like kennels, vets and grooms. This site promises that if you place an online order by noon, it will be dispatched that day. If not, they'll apologise and credit your account with £10.

Petz   **http://www.petz.co.uk/**

This site can be displayed in French, German, Italian, Spanish and Portuguese. There is a huge range of products for dogs, cats, rodents, birds and fish. Find the items you want and pay for them online using your credit card.

If you're thinking of getting a pet, you have an obligation to care for it for life.

Pet's Pyjamas   **http://www.petspyjamas.com/**

This website has a huge choice of food, treats, books and toys for sale online and links to a wide range of services like vets and grooms. When you get into this site, choose the type of animal you have and then select the item you want to buy from the drop-down menus, or enter a word into the search engine. When the list of suitable products is displayed, clicking on the catalogue number will provide additional information about it including its suitability for a particular type of animal.

Petopia   http://www.petopia.com

There's free-delivery and some free gifts at this US site, where you'll find pet food, toys, treats and advice. Products are indexed in six categories – Dog, Cat, Fish, Birds, Reptiles and Small Animals.

Pets.com   http://www.pets.com/

This US site offers US$10 off any order from a new customer. There are items for dogs, cats, reptiles, fish and birds which can be purchased online.

Financial services

However much or little we earn, we need to manage our money carefully to get the most from it. Whatever aspect of financial management you need, you'll find it on the Web.

Current (cheque) accounts

Several Banks and Building Societies offer their customers banking via the Internet. The advantage is that you can make transactions, order statements and carry out a variety of other banking tasks from the comfort of your home and at any time of the day or night, 365 days a year. The only thing you can't do is actually withdraw cash – you still need to go to a 'real' bank for that.

As yet, nobody has come up with a way of squirting dollar bills down the phone line.

First Direct   **http://www.firstdirect.co.uk/**

First Direct is a branch of HSBC which began offering a very successful 24 hour telephone banking service where customers simply dial a local telephone number and get balances, move money, arrange loans and generally do most things they would do in a traditional bank.

Many of the financial institutions listed here provide more than one service.

This success was followed when First Direct introduced Internet banking to run alongside their telephone service and this too has become very popular. Once enrolled, you will be provided with a CD ROM containing all the software required which is installed on your PC. When the software has been installed and you've registered, you'll have access to your bank account.

There is a link from the First Direct homepage which will provide you with information about opening a First Direct bank account.

Internet banking has had some bad press, unfairly in my opinion. Stories abound about hackers intercepting individuals' bank accounts and moving money, but these stories are largely bogus. Internet banking sites like First Direct are as safe as any traditional banking method. Some would argue that they are safer.

Needless to say, all online banking is through a secure connection.

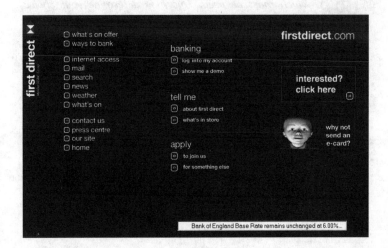

Probably more so than with any other Internet service, banking MUST be through a secure server. You should see the locked padlock at the bottom of your browser. Always look out for the symbol and don't proceed if it's not there.

Other current accounts

More and more banks are offering their customers the chance to bank online. Like the First Direct online banking, most of these are browser based. Simply, the software runs in your Internet browser which means there's no new software to learn.

Some Internet banking services specify a particular browser which must be used. This may determine your choice of browser.

For the customer, it means that you can:

- get a balance at any time of the day or night
- get a complete statement of your transactions at any time
- make payments
- set up standing orders
- transfer money between accounts
- all from home, and at any time throughout the year. The only thing you need to leave your armchair for is actual cash.

Alliance and Leicester   http://www.alliance-leicester.co.uk/

Formerly a Building Society, the services available via an Alliance & Leicester Internet Banking account include balance information, payments and fund transfers.

There is a good demo available on this site which clearly shows what banking services are available to you and how they operate.

You can order stationery and make currency or travellers cheque requests.

Barclays   **http://www.barclays.co.uk/**

One of the UK's big four banks, Barclays offer their personal and business customers free online banking. If you're not sure whether you want to try online banking, go to the Barclays website and follow the links to the demonstration. You can also trade shares online and Barclays online customers get free Internet access for life.

Citibank   **http://www.citibank.com/**

Citibank's Direct Access is a convenient and secure way to manage your money online. Provided certain conditions are met (like staying in the black) the service is free. There is no monthly fee and payments, transfers and stock quotes are free.

If you already have a Citibank account, click on the 'Sign-In' link to start banking online immediately.

Commonwealth Bank of Australia   http://www.commbank.com.au/

To find out about the online banking facility, follow the NetBank links. You can view up-to-date account balances for any of your Commonwealth Bank accounts including linked credit-card accounts, and view any fees charged to your account. You may still need a cheque book if the person you are paying is not so technologically advanced, and this too can be ordered online.

Information and receipts for all transactions can be printed to your local printer and transaction details can be exported to other applications, such as Microsoft Money 98, Quicken 99 and Microsoft Excel.

Halifax   http://www.halifax-online.co.uk/

This site is intended for UK residents and must be accessed only from within the UK unless otherwise stated.

With a Halifax account you can see all of the funds available to you, including your available overdraft. You can also see items still awaiting clearance, such as cheques. You can view the last 12 transactions.

Lloyds TSB   http://www.lloydstsb.co.uk/

The famous Black Horse provides online banking which, using your PC, gives direct access to manage your day-to-day banking. The service is currently only available between 4am and midnight throughout the week. It's open to all personal customers as well as business customers who have an account from the Lloyds range.

Trust Bank of New Zealand   **http://www.trustbank.co.nz/**

To be able to get started with online banking, your browser will need to meet stringent security requirements. The safest bet is to use either Internet Explorer version 4.0 or higher, or Netscape Navigator version 4.05 or higher. If you don't have either of these browsers, you can download them free from this site.

Royal Bank of Canada   **http://www.royalbank.com/**

The online banking arm of The Royal Bank of Canada offers the usual online features through your web browser. The display of your account looks a little primitive compared to some of the others.

National Westminster   **http://www.natwest.com/**

NatWest online banking has been designed for ease of use and is supported by a 24 hour customer helpdesk, which is charged at local rate unless calling from abroad.

With NatWest online banking you can see what is going through your account, pay bills and transfer money all through the year. You can have up to 20 accounts and see the last 40 entries on each of your accounts (50 for card accounts) and schedule payments or transfers in advance.

Royal Bank of Scotland   **http://www.rbos.co.uk/**

With a Royal Bank of Scotland account you can check the balance of your accounts online, transfer money between your RBoS accounts and much more. Payments can be made immediately or set-up to be paid in the future. They can also be amended and cancelled. You can set up and cancel standing orders, and cancel Direct Debits that have previously been set up.

Your statements can be viewed and then printed as often as you like and your financial details can be exported into a package such as Microsoft Money, Quicken or a spreadsheet like Excel.

Smile   **http://www.smile.co.uk/**

Smile has been designed and built for the Internet and is part of the Co-operative Bank plc. Currently it's the only Internet bank in the world to be accredited to BS7799 for Information Security Management by the British Standards Institution. Everything you need to know about banking with Smile can be found at this website.

Smile requires IE4 or Netscape 4.06 (or greater) and there are links to the appropriate sites so that you can freely download them.

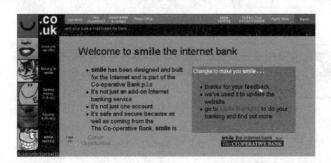

Standard Life   http://www.standardlifebank.com/

Standard Life offer Direct Access, 50 Day Notice, Fixed Rate Bond or Individual Savings Accounts account holders the opportunity to bank online.

You can check your balance and get a print out from any of your accounts at any time.

Woolwich   http://www.woolwich.co.uk/

If you are a Woolwich account holder and you are interested in finding out more about Open Plan Services including a working demo of the Home Banking service, visit the Woolwich home page.

Building societies

The UK building societies are an endangered species. Although the names remain, more and more are losing their mutual status and becoming public limited companies. Banks, in other words.

Nationwide   http://www.nationwide.co.uk/

Nationwide is the largest building society in the world, the UK's fourth largest mortgage lender and ninth largest retail banking, saving and lending organisation by asset size.

If you're unsure as to the benefits of Internet banking, visit this site which features an interactive demo clearly showing what is possible.

A recent addition to Nationwide's armoury of services is online banking. A Nationwide online account provides access to all Nationwide accounts including FlexAccounts, and Saver accounts.

Their website features online application forms for personal loans, credit cards, mortgages, savings and current accounts, and a secure online messaging facility.

There are several other Building Societies, most of which have websites but few offer online banking.

Credit cards

As if to endorse the security of the Internet, one major finance company is offering a credit card which can only be ordered over the Internet.

Egg   http://www.egg.com/

Egg launched their plastic card at the end of 1999 and offers users a 2% cash-back in the Egg Shopping Zone and 1% cash-back on all other purchases. As a bonus, there is no annual fee and no monthly statements. All payments are carried out online.

When you log on to Egg's website you can visit the card ordering page and complete all of your application details online. You will then be given an immediate response as to your recommended credit limit on the card. If you agree, the card will be sent, usually within 7 to 10 working days.

Marbles   http://www.marbles.com/

You won't be liable for any fraudulent use of your Marbles card, or card number, on the Internet if you or your additional cardholder give your card details to a retailer and they use it or someone steals your card or your details and uses them online.

You can view your account online wherever you happen to be in the world. You can check what you've spent and pay the balance without leaving home. If you want a Marbles card you can apply online and get a decision within 60 seconds.

Some credit card companies charge an annual administration fee. If you are considering getting a new credit card, opt for one that does not have an annual fee.

Yahoo   http://www.yahoo.com/

The name more commonly associated with the Internet search engine and recreational website also has a credit card bearing its name. The purple Yahoo Visa card offers 1% cashback on all purchases and a guarantee to protect you against fraudulent use of your card on the Internet. Statements will be sent each month, but you can also keep track of your account online.

Life Quote also offer income protection, accident sickness & redundancy and low cost endowments.

ISAs

Individual Savings Accounts, or ISAs as they are more commonly known, provide a high tax-free return. Typically, a UK£7000 investment could become as much as £20000 over 5 years. You may take out a maximum of UK£7000 per annum, and the advice is to keep them for at least 3 years and preferably 5. Although ISAs generally do very well, there is a risk – markets do collapse and you could lose.

Aberdeen Technology   http://www.aberdeen-asset.com/

If you invested UK£7000 five years ago, today it would be worth over UK£47000. This fund invests in technology related companies and, since it began in 1982, has become the best performing fund. Aberdeen is a global investment trust.

Fidelity   http://www.fidelity.co.uk/

Fidelity is the largest independent fund management organisation in the world. Although not quite up to the performance of Aberdeen, nevertheless a UK£7000 investment 5 years ago would now be worth almost UK£21000. Fidelity is also a global investment trust.

The value of investments can fall as well as rise. Past performance is no guarantee of future performance.

Invesco GT http://www.tel.hr/investco/

This European fund has also performed well in the last five years, turning UK£7000 into UK£28000.

Jupiter Income Trust http://www.jupiteronline.co.uk/

For those wishing to opt for a UK based ISA, Jupiter Income Trust has performed well in the past. UK£7000 invested five years ago would now be worth just over UK£19000.

Save & Prosper http://www.prosper.co.uk/

This is a UK based investment and has shown a good performance over the last five years making over UK£10000 from the original UK£7000 investment.

Threadneedle http://www.threadneedle.co.uk/

This European based investment would have turned your UK£7000 investment into almost £30000 over five years.

All statistics sourced Standard and Poor's Micropal offer to bid 1.12.99. Save & Prosper, Jupiter, Threadneedle, Invesco GT, Fidelity and Aberdeen ISAs recommended by The Daily Telegraph's Complete ISA Guide February 2000.

Insurance

Life insurance, it seems to me, is a form of betting. You're betting on how long you're going to live. The interesting feature is that if you win, it means you've died – so you've lost. If you live, you don't collect the money, so you've lost. The winners are, of course, those who survive you and pick up your winnings because you've popped your rivets.

Life Quote   http://www.lifequote.co.uk/

This site features one of the first independent online quotation services in the UK. You can enter your life insurance details and have a premium returned to your screen whilst you wait. If you wish you can request a written quotation.

Life Quote also offer income protection, accident sickness & redundancy and low cost endowments.

Saga   http://www.saga.co.uk/

The older you get, the more expensive life insurance becomes because there is a greater chance of you expiring. Saga offers low-cost deals for the over 50's. Visit their website for a competitive online quotation.

Mortgages

This is another relatively new service which looks set to become very popular. Most people who own a home have a mortgage. The question everyone is asking is "Am I paying too much?" Websites which provide instant answers are likely to become more widespread over the next few years.

EMFinance   http://www.emfinance.com/

A visit to EMFinance could provide you with the answer. Within seconds.

From the home page, there are links to help you calculate what you should be paying for your mortgage. You'll be required to enter some basic details about your home and the length of mortgage remaining and within a very short space of time, a response will come back telling you if it's worth changing your mortgage lender.

Every variation of mortgage is considered and all from the comfort of your own home.

I Promise   **http://www.ipromise.co.uk/**

In 10 minutes, the advert claims, you could secure a competitive re-mortgage quotation. In many cases, they can offer substantial savings on your existing mortgage repayments.

Nationwide   **http://www.nationwide.co.uk/**

To find out how much mortgage you can afford, enter the Nationwide site and click on Mortgages. You'll be presented with an online form into which you must enter details of income and expenditure. You will then be told how much you can safely afford to borrow.

Northern Rock   **http://www.northernrock.co.uk/**

Fixed rate? 5 Year option? 2 Year capped? If you're looking for a mortgage, it's worth visiting this site as it provides an excellent comparison table for the various types of mortgage. Full details of Northern Rock's various mortgage schemes are available online.

Standard Life   **http://www.standardlifebank.com/**

The Standard Life website includes a useful mortgage calculator to determine how much you can afford and how much you'll be repaying. There's also a very useful section about how to switch your mortgage.

Pensions

The trouble with putting money away for your pension is that there always seems to be something better to spend it on, and retirement seems a long way off. But the sooner you start, the better off you'll be when you retire.

Legal & General http://www.legal-and-general.co.uk/

In addition to mortgages and insurance, Legal & General's umbrella also covers pension plans. You can even get a quick online quote.

Marks & Spencer http://www.marksandspencer.co.uk/
financial-services

Stakeholder pensions are based on a Government Plan to make it easier and more affordable to invest money for your retirement. All the information you require about Stakeholder pensions is on the M&S home page.

Many of these companies offer more than one financial service.

Scottish Widows http://www.scottishwidows.co.uk/

The Scottish Widows' website contains a great deal of information about pensions, including some case studies which help to illustrate the need for a personal pension.

Advice and information

You don't only need advice when you go into the red. It pays to seek advice before you get into debt not only to prevent you getting into debt, but to ensure you get the maximum from your money.

The most important piece of advice is quoted on every financial website - "your home is at risk if you do not keep up repayments on a mortgage or other loan secured on it".

Moneysense   http://www.moneysense.co.uk/

Once you're into this site, click on the Financial Planning button to go to a section which gives advice about mortgages, loans, pensions and all manner of financial services.

Health Check   http://www.moneysupermarket.com/

You can use this site to shop for a mortgage, loan or credit card. The brilliant comparison section allows you to compare the benefits of different mortgages, loans, credit cards, life insurance and ISAs, but, as a bonus, you can also check out the different electricity, mobile phone, gas and water deals.

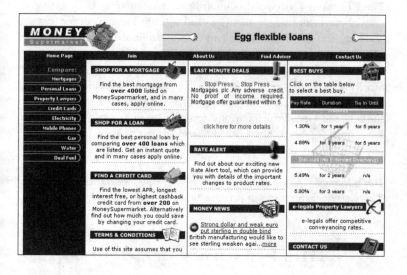

Hemscott   http://www.hemscott.com/

The Hemscott website provides news and information on listed companies.
You can also access share prices on this well presented UK site.

Some of Hemscott's content is chargeable.

FT Money   http://www.FTyourmoney.com/

This FT site provides a wealth of information about choosing ISAs, sorting out
loans, how to organise a mortgage and a really inviting section entitled
'Creating Wealth'. There's also plenty of information about getting a financial
advisor, sorting out your tax and saving.

Stock Alerts   http://www.stock-alerts.com/

For residents in the US, UK, Germany, France, Switzerland and Canada, this
site will send a free email if one of your stocks has moved by a given amount.
For a small fee, Stock Alerts can also send an alert to your pager or cellular
phone, anywhere in the world.

This is Money   http://www.thisismoney.com/

This website features lots of personal financial news and analysis.

Shares

Buying shares in companies seems to be a good way of making money, but it's not without risk. As many people have lost money as have made it. The Internet provides a fast way of dealing in shares and also provides plenty of online help.

Share People   **http://www.sharepeople.com/**

Share People is an online stockbroker that uses the Internet to bring shares and people together.

> *Share People is a member of the London Stock Exchange and regulated in the UK by the Securities and Futures Authority.*

If you are a UK resident over 18 years of age, you can apply for a Share People account online or simply register your interest. As soon as you complete and submit the online forms you will get access to the Share People website.

This site has been carefully designed to make investing in stocks and shares easy and convenient.

> *This Internet site is directed to UK residents only.*

National Westminster   **http://www.natwest.com/**

Online Share Dealing services are provided by NatWest Stockbrokers Limited which is a member of the London Stock Exchange and regulated by the Securities and Futures Authority.

Halifax   **http://www.halifax.co.uk/**

You can deal online using Halifax ShareXpress accounts. When you've logged on, should you have more than one account, you will be required to select which one you wish to deal on. Next you select the dealing option which will be either buying or selling shares, investing or raising money.

The software allows you to enter the first few letters of a company name and it will search for the stock. If you had selected to sell or raise you would get a list of the stocks available for selling. You enter the quantity of shares you wish to trade and, after confirmation of the transaction, details.

If your order is acceptable (and it's during market opening hours), the current price for the stock will be displayed and you'll have 15 seconds to confirm that you wish to deal. Outside market hours you may still place an order, but no price will be confirmed.

If your order has been successfully processed you will be presented with a transaction reference.

Make a note of the transaction number as it may be required if there is a query about the transaction.

Interactive Investor   **http://www.iii.co.uk/**

You can get quotes, real-time news, performance and advice on the Internet Interactive Investor website. You'll need to register which only takes a minute, after which you'll receive immediate access to their comprehensive range of facilities for personal investors. The Portfolio facility allows you to monitor all of your holdings, whether they are equities, unit trusts or pensions.

Other features include interactive calculators, links to providers and information about investment trusts, online banking, building society savings, tax, mortgages, pensions, credit cards and home insurance.

Ways to raise money

It seems that the more we have, the more we want. Our 'must have' mentality has been superseded by a 'must have now' approach. Unless we inherit a gold mine from some long-lost aunt, we've either got to work or try some other ways to raise money.

Loans

It's difficult to get through life without borrowing at some stage. Indeed many people actually advise borrowing as a way of easing their cashflow. Other borrow because they need to make a large purchase like a house or car.

Bibby   **http://www.bibby-group-factors.co.uk/**

This organisation claims to be able to free your cashflow and help your business prosper in a friendly and flexible way.

Car Credit   **http://www.yescarcredit.net/**

If you want a loan for a car, Car Credit will usually give you a quote by email. Car Credit will consider a loan application for a car regardless of your personal financial situation. There will be no arrangement fees, no complicated forms and all applications are in confidence. The loan will be secured on the car and not on your home.

Foster & Cranfield   **http://www.foster-and-cranfield.co.uk/**
Visit this site if you want to auction off your 'with profits' endowment policy.

The services offered by Foster & Cranfield are not available to US or Canadian citizens.

Express Loan   **http://www.expressloan.co.uk/**
To apply for a loan, complete the online form and you'll get a reply usually within 24 hours.

Your home is at risk if you do not keep up repayments on a loan secured on it.

HFS Loans   **http://www.hfsloans.com/**
I love the opening shot of what is many people's idea of what a bank manager is like. HFS offer a wide variety of financial services including a wide range of loans.

Midland General   http://www.midland-general.co.uk/

Complete the online application form and you could get a proposal within 24 hours.

Only take out a loan if you are sure you can make the repayments.

Nationwide   http://www.nationwide.co.uk/

Enter the Nationwide site and click on the Personal Loans button. Enter the amount you want to borrow and the repayment period and it will calculate the monthly repayments both with and without protection.

Ocean Finance   http://www.ocean-finance.co.uk/

As the UK's largest finance broker, Ocean can arrange loans for a variety of different purposes. You can pay off all your existing credit cards, overdrafts and unsecured loans and replace them with just one manageable monthly payment.

Ocean Finance is a registered member of both the Corporation of Finance Brokers and The Finance Industry Standards Association.

Purple Loans   http://www.purpleloans.com/

Complete the online application form and you could get a reply within 24 hours.

Smile   http://www.smile.co.uk/

To get an overdraft of £500 with no fees, visit Smile, from the Co-operative Bank.

Vivid   http://www.itsvivid.co.uk/

You can use the online calculator to work out how much the repayments will be. If you think you can do it, and you want to do it, apply online for a loan.

Betting

Betting is basically trying to predict the outcome of an event. I'm not sure that betting can be regarded as a financial transaction, but as I couldn't think of anywhere else to put it, here seemed as good a place as any.

In most cases, your stake money will be taken out of your bank account. Only bet what you can afford to lose.

Eurobet   http://www.eurobet.co.uk/

Eurobet is part of the Coral Group and as such is one of the most trusted and respected names in bookmaking. You can bet on most sports including athletics, basketball, boxing, football, cycling, golf, motor sport, rugby, skiing and tennis.

You must begin by opening an account using a debit card like Switch or Delta. When you make a bet the money is taken from your account and when you win, the winnings are put into your account.

This site offers some help for the novice including an explanation of the different types of bet.

Blue Square   **http://www.bluesq.com/**

As with most betting sites, you'll need to register, but you can browse around as a guest if you wish. This betting shop is at present the UK's largest and accepts payment with Visa, Mastercard, Delta and Switch cards. You can bet on all manner of events, not just sporting. For example you can place a bet on the closing prices of the Wall Street index.

Ladbrokes   **http://www.bet.co.uk/**

You can place online bets on football, horse racing and golf via Ladbrokes' website. You must register and provide them with your Switch or Delta account number. If you want to bet on other sports with Ladbrokes, you can telephone using the same account.

William Hill   **http://www.willhill.com/**

Although William Hill take bets on most sports, top of the list is horse racing and dog racing. Followed by soccer. You can browse round this site to see what's on offer and, if you decide to join, you open an account with a debit card, but you must login to make a bet.

When you want to bet, locate the event you want to bet on and you'll get a table listing the competitors. You've got the chance to opt for all the usual variations like each way. Place the amount you want to bet alongside the competitor and click on the 'Place bet' button.

Then all you need to do is keep your fingers crossed. UK residents can also use *http://www.williamhill.co.uk/*.

Inland Revenue   **http://www.inlandrevenue.gov.uk/e-tax/**

UK residents who belong to this exclusive club can now make their contributions online. This service allows contributors to send their completed Self Assessment tax returns to the club's HQ over the Internet. You will get immediate acknowledgement that your contribution has been received. Free software is provided for the most frequently used parts of the tax return and you may qualify for a discount if you send your return over the Internet and pay any tax due electronically on time.

Index

B

D

G

H